Martin Heidegger

The Metaphysical
Foundations
of Logic

Translated by Michael Heim

Translator's Introduction
by Michael Heim

Indiana University Press
Bloomington

Preparation of this book was aided by a grant from the Program for Translations of the National Endowment for the Humanities, an independent federal agency.

Published in German as *Metaphysische Anfangsgründe der Logik im Ausgang von Leibniz*
© 1978 by Vittorio Klostermann

Library of Congress Cataloging in Publication Data

Heidegger, Martin, 1889-1976.
    The metaphysical foundations of logic.

    (Studies in phenomenology and existential philosophy)
    Translation of: Metaphysische Anfangsgründe der Logik im Ausgang
von Leibniz.
    Includes bibliographical references and index.
    1. Leibniz, Gottfried Wilhelm, Freiherr von, 1646-1716—Logic—
Addresses, essays, lectures. 2. Logic—Addresses, essays, lectures.
3. Reason—Addresses, essays, lectures. 4. Metaphysics—Addresses,
essays, lectures. 5. Transcendence (Philosophy)—Addresses, essays,
lectures. I. Title. II. Series.
B3279.H48M4713   1984   160   83-48649

ISBN 0-253-33783-6
1 2 3 4 5 88 87 86 85 84

Translator's Introduction

Michael Heim

Much recent philosophy is a debate over whether or not the necessities of logic are indicative of necessary traits of reality. Does the modern logical system have implications for describing what is ultimately real? Or can languages be developed, both natural and artificial, which have no more ontological commitment than is required for internal self-consistency? Positions in the debate range from Quine's minimalist nominalism to Russell's mathematical Platonism (a commitment to the existence, or "subsistence," of abstract entities such as universals or real sets); sometimes a Kantian approach is urged, to establish the conditions necessary for any reference to extralinguistic reality, as in Kaminsky and Strawson.

The debate arises along with a deep underlying uncertainty, the uncertainty accompanying the success of the logical calculus early in the twentieth century. With the rapid growth of modern logic, a full system of proof is offered in which great scope and consistency are attained with unprecedented rigor. A powerful symbolic system of crystalline clarity seems to have absorbed the previously dominant logic based on the syllogistics of Aristotle. Yet mathematical language, the calculus of propositions, is a system of symbols equally applicable to electronic switching-circuitry as to assertions made in natural language. The symbolic logic of propositional and predicational relations seems to prescind from any intrinsic connection with direct assertions or general truths (premises based on species-identities, as in Aristotle's *eidei*). The formalism achieved by relational logic seems to render irrelevant any

iii

specific enbeddedness in any particular domain of reasoning. Just as geometrical axioms are no longer bound to the domain of real circles (physical figures) but are operable with contrary postulates, so too logic is now gradually freed of any naturally given syntax.

The result is philosophical uncertainty. Is traditional syllogistics still a feasible model for rational discourse and for the explanatory elaboration of proof or is it merely an interesting variant of a larger system based on widely accepted but contingent postulates? Further, is logic in an essential way largely irrelevant to our everyday nonscientific argumentation?

This philosophical uncertainty can be seen in the pedagogical chaos of logic textbooks. While generally reluctant to revive Aristotelian syllogistics, textbooks become increasingly experimental in an effort to bring forth a model for rationality. There are texts which put forward unadulterated mathematical logic, a branch of pure mathematics, and ignore the intelligent student who winces at the excruciating violence done to language in the name of "translation" and "well-formed formulas." Other texts subscribe to an amorphously "informal" logic aimed at detecting fallacies, thus providing merely a negative model for rationality. And then there are numerous attempts at "rhetorical" approaches to material logic, efforts that demonstrate great ingenuity but begin from arbitrary starting points, and in which complex rules for diagramming arguments are proliferated, but with no foundation in systematic intellectual principles.

It is not therefore surprising when a philosopher comes boldly forth and declares provocatively that we have "two logics" (Henry Veatch's book by that title in 1969): first, a traditional (Aristotelian) logic with rules for the predicative inferences "natural" to the spoken and written word; and second, a "spider-like" calculus which weaves logical relations of great technical power and abstraction without, however, being grounded in any particular human purposes or without being interpretive of a definite experiential domain. To point out such a state of affairs or *quid facti* is troubling not only on account of the pedagogical perplexity. We are left philosophically uneasy with the existence of "two logics" until we can answer the question *quid iuris*: By what right do we advance one over the other as a standard or model for reasoning? Is it possible philosophically to *ground* the primacy of one over the other?

The question is exacerbated by recent developments in combinatorial logic systems. Artificial languages are springing from formal systems and are increasingly widespread in computational and cybernetic applications. The formalized logic of these systems is rapidly becoming a "second language" throughout the global culture. Is rationality thus unitary, homogeneous insofar as we abstract from natural language with its heavy baggage of historical accretions and organic growth? Or are we permanently involved with two or more logics, it being necessary to work out each formal system from the perspective of the language we inherit as members of a historical culture? Is mathematical logic a culture-neutral opportunity to shed the blind accumulations of history? Or is it the intellect's most dangerous game to weave a free-floating rationality that is no longer rooted in the communication that occurs among certain mammals in cultural situations?

Put simply, the crisis arising from the current plurality of logics is how to ground a logic as a model of rationality or whether or not to ground logic at all. A logic may be grounded by demonstrating its *rootedness* in reality, through a theoretical metaphysics that shows the necessity of logical truth. Besides establishing metaphysical rootedness, another way of grounding logic is to argue for the ontological commitments of a given logical system, by showing what reality structures the logic refers to by *implication*. These two ways of grounding, rootedness and implication, differ in their respective directions: metaphysical rootedness grounds by proceeding from an account of reality to the rationality of a logic; the way of implication begins with a rational system and proceeds to the structures of reality implied by that system. For instance, the traditional predilection for Aristotle's syllogistics rests on the rootedness of that logic in an orderly structure of being: reasoning through inferences based on increasing generality and ontological intelligibility (i.e., permanence and hierarchical integrity of being) provides a scheme in which arguments can be adjudicated by referring finally to higher and qualitatively more valuable "first principles," even to the ultimate appeal to a Prime Mover or originary principle (first premise). Aristotelian logic is an example of logic grounded through its rootedness in ontology.

The Metaphysical Foundations of Logic (hereafter *MFL*) by Martin Heidegger is a study of the ontological commitments of a system of logic as that logic is rooted in a theory of reality or metaphysics. But in Heidegger's work neither "ontology" nor "commitment" pass for self-evident or unanalyzable assumptions. In fact, the chief endeavor of the volume of lectures is to patiently develop a rich notion of commitment as it pertains to the grounds of inferential reasoning, as well as a rich notion of ontological grounding as it involves an inherent commitment. And the book as a whole is yet another facet of Heidegger's sustained attempt to question the ramified significance and current potential of the traditional term "ontology." One will be therefore disappointed if one seeks here a founding of logic upon naked appeal to "what there is," or to "actual existence," or to "mathematical Platonism" as mythical belief in the "reality of abstract entities." Heidegger's discussion does indeed touch on Platonic ontology, but does so by raising questions regarding the implicit temporalization of "being" in Plato's sense of the term. In other words, mathematical Platonism is here treated less as a commonplace "ism" than as an opportunity to re-think Plato's point of departure.

The original German title of *MFL*, *Metaphysische Anfangsgründe der Logik im Ausgang von Leibniz*, makes explicit reference to Gottfried Wilhelm Leibniz (1646–1716). The entire first half of *MFL* is a meticulous exegesis of Leibniz's notion of propositional truth. In it Heidegger claims to have proven the rootedness of Leibnizian logical theory in the monadological metaphysics of Leibniz. The *Anfangsgründe* of the title is virtually untranslatable, as is also *im Ausgang von*. *Anfangsgründe* covers meanings such as "elemental bases," "initial premises," and "principial grounds." *Im Ausgang von* can mean "beginning with," as well as "proceeding from." So the original title refers to the foundations or grounds of logic as it is found in and as it develops out of Leibniz. The specific nature of that foundation, whether of rootedness or of implication, is the matter elaborated in the volume, though these terms are not Heidegger's.

Leibniz pioneered, among other things, the logical calculus. Both Bertrand Russell and Alfred North Whitehead, co-authors of the epochal *Principia Mathematica* (1910–13), were indebted to him. Whitehead's metaphysics is a striking parallel to the monadology, and Russell's first major book is *A Critical Exposition of the Philosophy of Leibniz* (1900). It was Leibniz's peculiar approach to inferential reasoning which made him the shaper of modern logic. As early as the *De arte combinatoria* (1666), he believed inferential reasoning to be assimilable to a universal calculus of human knowledge. Such an exhaustive calculus would require a "universal grammar," a *characteristica universalis*, which would serve to formalize in a deductively rigorous way all reasoning and scientific proof. The science of symbols proposed by Leibniz was to establish and foster the organized unification of scientific research within a single system of combination and permutation. To this end also, Leibniz worked on different models of the calculating machine throughout his lifetime. Appropriately enough, it was Leibniz's binary number system which was to be used centuries later by John von Neumann in developing electronic computers at Princeton.

But Leibniz was more than a logician. His contributions go beyond mathematics to include physical science, theology, politics, and history. As a courtier, diplomat, and ecumenical theologian, Leibniz worked constantly toward the harmonious unification of the European world—he was even a pioneer Sinologist. His creative advocacy of a universal symbolics seems to have had as much to do with furthering international cooperative work in the sciences as it did with the "pure" invention of a formally rigorous language system. In an age of religious wars and with the inception of national states, Leibniz devoted his energies to the formation of a harmonious world-federation based on the context-neutral language of scientific understanding. For Leibniz, scientific understanding contravened neither theology nor ancient philosophy; all could be conciliated within a single ordered system. As a proponent of organized research, Leibniz developed a modern theory of rationality to unify the civilized world, and his monadological metaphysics may be viewed as a projection of the first principles of a diverse but homogeneous world-order.

In his book on Leibniz, Bertrand Russell completely dissociates Leibniz the logician from Leibniz the metaphysician, suggesting that the metaphysical and theological writings represent not the real views of Leibniz but merely the public mask shaped under social and political pressures. Countering this once-dominant assessment, Heidegger's lectures on Leibniz in *MFL* show step-by-step the rootedness of Leibnizian logic in the ontology of the monad. Proof for the interdependence of logic and ontology is a detailed demonstration of the intrinsic correlation between the truth structure of the proposition and the metaphysical structure of the monad. Issuing from this demonstration is Heidegger's claim that the philosophical consideration of logic is properly a "metaphysics of truth." In other words, philosophical logic is of a piece with the philosophical questions of metaphysics. And to sever Leibniz the logician from Leibniz the metaphysician is to prevent a properly philosophical understanding of the model of modern rationality initiated by Leibniz.

Yet it would be misleading to introduce *MFL* as a mainly destructive attack on the prevailing picture of a dichotomized Leibniz. Like Heidegger's *Kantbuch*, his *Leibnizbuch* is a critical destruction in another sense. *MFL* constitutes another part of the larger project begun in *Being and Time*, another facet of the endeavor to raise again the question of being through a critical re-examination of the philosophical tradition. Just as the *Kantbuch* challenges the isolation of an epistemology presumably freed of ontological assumptions, so, similarly, the *Leibnizbuch* questions the isolation of a formal logic independent of ontological truth. Heidegger shows, through the specific analysis of Leibniz and through other more general arguments, that logic is grounded in a definite conception of being.

It is not that Heidegger calls attention to the ontological foundations of logic in order to insert under logic some preconceived ontology of his own. While the critical destruction of logical formalism does indeed belong to the "fundamental ontology" developed in *Being and Time,* the work of fundamental or foundational ontology is itself directed not at producing yet another and different ontology but it aims at reawakening a sense for the meaning of "being" as a question. The "fundamental" ontology of Dasein is therefore part of Heidegger's exploration of foundational problems, and that is why the discussion of *Being and Time* and the clarification of his descriptive ontology of Dasein play such an important role in *MFL.* Strong evidence for the foundational nature of the ontology Heidegger develops—as opposed to an ontology to rival that of Leibniz—is the frequency with which the formulations of the foundational ontology reflect the influence of the Leibnizian conception they are to illuminate. This reciprocity is at times uncanny, especially in the original German, and Heidegger explicitly refers to this hermeneutical circularity near the end of the book.

What the second half of *MFL* explores is the very nature of foundations or grounds. The reader who was once perplexed by the gnomic succinctness of *Vom Wesen des Grundes* (translated by Terrence Malik as *The Essence of Reasons*) or by the poetic reaches of *Der Satz vom Grund* will find here much light, because the lectures spell out every, or nearly every, step of an intricate argument. The progressive discovery of the metaphysical foundations of Leibnizian logic leads to the meta-foundational questions about the *meaning* of "grounding," of "commitment," of the substantive "being" referred to by metaphysics. Here Heidegger analyzes "ontological commitment" as something considerably more weighty and fateful than the mere implications of a form of "discourse" or "theory." He takes apart the ontological root of Leibnizian logic to exhibit temporal ecstases of Dasein's understanding-of-being, and he explicates commitment as the freely self-obligating structure of finite existence. To state it preemptively as a conclusion or "result," ontology or an understanding-of-being is the intrinsic free movement of Dasein to commit itself to a "world" or complex of involvements.

The metaphysics, then, which Heidegger finds at the foundation of modern logic is not simply an ontology of things, of substances and their relations, of individuals and their predicable properties. It is rather a pre-theoretical and implicit projection of a "world" by finite freedom. Such is the meaning of metaphysical statements; they are expressive of world or of a context of involvements. The world, in this sense, is an existential matrix for the generation of things, of individuals and their predicates. So it is the process of grounding that is to be observed in the world-disclosing significance of metaphysical statements and not simply some absolute referent of a metaphysical principle. Rather than a fixed set of conceptions, the metaphysics uncovered reveals the historical world or implicit contexture of meaning of the logic in question, what historians call the *Sitz im Leben* or "life-setting" of the logic. There is some resemblance here to John Dewey's efforts to deconstruct the theoretical independence of formal logic by finding logic to be an immanent procedure for solving "problematic situations." In the pragmatic understanding, logical formalism is a reconstructed version of the historically concrete logic-in-use. But the resemblance ends at the point where Dewey proposes the scientific model of inquiry as continuous with "how we think," whereas Heidegger regards thinking as an epochally transformative process based on a finite cultural project or ontological understanding of reality.

What then is the existential meaning or historical world discovered in Leibnizian metaphysics as the root of modern formal logic? *MFL* is a complex work of symphonic intelligence and any brief answer must necessarily impoverish Heidegger's polyphony of themes. But part of the answer has to do with the projection of a model for a universal modern rationality. The ontological commitment that grounds the Leibnizian calculus of propositions does project a certain world-meaning or way of involving oneself with things.

The foundational terms Heidegger employs for the analysis of metaphysical structures include "being-in-the-world" and the "temporal ecstases" of being. Being-in-the-world is itself a primal temporalization or movement of transcendental time. Within the trajectory of time—which is "transcendence" or the original "place" within which the relation between subject and object appears—all things are shaped, including the substantivization of things, the consciousness of subjectivity, and the coherence of systems. The self-grounding, self-initiating trajection of temporality is the paradigmatic ground for all other forms of ground: causes, reasons, proofs, and essences. Thus each "world" has its own peculiar temporalization of things, where everything is gathered within the circumscription of a characteristic "mood" or type of *Befindlichkeit* ("disposition" or state-of-mind, the way we for the most part find ourselves).

The temporalizing mood peculiar to Leibniz's analytical formalism, i.e., to mathematical logic, is the all-at-once simultaneity of totalizing presentness. Heidegger shows how the Leibnizian analycity of formal truth is grounded in an existential project to shape rationality along the lines of a distinct metaphysical model. The model is that of the *visio Dei*, the deity's intuitive cognition which was put into the philosophical tradition by the Aristotelianizing Scholastics. It is the knowledge of God, at least in its temporalizing simultaneity, that serves as model for human cognition in the modern world as projected in the metaphysics of Leibniz.

It is not unusual to connect the origin of logical operators and syntactical structures with the awareness of moods. For instance, H.H. Price in his *Thinking and Experience* (Cambridge, 1953, p. 124) asserts: "Disappointed expectation is what brings NOT into our lives," and Price goes on to connect the syntax of existential quantification and material implication to other experiential conditions. In his "What Is Metaphysics?" of 1929, Heidegger considers logical negation to be more derivative than basic kinds of negative experiences, such as harsh opposition, refusal, painful failure, and prohibitive strictures; these experiences open us, through anxiety, to a primal dimension of the world which can then be the basis for the understanding of logical negation in a formal sense. The philosophical priority of "annihilative experiences" would be obliterated or at least concealed if it were necessary first to subject them to a clean and rigid notion of formal negation, as Carnap tries to do—in his harsh *opposition* to Heidegger's study of nihilation.

But in *MFL* the moodful dimensions of the world are additionally temporalized in the ecstases of primal time, and the temporalized world-project is the root from which formalized *systems*, and not only logical operations, as such grow. Thus Heidegger finds the ontological commitment of modern formalism not in some presumptive referents of a system. Ontological meaning is not to be found merely in the suppositions a developed formal system makes about what there is. Rather, formalism displays a contraction of the temporalization process that gathers things into a certain kind of presence. The Leibnizian ideal of complete analycity in a systematic totality of true propositions is, culturally or *seinsgeschichtlich,* the continuation of the absolute presentness of the medieval divinity. Later on in his work Heidegger describes the modern period as epochal displacement of the medieval search for the salvation of the soul by the quest for mathematical certitude in a homogenized world-culture. There are startling breaks in the epochal history of being, but there is also an unforeseen and unlikely continuity in retrospect.

These introductory remarks began by referring to two questions: Do the necessities of a logical system reflect, or correspond to, necessities in reality? Do we need a single logic to provide an accurate model of rationality? In conclusion, answers to these questions can only be adumbrated in the briefest possible way.

In the *MFL* we find that Heidegger argues: (1) propositional logic is founded on a metaphysics of truth which is in turn founded on a general metaphysics—though the general metaphysics may not be immediately accessible and may require an excavation of latent principles; (2) the meaning of metaphysical statements needs clarification through an existential analysis which describes the experiential being-in-the-world derived from a finite world-project. To say that logic is rooted in metaphysics eliminates the problem of how to get logic to "picture" or "correspond to" reality; as an outgrowth of metaphysics, logic is a branch organically expressing the whole of an understanding-of-being. Other branches of that understanding include painting, architecture, and politics—all various world-disclosures of being. The necessities envisioned in a system of logic are founded in the self-obligating freedom that projects a world to which one is committed. And "commitment" means the determinate way in which transcendental time is contracted into a definite presencing of beings. Furthermore, understanding-of-being is not an arbitrarily manageable human capacity, but is the existential structure (Dasein) of the transcendence that characterizes human beings in their freedom and unfreedom.

Through his existential analysis of "world," Heidegger undercuts the question concerning the universal model of rationality. Grounding is not only inferential; it is also existential. Since world, in the existential sense, admits of a plurality, the analysis of the Leibnizian metaphysics supporting modern logic highlights the finitude of the project to homogenize a planetary culture through a unified symbolics. Such a world represents indeed a unified oneness, but it remains, existentially, one of many possible worlds. In terms of its metaphysical meaning, however, the projection of a unitary world may be a European destiny that has been overcome from within by Heidegger's own inquiry into the existential meaning of metaphysical truth. The European search for an absolute foundation, the *fundamentum absolutum et inconcussum* of Descartes, may be regarded as a great "Event" in which we still move, but from which we are now moving away. We are increasingly aware of the delightful and abysmal freedom to create a plurality of logical systems, and there is a growing critical awareness that claims to completeness are deluded, even though such claims necessarily haunt every act of systematizing.

What then of the new "philosophical logic" Heidegger calls for? How would such a postmodern logic take shape in the developing and teaching of a postmodern model of rationality?

If we take our bearings from the later work of Heidegger, we can surmise that such a logic-in-the-making would emphasize the place or *topos* where two or more different worlds meet, where an exchange takes place over the gap of mutually divergent domains of meaning and involvement. Such a logic or *logos* would be self-opening and inherently translucent to that which lies beyond its own incompleteness. The later works suggest the model for postmodern logic by portraying the paradigm of conversation: philosophy converses with poetry; the philosophy of technology converses with Parmenides; the German philosopher has a dialogue with the Japanese philosopher. Fittingly enough, the give-and-take of conversation was the original locus within which the logic of argumentation was first studied and formulated by Aristotle. But more than argumentation is required in postmodern logic. In "A Conversation about Language between a Japanese and an Inquirer," Heidegger has written in and emphasized the silences and intermittent hesitancies before what is unsayable between East and West, between two (or more) worlds. It may be necessary for logic, as a model of rationality, to protect the interstices of the unsayable, to affirm the fragile finitude of cultural symbolics. For without the patient protection of the plurality of worlds and of what is unsayable between them, there may be less likelihood of nurturing a diversified planetary culture as a response to the threat of the unspeakable.

The Metaphysical Foundations
of Logic

Studies in Phenomenology and
Existential Philosophy

Martin Heidegger

The Metaphysical Foundations of Logic

Translated by

Michael Heim

Indiana University Press

BLOOMINGTON

Preparation of this book was aided by a grant from the Program for Translations of the National Endowment for the Humanities, an independent federal agency.

Published in German as *Metaphysische Anfangsgründe der Logik im Ausgang von Leibniz*
© 1978 by Vittorio Klostermann

Library of Congress Cataloging in Publication Data

Heidegger, Martin, 1889-1976.
   The metaphysical foundations of logic.

   (Studies in phenomenology and existential philosophy)
   Translation of: Metaphysische Anfangsgründe der Logik im Ausgang
von Leibniz.
   Includes bibliographical references and index.
   1. Leibniz, Gottfried Wilhelm, Freiherr von, 1646-1716—Logic—
Addresses, essays, lectures. 2. Logic—Addresses, essays, lectures.
3. Reason—Addresses, essays, lectures. 4. Metaphysics—Addresses,
essays, lectures. 5. Transcendence (Philosophy)—Addresses, essays,
lectures. I. Title. II. Series.
B3279.H48M4713   1984   160   83-48649

ISBN 0-253-33783-6
1 2 3 4 5 88 87 86 85 84

Contents

Key to References Cited in the Text

Throughout the text, references to Leibniz's works have, whenever possible, been referred to in the English-language edition of Leibniz's papers and letters translated by Loemker. The English translations from Leibniz have, on occasion, undergone slight modifications so as to correspond to Heidegger's German version, and deviations in meaning are noted in the translator's notes. Along with the English-language texts, Heidegger's own German references are also given; the English and the original references are identified by the following code letters:

C.= Louis Couturat, *Opuscules et fragments inédits de Leibniz*, Paris, 1903. Latin and French.

E.= Joh. Ed. Erdmann, *Leibnitii Opera Philosophica quae extant Latina, Gallica, Germanica Omnia*, 2 vols., Berlin, 1840.

G.= C. I. Gerhardt, *Die philosophischen Schriften von Gottfried Wilhelm Leibniz*, 7 vols., Berlin, 1875–90.

L.= Leroy Loemker, *Gottfried Wilhelm Leibniz: Philosophical Papers and Letters*, 2nd edition, D. Reidel Publishing Co., Boston, 1969.

F.= L. A. Foucher de Careil, *Nouvelles Lettres et Opuscules inédits de Leibniz*, Paris 1857; reprint, Hildesheim, 1971.

B.= A. Buchenau, translator, *G. W. Leibniz, Hauptschriften zur Grundlegung der Philosophie*, edited by E. Cassirer, 2 vols. (Philosophische Bibliotek, vols. 107 and 108), Leipzig, 1904–06.

The Metaphysical Foundations
of Logic

Introduction

I. On the traditional conception of logic

The expression "logic" is an abbreviation of the Greek λογική. To complete it ἐπιστήμη must be added: the science that deals with λόγος.* Here *logos* means as much as "speech," specifically in the sense of *statement,* predication. The latter consists in saying something about something: the body is heavy, the triangle is equilateral, Kant died in 1804, "king" is a substantive noun, nature is objectively present. Such statements express a *determining something as something,* a *determinatio.* We call this determining *thinking.* Accordingly, logic, the science of the λόγος, is the science of thinking. But the thinking which determines is at the same time, as a determining of something as something, a determination about X.† Something, a body for example, is determined as something, as, for example, heavy. The "relationship," something (asserted) of something, the predication, is at the same time intrinsically related to a being about which a determination is given in these determinations. That about which determinations are made

---

*"Science" is used here to translate the German *"Wissenschaft,"* which is in turn used by Heidegger to translate the Greek *episteme.* Both German and Greek terms have a somewhat broader meaning than the English "science" and are by no means restricted to a knowledge of facts or a theoretical grasp of nature. *Wissenschaft* refers to any organized body of knowledge.

†The German reads "eine Bestimmung über. . . ." I add here the generalized variable symbol to facilitate reading, but at the same time wish to warn the reader that, due to Heidegger's ontological intent, we must be cautious in our use of logical-mathematical formalism at the level of examining a phenomenon such as assertion.

1

is the being itself. That of which something is said is that about which something is said as object of predication. We are thus dealing with the articulating disclosure and determination of the being itself. We can represent it like this:

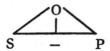

Of its own accord, a determining so understood tries to measure up to that about which the statement is made. This measuring up to that about which the determination and statement are made, the *adaequatio,* characterizes what we generally mean by the truth of statements. Λόγος can be adequate or inadequate, true or false. Every factically* performed λόγος is necessarily either true or false, because it is always essentially a statement about something. (A claim, to be sure, which will occupy us in great detail later.)

Now logic as science of λόγος does not investigate all the factical statements that have ever been made about everything possible and impossible, both true and false. Nor does it investigate only all the true statements. Rather, logic asks about the properties in general of λόγος, of statement, of that determining where the essence of thinking as such resides.

But thinking is a thinking *about* something. All real thinking has its theme, and thus relates itself to a definite object, i.e., to a definite being which in each case confronts us, a physical thing, a geometrical object, a historical event, a "linguistic phenomenon." These objects (of nature, of space, of history) belong to different domains. They differ in their subject-matters, each differing completely in the kind of thing it is. Plants are something other than geometrical objects, while the latter are completely different from, say, a literary work. But these things are also different in the way they are, as things existing either naturally or historically. The determinative thinking which is to measure up to the particular being in question must also take into account a corresponding di-

---

*"Faktische Aussagen" does not, in this context, mean "factual statements" in the sense of statements of fact, nor does "faktisch vollzogene Aussagen" mean "factually performed statements" in the sense of statements performed as a matter of course. Instead, *faktisch,* here and elsewhere, means something like "having actually transpired" or "having historical reality." In order to allow this meaning to come through with the least amount of syntactical complexity, I have allowed the Germanism "factical" to carry this somewhat special meaning. Cf. also Hofstadter's Lexicon, p. 356, of his translation of Heidegger's *The Basic Problems of Phenomenology* (Bloomington: Indiana University Press, 1982).

versity regarding what and how the being in each case is. The thought determination, i.e., the concept formation, will differ in different domains. Scientific investigation of this thinking is in each case correspondingly different: the logic of thinking in physics, the logic of mathematical thinking, of philosophical, historical, theological, and even more so, philosophical thinking. The logic of these disciplines is related to a subject-matter. It is a *material logic*.

But a logic pure and simple—a "general" logic, which relates neither to a thought determination of nature nor to one of space or of history—logic pure and simple has for its theme thinking about X. But about what? Its theme is indeed thinking about X in general, but the object of thinking is always a definite object. Yet logic's theme is not the thinking about this or that. Is its theme then a thinking about nothing? "Thinking about nothing" is ambiguous. First of all it can mean "not to think." But logic as the science of thinking obviously never deals with not thinking. Secondly, it can mean "to think nothingness," which nonetheless means to think "something." In thinking of nothingness, or in the endeavor to think "it," I am thoughtfully related to nothingness, and this is what the thinking is about.

All thinking is, qua thinking, related to X. If I now consider thinking in general, then what the thinking is about is irrelevant. Yet the irrelevance of an object does not mean no object at all. Rather in each case there is an object, but it does not matter which object. It is anything that can be thought. That to which thinking relates is—from the viewpoint of logic—anything and cannot be decided from the idea of thinking as such. As science of thinking in general, logic simply does not consider thinking qua thinking of this or that object of such-and-such properties. It does not attend to the special what and how of that to which thinking relates. But this disregard of the particular subject-matter and way of being of the thing thought about never implies that thinking in general does not relate to anything. It only implies that the object of thinking is irrelevant—as long as that about which thinking thinks confronts us, as such, only as *something*. Because of this irrelevance, the specific subject-matter plays no role; the "material," the what of the objects, is indifferent. It is only important that something be intended in thinking. "Anything at all"—without regard to its what (its matter)—is not a definite content-relevant object, but only the "form" of an object. Thinking taken as thinking about something, with any subject-matter, is formal thought, in contradistinction to material, content-relevant thought. This formal thinking is not without an object, but is very much object-oriented, though neutral with respect to content. General logic, as knowledge of formal thinking, is thus *formal logic*.

This general logic, logic simply, treats then whatever belongs to a thinking about anything at all, treats that which makes thinking, as such, intrinsically possible, treats the lawfulness that every thinking, as thinking, must satisfy. Thus logic is also characterized as the science of the formal rules of thought. Yet this characterization remains unclear. Not only the problem of correctness, but also the problem of "truth" belongs to logic, albeit only in a formal way. Correctness and "formal truth" (i.e., the form of truth in general) are not really the same; this is unclear in Kant.

The rigorous conception of a formal logic has been developed only infrequently, and never in its principle. However, that which is to comprise such a logic is partially, though confusedly, the content of the logic that developed under the impetus of Aristotle and solidified into an academic discipline since the Stoa in the last centuries before the Christian era. Kant has this logic in mind when in the preface to the second edition of the *Critique of Pure Reason* (B VIII, f.), he expresses his opinion of logic:

> That logic has already, from the earliest times, proceeded upon this sure path is evidenced by the fact that, since Aristotle, it has not required to retrace a single step, unless, indeed, we care to count as improvements the removal of certain needless subtleties or the clearer exposition of its recognized teaching, features which concern the elegance rather than the certainty of the science. It is remarkable also that, to the present day, this logic has not been able to advance a single step, and is thus to all appearance a closed and completed body of doctrine. . . . That logic should have been thus successful is an advantage which it owes entirely to its limitations, whereby it is justified in abstracting—indeed, it is under obligation to do so—from all objects of knowledge and their differences, leaving the understanding nothing to deal with save itself and its form.

We will not as yet address ourselves to the fact that Kant himself, though quite unclearly and uncertainly, took a step which turned out to be the first step forward in philosophical logic since Aristotle and Plato.

What we have just described as formal logic is also, however, what floats vaguely enough before the mind when someone speaks of "logic." To this day, albeit with some reservations, it is said that this logic is the propaedeutic to academic studies, as well as an introduction to philosophy.

But this estimation of logic—perhaps at bottom correct—conflicts with an all-too-frequent experience we may not conceal from ourselves. This logic stalwartly taught by philosophy professors does not speak to its students. It is not only dry as dust; it leaves the student perplexed in the end. He finds no connection between this logic and his own academic study. And it certainly never becomes clear what use this logic is supposed to have, unless it be so paltry and basically unworthy a use as the preparation of more-or-less convenient material for an examination. Nor does this technical and academic logic furnish a conception of philosophy. Its pursuit leaves the student outside philosophy, when it does not actually drive him from it.

On the other hand, it is surely no criterion for the genuineness and intrinsic legitimacy of a science or philosophical discipline that it does or does not appeal to students—least of all today, when the inner rebellion against knowledge, the revolt against rationality, and the struggle against intellectualism have become fashionable. There is need for another logic, but not for the sake of providing more entertaining and appealing classroom material. We need another logic solely because what is called logic is not a logic at all and has nothing in common anymore with philosophy.

In the end, logic is in fact a propaedeutic to academic studies in general and is, at the same time, quite correctly valued as an essential entry into philosophy—assuming that logic itself is philosophical. So this is the challenge: logic should change; logic should become philosophical!

But what sort of enterprise is it to want to shift the foundations of a bimillenial tradition? Is not the very intention then absurd? Should something like a new logic be created, new laws of thought invented and the old ones overturned? Can, for instance, the principle of non-contradiction—in Kant's formulation: "no predicate contradictory of a thing can belong to it" (*Critique of Pure Reason*, A 151, B 190)—be replaced by a better one? Or is the principle of sufficient reason (*nihil sine ratione*: nothing without a reason)—which among other things implies that every true statement requires its grounds—to be made dispensable by a new logic? If not, what then is the intention? Are there any new, or better, more radical possibilities of philosophical questioning with regard to, for example, the aforementioned basic laws of thought? Are not these laws completely self-evident, immediately intelligible and convincing to everyone? Can anything more be said of them than that they can be so "formulated": A=A; non-A≠A?

Only if it belonged to the essence of philosophy to make the obvious incomprehensible and the unquestioned something questionable! Only if philosophy had the task of shocking common sense out of its presumptive self-glorification! Only if philosophy had the function of arousing us so that we become awake to see that, with a lot of hullabaloo and expenditure of activity, we wander around for the most part exclusively in the superficial regions of our existence, in intellectual matters as well! If philosophy had such a task, then the idea of what we call logic would, finally and directly, become fundamentally intelligible. It would become clear that we have tasks before us which in no way fall short of the tasks taken up by the philosophers of ancient times.

If we succeed in clarifying the idea of a philosophical logic, then the genuine history of logic will also become transparent. Then it will be clear that the thread of logic's "development" was already broken with Aristotle and Plato and could not be picked up again—despite all the new impulses that entered logic through Leibniz, Kant, and Hegel, and finally through Husserl.

II. Introduction to the idea of philosophy

But how should a *philosophical* logic be set in motion? Where can we get even an idea of such a logic?

The way seems simple: All we need to do is delineate the concept of philosophy and define what logic is in the light of this concept. This way, however, is a long detour. We are confronted, in particular, by the following question: Where do we get our concept of philosophy? Philosophy is not of course something objectively present and at hand, about which we can have and exchange opinions. Surely the idea of logic will have its origin in the idea of philosophy. But this says nothing about the mode and manner, how and in what order we conceive this dependence by origination.

We choose another path for characterizing the idea of philosophical logic. We shall try to loosen up the traditional logic in such a way that central problems in it become clear, and from the content of these very problems we shall allow ourselves to be led back into the presuppositions of this logic. In this way we shall gain immediate access to philosophy itself. We shall then not have to ask how these logical problems relate to philosophy. Such a procedure has manifold advantages. First, we shall become familiar with what the traditional logic treated. Be its contents ever so dead, it once arose from a living philosophy. The task now is to release it from petrifaction. But at the same time we are acquiring a familiarity by which the traditional material is brought within the horizon of problems that are not arbitrary but central to philosophy. We thus finally arrive at a concept of philosophy in a concrete way. We obtain an "intro-duction" to philosophy which does not stand outside of philosophy and spin yarns about what was thought about philosophy and could possibly be thought about it today, but an "intro-duction" which leads into philosophy itself. One can never philosophize "in general," but rather every genuine philosophical problem is, in each case, a single specific problem. But, on the other hand, no genuine philosophical problem is a so-called specialized problem. Every genuine problem is a fundamental problem.

N.B. The widespread sterility of academic philosophy courses is also caused by the attempt to instruct the students with the well-known broad brushstrokes, in possibly one semester, about everything in the world, or about even more than that. One is supposed to learn to swim, but only goes meandering on the riverbank, converses about the murmuring of the stream, and talks about the cities and towns the river passes. This guarantees that the spark never flashes over to the individual student, kindling a light in him which can never be extinguished in his Dasein.*

In short, we can gain access to philosophy through the concrete problems of logic. True, one might say that this very process of loosening logic in its philosophical roots and problems likewise already presupposes an understanding of philosophy. For only then can the loosening produce an occasion for establishing and maintaining a direction toward philosophy and staying on course. That is indeed indisputable. But from this we can only immediately infer that the teacher of a certain way must already have in view the way's direction, that he really must have, as it were, already been where he wishes to take us. The manner in which he leads must betray whether he has already really been there, or whether he is only relating what others surmise about it, who have not themselves been there either. But to provide the student with a preliminary glimpse, we had best come to an understanding about the idea of philosophy, though in a very provisional way. This is not required merely in consideration of the particular steps of this lecture course, but even more so in consideration of your having devoted your current Dasein to academic studies, and that always means, explicitly or not, to philosophy. To what extent this

---

*"Dasein" does not necessarily carry the full theoretical content of a terminus technicus at this point, but may have the usually vague general denotation of "existence." Here it is left in German, as it is throughout the translation, to indicate the wide range of Heidegger's language, which is rooted in everyday usage even in its most creative elaborations of meaning.

is happening and has happened out of an inner freedom, whether there is an actual will behind this decision, how far the compass of this form of existence at the university as such is clear or is deliberately left in darkness and indifference, all that is a matter for the individual.

When we attempt to characterize the idea of philosophy in a provisional way, that is, to find for ourselves where and in what way anything like philosophy is to be attained at all, then we can adopt various paths which are not arbitrary and accidental, but which are simply the reflection, as it were, of philosophy itself.

For reasons which will first become intelligible on the basis of a clear conception of philosophy, the following is important for all the ways of characterizing the idea of philosophy: Philosophy can be characterized only from and in historical recollection. But this recollection is only what it is, is only living, in the moment of self-understanding, and that means in one's own free, productive grasp of the task harbored in philosophy.*

The ways of historical recollection and of reflection on the present are not two ways, but are both essential elements of every way toward the idea of philosophy. This idea is to be defined not by our devising, say, a so-called modern notion of philosophy, so that we may then consult the history of philosophy in retrospect to find out what has already been thought and intimated of our idea and what has not. Nor is it an appropriate procedure for us to pick out a philosophy from history, be it the philosophy of Plato or Aristotle, or of Leibniz or Kant, and simply install ourselves in it as in the presumptive truth, in order then to tailor and supplement it, as it were, for modern needs. There is not a historical definition of philosophy and next to it a so-called systematic definition, nor conversely. What is needed, rather, is a definition "from historicity."† Historical description is dead if it is not systematic, and sys-

---

*The notion here of the *geschichtliche Erinnerung* that takes place *im augenblicklichen Sichselbstverstehen* or *augenblicklichen Besinnung* is of course the theme of a large part of the analysis in *Being and Time,* where the "self-reflective moment" or "reflection on the present" is a key to the three temporal ecstases. *Augenblickliche Besinnung* is translated as "present-focused reflection" or "reflection here and now" or "moment-focused reflection."

†Here Heidegger calls for a "geschichtliche Bestimmung," a "historical definition," in the sense of one which takes the temporal happenings of being seriously. He goes on to say that a "historische Kennzeichnung," a "historical description," in the sense of a characterization based on ascertainable historical facts and texts, is dead if it is not systematic. Hence the dichotomy "historisch-systematisch" is factitious as alternatives for describing philosophy in its essence; it is the "geschichtlich" definition of philosophy which overcomes this false dilemma. The translation uses "historicity" or "from historicity" to signal "historical" in the sense of *geschichtlich,* as opposed to *historisch.*

tematic description is empty if it is not historical. This shows the distinction is spurious and must be eliminated.

There is really only a single philosophical clarification of the idea of philosophy. This clarification is in itself *at once recollective and focused on the present.* There is here an original unity, that is, the unity of the temporality of the philosophizing factical Dasein itself; the full problematic must be unfolded from this unity. Only one's own free project is commensurable with what is recollected, and not the seemingly worthwhile but ultimately cowardly reliance on any tradition, even the most venerable.

The recollection from historicity is necessary not because we have already a long history of philosophy behind us, nor because piety demands that we also heed the ancients. Even if there were no explicit history of philosophy, it would still be necessary to go back and take up the tradition in which every human Dasein stands, whether it has a developed historical consciousness or not, and whether or not what it has to recollect is expressly called "philosophy."

III. The definition of philosophy according to Aristotle

Now the philosophical clarification of the idea of philosophy as recollecting and focusing on the present can itself follow various directions. Most proximate is the way of identifying philosophy by distinguishing it from the nonphilosophical sciences. After all, the connection philosophy has with the sciences has always been, for all its variations in details, a living one, because it is an essential connection. Yet we do not want to take this route, since the problem of the connection between philosophy and the positive sciences will occupy us within logic itself.

We will proceed, rather, from a direct "definition" of philosophy given by Aristotle. And we choose precisely this orientation because, in ancient thought, basic philosophical problems are intelligible in their elemental originality—which is not to say that all basic problems may have already been posed. In fact, ancient philosophy is a gigantic beginning, and as such it contains within itself a wealth of truly undeveloped and in part completely hidden possibilities. To this elemental originality and assurance of antiquity corresponds the disoriented psychologizing chattiness of contemporary philosophy. In short, the primordiality of antiquity corresponds to the *present necessity* of bringing problems back to simplicity; only in this way can they be given their full sharpness.

We furthermore choose Aristotle in ancient philosophy, since he represents the peak of the development of genuine ancient philosophy. But because philosophy is the most radically free endeavor of the finitude of man, it is in its essence more finite than any other. Aristotle is himself far from a fulfillment or even from a final clarity in what has been attained. This is seen in his very characterization of philosophy (*Meta. Γ* 1, 1003a 21f.): Ἔστιν ἐπιστήμη τις ἢ θεωρεῖ τὸ ὂν ἢ ὂν καὶ τα τούτῳ ὑπάρχοντα καθ' αὑτό. "There is a definite science which inquires into beings as being and into that which belongs to it as such." This science Aristotle calls φιλοσοφία πρώτη—first philosophy (*Meta.* E 1, 1026a 30), philosophy of what is first, philosophy of the first order and in the genuine sense. And he repeats this same characterization: καὶ περὶ τοῦ ὄντος ἢ ὂν ταύτης ἂν εἴη θεωρῆσαι, καὶ τί ἐστι καὶ τὰ ὑπάρχοντα ἢ ὂν (Ibid. 1026a 31f.). "And the task of this science would be to inquire into beings qua being, to clarify what it ⟨in this respect⟩ is and what belongs to it as such."

This description of philosophy seems extremely abstract and empty: the inquiry into beings as beings. What is meant is the investigation not of this or that being, this thing, this stone, this tree and this animal, this human being nor the investigation of all material bodies, all plants, animals, humans—that would in each case be the investigation of a specific region of that which is, of being. But neither does Aristotle say philosophy is inquiry into all beings taken collectively, all these regions taken together. Rather, what should be investigated is the τὸ ὂν ἢ ὂν—beings with regard to being, i.e., solely with regard to what makes a being the being it is: being. Knowledge of the first order, i.e., knowledge of the first, is knowledge of *being*.

But the meaning of "being" seems to remain obscure. We cannot imagine anything under this term. A being, this or that one, surely we can place it before our eyes—but being? Yet Aristotle certainly does not assert that what being is stands in full clarity; he says that this is precisely what is to be questioned. It is a problem. It is *the* problem of philosophy to pose this question in the right way and to explain what it is that belongs to being as such. Being as the theme of philosophy is indeed obscure. It can only be said negatively: the object of philosophy is nothing belonging among beings as a particular being.

At the same time, however, Aristotle speaks of genuine philosophy as θεολογικὴ (φιλοσοφία) (*Meta.* Ibid., 1026a 18ff.). This relates to the αἴτια τοῖς φανεροῖς τῶν θείων, the causes of what is superior manifesting itself in evident beings: . . . οὐ γὰρ ἄδηλον ὅτι εἴ που τὸ θεῖον ὑπάρχει, ἐν τῇ τοιαύτῃ φύσει ὑπάρχει, καὶ τὴν τιμιωτάτην δεῖ περὶ τὸ τιμιώτατον γένος εἶναι [it is clear that if the divine is present anywhere, it is present in this kind of entity: and also the most noble science must deal with the most noble type of being]; the highest science must be science of the highest, of the first. Τὸ θεῖον means simply beings—the heavens: the encompassing and overpowering, that under and upon which we are thrown, that which dazzles us and takes us by surprise, the overwhelming. θεολογεῖν is a contemplation of the κόσμος (cf. *de mundo* 391b 4). Let us keep in mind that philosophy, as first philosophy, has a twofold character: knowledge of being and knowledge of the overwhelming. (This twofold character corresponds to the twofold in *Being and Time* of existence and thrownness.)

Yet with this definition we have come to an initial orientation. For this science itself is not simply obvious. It is not a direct possession like everyday knowledge of things and of ourselves. The πρώτη φιλοσοφία is the ἐπιστήμη ζητουμένη: the science sought after, the science that can never become a fixed possession and that, as such, would just have to be passed on. It is rather the knowledge that can be obtained only if it is each time sought anew. It is precisely a venture, an "inverted world." That is, genuine understanding of being must itself always be first achieved.

It belongs to the essence of this science that it must be sought after. There is such knowing only if a search for and propensity toward it is alive, an inclination behind which there is effort and will. This knowledge is the voluntary leaning toward original understanding: φιλο-σοφία. Φιλεῖν means to love in the sense of to be concerned about something trustingly; σοφός means he who understands something, who can "under-stand" a matter, who surveys its possibilities, to whom the thing is transparent, who has grasped it; σοφία denotes the possibility of the correct conceptual understanding of what is essential. So in the *Nicomachean Ethics* (Z 7, 1141a 12) Aristotle defines σοφία as ἀρετὴ τέχνης, as the outstanding free disposition over knowing what one is about. "Wisdom," the usual translation, is in the main empty and misleading.

In the same passage it is said about the σοφός (Ibid., 1141b 3ff.): διὸ Ἀναξαγόραν καὶ Θαλῆν καὶ τοὺς τοιούτους σοφοὺς μὲν φρονίμους δ' οὔ φασιν εἶναι, ὅταν ἴδωσιν ἀγνοοῦντας τὰ συμφέροντα ἑαυτοῖς, καὶ περιττὰ μὲν καὶ θαυμαστὰ καὶ χαλεπὰ καὶ δαιμόνια εἰδέναι αὐτούς φασιν, ἄχρηστα δ', ὅτι οὐ τὰ ἀνθρώπινα ἀγαθὰ ζητοῦσιν.*

*"This is why people say that men like Anaxagoras and Thales 'may be wise but are not prudent,' when they see them display ignorance of their own interests; and while admitting them to possess a knowledge that is rare, marvellous, difficult and even superhuman, they yet declare this knowledge to be useless, because these sages do not seek to know the things that are good for human beings." Rackham translation.

We will comment on what is significant here for our context: Thus they say Anaxagoras and Thales and such people are σοφοί, understanding ones, because it is observed that these men do not look to their own interests and advantages but rather have an eye to the περιττά, to what lies beyond the everyday viewpoint of common sense—, for the θαυμαστά, for what arouses wonder, astonishment, i.e., what constantly impels toward new questions—, for the χαλεπά, the difficult, what is not attainable by the usual means of clever and quick ways of thinking—, for the δαιμόνια, that which pertains to humans as far as the ultimate and the whole are concerned and holds them in thrall (cf. *Meta.* A1&2). Things of this sort are the ἄχρηστα, useless for day-to-day necessities; these men do not seek after what humans commonly and on the average are interested in, pleasure and prestige.

Everything essential, however, which has decisive meaning without being conspicuous, is always attended by what only looks like the genuine and real thing, the *semblance*. This is why, in every period, philosophy must bring in its wake something that looks like philosophy and imitates it in manner and behavior, and even outdoes it—and yet at bottom poses an embarrassment. The semblance of the φιλόσοφος is the σοφιστής [sophist]. The latter does not strive for genuine understanding, has no perseverance, but only nibbles on everything, always just on the newest and usually on what is in fact even worthwhile, but he only nibbles on it and is seduced into mere curiosity and bluffing. He is not one who seeks to understand, i.e., not the one who truly understands. He is rather the rationalizer for whom nothing is certain, except those things he notices he cannot reach with his means. The latter he does not, however, simply leave alone but tries to show that just that sort of thing does not exist or is a fabrication of philosophers. For him it is all idle talk, regardless of whether it really exists or not. Οἱ γὰρ διαλεκτικοὶ καὶ σοφισταὶ τὸ αὐτὸ μὲν ὑποδύονται σχῆμα τῷ φιλοσόφῳ· ἡ γὰρ σοφιστικὴ φαινομένη μόνον σοφία ἐστί (*Meta.* Γ 2, 1004b 17ff.) [Dialecticians and sophists wear the same appearance as the philosopher, for sophistry is sophia in appearance only.]

φιλοσοφία differs from σοφιστική: τοῦ βίου τῇ προαιρέσει (Ibid., 1004b 24ff.), through existence already having been deeply moved in advance, i.e., through "seriousness."* The philosopher has

---

*Philosophy differs "durch das Im-vorhinein-ergriffenhaben der Existenz," where *Ergriffensein* means to be seized by a compelling affection and also implies the usual mental act of understanding connoted by *Ergreifen*. But "mental act" alone would suggest, too strongly, conscious control, where we are dealing with an a priori aspect of *Befindlichkeit*.

taken upon himself the seriousness of the concept, of fundamental questioning. Everything routine, everyday, average (fallenness) is the opposite of this endeavor. The sophist, on the contrary, as rationalizer and know-it-all, appoints himself to work on human beings, persuades them they must worry about one another's spiritual needs.

Φιλοσοφία is a striving for the possibility of genuine understanding. Thus it is really not the label for any sort of knowledge that could be freely circulated. It is not the possession of information and doctrines. Philosophy must essentially be sought after, that is, its object must be originally "earned." But where does philosophy find out which object it should take as object of its knowing?

The striving for the possibility of a correct understanding of the essential, or this understanding, has for its object *being*. This is what is essential. Understanding directed to this is *first* insofar as it is the understanding of what *precedes* everything else, what is earlier, prior to everything else, that is, prior to individual beings. But being is prior to individual beings, for it is what is first understood before anything like a being can arise anywhere and in any way.

Thus, philosophy is knowledge of being. Insofar as it strives for conceptual understanding and determination, for a λόγος of the ὄν ᾗ ὄν, it is *ontology*. This notion is not originally of Greek origin, but first appears late in the seventeenth century, for example in the Cartesian Clauberg. But little is achieved with this description as long as it is not made clear what sort of inner possibilities and tasks reside in such a science and what sort of bases it stands upon.

N.B. Philosophy tries to conceive being, not this or that being. Indeed, what do we mean then by being in contradistinction to beings? What is meant by the being of something present-at-hand? For example, the stone: it has a certain color, hardness, shine, spatial figure, weight, size. These belong to it as this being. It "is" all these, is such-and-such. But what is meant by its being—its being present-at-hand and its being such-and-such? The presence-at-hand of the stone is not itself present-at-hand in it, as is its color, hardness, etc. Proper to the stone is that on the basis of which I say it is present, even if I am not at the moment considering it, even if I myself am not. And what I mean by "myself" is also a being. Is that being also in being if I am not? Obviously not—"I" belongs to it. Yet these are not two, the being of a stone and of the ego. But it is the case that the being that can say "I" is such that it is committed to its being and is itself responsible for this being.

But philosophy is, in the first place, also ϑεολογική. What is meant by this, an appendage, a finishing touch, a world-view? Is φιλοσοφία a ϑεολογική only so as to have a conclusion? Or is philosophy either an ontology or a theology? Or is it both at once? Does that which is sought under the term "theology" in fact reside in the essence of philosophy understood totally and radically? Or is what arises in Aristotle as theology still a remnant of his early period? Is it the old metaphysics, and ontology the new metaphysics? And did an evolution take place from one to the other? These questions[1] cannot be resolved solely through historical-philological interpretation.[2] On the contrary, this interpretation itself requires that we be guided by an understanding of the problem which is a match for what is handed down. And we must first acquire such an understanding.[3] With the Aristotelian twofold description of philosophy as "ontology" and "theology," either nothing is said or everything, according to how we ourselves bring with us original possibilities of understanding. In what sense and to what extent then does theology belong to the essence of philosophy? To show this we would have to make clear what Aristotle quite vaguely, as ϑεολογική, crosses with philosophy. And we would have to make this intelligible in such a way that we would radicalize the notion of ontology. Thus we could also obtain a vantage point for answering the question about the relationship between philosophy and world-view. But with regard to our particular task, the important thing is to describe the general horizon within which a philosophical logic must move, a horizon which will become ours in more visible dimensions precisely through the concrete philosophical treatment of the basic problems of logic.

Our return to Aristotle will first become authentic recollection only when we philosophize here and now. But at the beginning of this lecture course we cannot yet think of pushing moment-focused reflection on the essence of philosophy so far as to be in a position to understand immediately how the Aristotelian definition and twofold characterization can become vital. At this point we can only suggest what is important with regard to moment-focused reflection.

1. Cf. Paul Natorp, "Thema und Disposition der Aristotelischen Metaphysik," *Philosophische Monatshefte* 24 (1888), pp. 37-65 and 540-74.

2. Cf. Werner Jaeger, *Aristoteles, Grundlegung einer Geschichte seiner Entwicklung* (Berlin, 1923) [*Aristotle: Fundamentals of his Development*, trans. Richard Robinson, (Oxford: Clarendon, 1948, reprinted 1960)].

3. Cf. Kant on this point: "Von dem transzendentalen Ideal," *Kritik der reinen Vernunft*, A 571-83, B 599-611.

IV. *The basic question of philosophy
and the question of man*

It is no arbitrary invention of Aristotle that philosophy has to ask about the being of beings; ancient philosophy was preoccupied with this question from its beginnings. It is not a question one can exchange at will for another, as is the case, for instance, when one considers whether to do research now on insects or on mammals.

And for the same reason, because the question of being is not arbitrary and not applied to man externally, but is more or less stirring in man insofar as he exists at all as human, and because human Dasein takes this question over, as it were, along with human existence, this question has, as a burgeoning problem, its own necessities. This is why the latter manifest themselves already in the first steps of philosophy. Here especially the *field* becomes visible, albeit still vaguely, upon which the γιγαντομαχία περὶ τοῦ ὄντος takes place, the battle of the giants over being.

For Parmenides the clarification of being takes place by way of a reflection on "thinking," νοεῖν, knowing what is (εἶναι), knowledge of beings. Plato's discovery of the "ideas," which are determinations of being, is oriented to the conversation the soul has with itself (ψυχή-λόγος). Guided by the question about οὐσία, Aristotle obtains the categories by reference to reason's predicative knowing (λόγος-νοῦς). In the search for *substantia,* Descartes founds "first philosophy" *(prima philosophia)* explicitly on the *res cogitans,* the *animus* [mind]. Kant's transcendental, i.e., ontological, problematic directed toward being (the question of the possibility of experience) moves in the dimension of consciousness, of the freely acting subject (the spontaneity of the ego). For Hegel substance is defined from the subject.

The struggle over being shifts to the field of thinking, of making statements, of the soul, of subjectivity. Human Dasein moves to the center! Why is this? Is it an accident that the battle gets shifted onto this field? Is it up to the whims of philosophers, according to each of their would-be world-views or ethics, according to just how important they, in each case, take the "I" to be? Is it a peculiar, irrational enthusiasm for the inwardness of the soul, or an especially high esteem for free personhood, or a blind subjectivism, which here in this basic problem selects human Dasein, as such, for the battlefield? None of these! Rather, the content pertinent to the basic problem itself, and this alone, requires this battlefield, makes human Dasein itself into this privileged field. For this is not an indifferent theater of action on which the battle was once placed, rather the battle grows from the soil of this field itself, breaks out from human Dasein as such—specifically because the question of being, the striving for an understanding of being, is the basic determinant of existence.*

Once this is understood, then the sole task, first of all, is to realize that this human Dasein is itself a being and thus also falls under the question of the being of beings. But if Dasein, as such, constitutes the battlefield for the central philosophical problematic, then this problematic should unfold ever so much more clearly, pointedly, and originally the more the battlefield itself is worked out clearly, pointedly, and originally—*with regard to the guiding problem of being.* But this means that that being which is essentially the basis and ground for the problem, human Dasein, must be first defined sufficiently in its specific being with regard to the guiding problem of being.

In the direction of this basic problem, the decisive determination of human Dasein lies in the insight that that which we call the *understanding-of-being* belongs to Dasein's ontological constitution. Human Dasein is a being with a kind of being to which it belongs essentially to understand something like being. We call this the transcendence of Dasein, primal transcendence (see the second major part of the lecture course). It is on the basis of transcendence that Dasein comports itself to beings, is always already thrown onto beings as a whole.

Its understanding of being is not one capacity among others, but the basic condition for the possibility of Dasein as such. Because it belongs to the essential constitution of man to understand being, the question of being, taken in the way mentioned, is a question, even *the* question, about man himself. Human Dasein bears in itself, in its ownmost history, the fate of philosophy along with it. Only Dasein hands this fate on and commits it again and again to human possibilities.

The basic question of philosophy, the question of being, is in itself, correctly understood, the question of man. It is, correctly understood, a question about man which lives hidden in the history of philosophy and in this history will move onward, but which will have to be brought to light afresh in every moment. Yet the important thing is to raise the question of man in view of the problem of being. Then the question is far removed from any noisy

---

*Here the word "Existenz" already carries with it the full weight of being-in-the-world, which was developed in *Being and Time* and which was developed by others into Existentialism and *Existenzphilosophie.*

self-importance concerning the life of one's own soul or that of others.

This fundamental philosophical question about man remains prior to every psychology, anthropology, and characterology, but also prior to all ethics and sociology. The fact that the aforementioned appear wherever this question is more or less explicitly alive, and are even taken for essential in its stead, only demonstrates one thing: that this question, and with it the basic problem of philosophy, is not and never does become easily accessible. For this reason also it is constantly threatened by sophistry. What is easier than, in a comfortable and interesting way, to interest a human being in human beings, to enumerate for him his complexes, potentials, standpoints, one-sidedness, and failings, and to say this is philosophy? It is crucial that the human being, in this sophistical sense, become completely irrelevant in the rightly understood fundamental philosophical question about man. Philosophy never "busies" itself with man in this hustling sense in which man can never take himself to be important enough.

One of the basic errors of our times is to believe a "deep" understanding of the human being is to be obtained by groping around in trivial shallows. Human Dasein gains depth only if it succeeds for itself, in its own existence, in first throwing itself beyond itself—to its limits. Only from the height of this high projection does it glimpse its true depths.

That the basic ontological question of philosophy has somehow to do with beings as a whole, as well as thereby with human existence and in such a way that the existence of the one philosophizing is in each case decided, this is expressed in Aristotle by the fact that "first philosophy" is, at the same time, θεολογική. Philosophy, in its innermost ground, is the most radical, universal, and rigorous conceptual knowledge. But the truth of this knowledge is not the truth of free-floating, arbitrarily knowable propositions about any matters-of-fact. The proofstone of philosophical truth consists solely in the loyalty the philosophizing individual has to himself.

We do not philosophize in order to become philosophers, no more than to fashion for ourselves and others a salutary world-view that could be procured like a coat and hat. The goal of philosophy is not a system of interesting information, nor a sentimental edification for faltering souls. Only he can philosophize who is already resolved to grant free dignity to Dasein in its radical and universal-essential possibilities, which alone makes it suitable for withstanding the remaining uncertainty

and gaping discord, while at the same time remaining untouched
by all the idle talk of the day. There is, in fact, a philosophical
world-view, but it is not a result of philosophy and not affixed to it
as a practical recipe for life. It resides rather in the philosophizing
itself. Nor is it, therefore, ever to be read off from what the philosopher may say expressly about ethical problems, but it becomes
manifest in what the philosophical work is as a whole.

Thus also the result of a philosophical effort has a character fundamentally different from the acquisition of particular sciences. To
be sure, philosophizing—and it especially—must always proceed
through a rigorous conceptual knowledge and must remain in the
medium of that knowledge, but this knowledge is grasped in its
genuine content only when in such knowledge the whole of existence is seized by the root after which philosophy searches—in
and by *freedom.*

The question of being and its variations and possibilities is at
heart the correctly understood question of man. Compared with
the duration of cosmic galaxies, human existence and its history is
certainly quite fleeting, only a "moment." But this transiency is
nevertheless the highest mode of being when it becomes an existing out of and towards freedom. The level and type of being does
not depend on duration!

V.   *Basic problems of a philosophical logic*

The rough indications about philosophy should make two things
clear: (1) Philosophy is the rigorous conceptual knowledge of
being; (2) It is this, however, only if this conceptual grasp is in
itself the philosophical apprehension of Dasein in freedom.

N.B. You do not get to philosophy by reading many and multifarious philosophical books, nor by torturing yourself with solving the riddles of the universe, but solely and surely by not evad-
ing what is essential in what you encounter in your current Dasein
devoted to academic studies. Nonevasion is crucial, since philosophy remains latent in every human existence and need not be first
added to it from somewhere else.

But what does "logic" have to do with all this? What does logic
have to do with the freedom of existence? How does the basic
question of being belong here? Logic does not treat being directly,
but deals with thinking. "Thinking" is of course an activity and
comportment of humans, but still only one activity among others.
The investigation into thinking as a form of human activity would

then fall under the science of man, under anthropology. The latter is, of course, not philosophically central, but only reports how things look when man thinks. It reports the various forms in which man can think, how primitive peoples "think" differently than we do and follow different laws. These anthropological and psychological questions about forms and types of thinking are certainly not philosophical. But it remains open whether these are the only questions and even the only radical questions.

If thinking is a mode of Dasein's comportment and if it is not abandoned to arbitrariness but stands under laws, then the question must be asked: What are the fundamental laws belonging to thinking as such? What is, in general, the character of this lawfulness and regulation? We can obtain an answer only by way of a concrete interpretation of the basic laws of thinking which belong to its essence in general.

What is meant by "basic principles," and what is their essence? What principles are there? The tradition gives us the principle of identity, the principle of non-contradiction, the principle of the excluded middle, the principle of sufficient reason, *principium identitatis, principium contradictionis, principium exclusi tertii, principium rationis sufficientis*. Are these all? In what order do they stand? What intrinsic connection do they have? Where do they find their foundation and their necessity? Are we dealing here with laws of nature, with psychological or moral laws? Or of what sort are they that Dasein is subject to them?

But the account of the laws governing thinking pushes us back into the question of the conditions of their possibility. How must that being which is subject to such laws, Dasein itself, be constituted so as to be able to be thus governed by laws? How "is" Dasein according to its essence so that such an obligation as that of being governed by logical laws can arise in and for Dasein?

These basic principles [Grund-Sätze] are not rules alongside a thinking that would be determined from elsewhere, but they are the grounds [Gründe] for statements [Sätze] in general, grounds which make thinking possible. And they are this, furthermore, only because they are the bases [Gründe] for understanding, existence, the understanding of being, Dasein, and primal transcendence.

It is becoming clear that with such problems we are already immediately in the realm of the question concerning the constitution of Dasein's being. Even more, obligation and being governed by law, in themselves, presuppose freedom as the basis for their own possibility. Only what exists as a free being could be at all bound by an obligatory lawfulness. Freedom alone can be the source of obligation. *A basic problem of logic, the law-governedness of thinking, reveals itself to be a problem of human existence in its ground, the problem of freedom.*

Let us review our opening account of the idea of formal logic and its object. In thinking as thinking about something, there is the intent to measure itself up to that about which it thinks and which it determines in thinking, i.e., to make manifest in itself that about which it thinks, to uncover it and let what is uncovered become accessible. Determinative thinking is uncovering or concealing. That is, it is either true or false. To be false is a negative mode of being true, to be un-true. Thinking is as such always in some form an uncovering, a being-true.

How is this possible, how can anything of this sort be applicable to thinking as an activity of Dasein: to be true, to move within the either-or of being true or being false? What is truth? In what way "is" truth at all, for it is neither a thing nor anything like a thing? And how does it belong to human Dasein itself? This question about being-in-the-truth leads us back to the problem of Dasein's transcendence. And insofar as the truth of thinking is co-determined by lawfulness, the problem of truth is conjoined with the problem of lawfulness and, that means, with the problem of freedom.

In measuring itself up to that about which it thinks, true thinking seeks in the being itself that on which it supports and grounds itself. All true thinking finds grounds and has definite possibilities of grounding. There is thus the further question, How is it that the truth of thinking and thinking itself must have something like a *ground*—and can have a ground? What does ground as such mean? How are ground and Dasein related to one another? How are ground, truth, lawfulness, freedom connected with one another with regard to thinking?

To think, we said, is to determine, *determinare;* in its simplest form: determining something as something,—"as" something: as such-and-such. The question is, What does this "as something" imply, this reference to another from which something given is supposed to be determined? To what extent is there presupposed here the basic form of that kind of grasping we call conceiving and the *concept?* How is conceptualizing related to grounding and thus to truth and lawfulness? How are concept and freedom connected?

And finally, determinative thinking, as thinking about beings, brings, in its own way, the being of beings to expression. The simple statement "A *is* b" shows this in the most rudimentary way.

The "is," nevertheless, need not be expressed in language. It is also contained in such statements as "the car goes," "it rains" (*pluit*). The "to be" that appears expressly in the sentence is termed the *copula*. The fact that determinative thinking is, in its basic form, tied directly to the "is," to being, indicates that there must be a special connection between thought and being—not to mention that thinking itself is a being and as such is directed toward beings. And the question will arise, How is this being as copula related to concept, ground, truth, lawfulness, freedom?

A rather rough consideration of thinking thus already provides us with a preliminary glimpse into many extremely important connections pointing directly to the dimension of basic philosophical problems. The possibility and necessity of a *philosophical* logic becomes more familiar.

But it becomes clear too that only when we prepare ourselves first for a truly philosophical understanding of what is meant by the terms truth, ground, lawfulness, freedom, concept, being, only then can we understand the form of Dasein in which we act as humans committed to science.

Whether we learn to think, in the real sense, by way of logic depends on whether we arrive at an understanding of thinking in its intrinsic possibility, that is, with regard to lawfulness, truth, ground, concept, being, and freedom. When we acquire this understanding for ourselves, even if only in a few basic outlines, then we will have warrant to clarify the particular positive science we are working in from out of its intrinsic limits, and only then do we take possession of a science, as a free possession. And science, thus appropriated, and only such a science, is in each case the genuine school for thinking.

VI. *The traditional classification of logic and the task of returning to the foundations of this logic*

In going back to matters like truth as such, ground, concept, lawfulness, and freedom, we are seeking a philosophical logic, or better, *the metaphysical foundations of logic (initia logicae).*

We seek a return to these basic problems, and thereby a concrete entrance into philosophy itself, by way of a critical dismantling of traditional logic down to its hidden foundations.

Now the history of logic, however, precisely if one looks not only at results but at its more-or-less-explicit emergence from philosophy in each case, is not only vast and complicated. It also manifests several important stages which we designate mainly by the names: Plato, Aristotle, the Stoa, the Middle Ages, Leibniz,

Kant, Hegel, and in the nineteenth and in the transition to the twentieth century: Lotze, Sigwart, Husserl. It is impossible in this lecture course to develop a picture of this history of logic along with the treatment of the problems themselves. Taking our bearings from the central problem we are striving toward, we must try to reach a place appropriate for the recollection from historicity.

An appropriate place means we must, as it were, find there an arrangement of the traditional themes of logic such that it will, at the same time, enable us to proceed consistently from them back to the several basic problems mentioned earlier. Such a historical place can in fact be found in *Leibniz* (1646–1716). Not only does the ancient and medieval tradition of logic converge in him in an independent new form; he becomes at the same time the stimulus for posing new questions, providing suggestions for tasks which are in part taken up only in recent times. From Leibniz we can create for ourselves perspectives reaching back to the ancients and forward to the present, perspectives important for the foundational problems of logic.

To be sure, in Leibniz we have no systematic presentation of logic, for even the important things he left behind are dispersed in letters, small treatises, occasional writings, and programs. So we cannot think of constructing an exhaustive exposition of his teachings. Nor do we desire a historical report, but we want to seize the occasion for a breakthrough into the problems themselves.

But even if we want first to focus on Leibniz, the question still remains: Which traditional objects of logic should we select? What does logic as such deal with?

Let us go back to the notion of formal logic as already described. According to it, logic is a science of the λόγος, of the statements which determine something as something. "Statement" here is ambiguous. It can mean to make a statement, *to communicate* in contradistinction to remaining silent and keeping something to oneself. This kind of stating is always necessarily a linguistic utterance. "Statement" also means, however, and here it means primarily, to say something about something, "A is b," to determine b as belonging to A. This is statement in the sense of *predication*. This propositional character of λόγος comes out most clearly in Aristotle's description of it.

Aristotle's explicit treatment of λόγος is in a small and difficult treatise entitled περὶ ἑρμηνείας (de interpretatione), "On Interpretation." Here Aristotle says (Chap. 4, 16b, 26ff.): Λόγος δέ ἐστι φωνὴ σημαντική, ἧς τῶν μερῶν τι σημαντικόν ἐστι κεχωρισμένον, ὡς φάσις ἀλλ᾿ οὐχ ὡς κατάφασις. λέγω δέ, οἷον ἄν-θρωπος σημαίνει μέν τι, ἀλλ᾿ οὐχ ὅτι ἔστιν ἢ οὐκ ἔστιν· ἀλλ᾿ ἔσται κατάφασις ἢ ἀπόφασις, ἐάν τι προστεθῇ. We translate this: speech, statement, is a vocal-linguistic articulation which means something, contains in itself a meaning-content in such a way that in each case a part of this statement, when taken separately by itself, still has a meaning as a mere saying something (φάσις) but not as a positive assertion (κατάφασις, "the man there is excited"; κατά means "from above down toward" something). Thus, for example, the expression "man" means something by itself (we say that we are able to think something when we hear the word), but by this mere saying of the isolated word it is not stated whether a man exists or not. But when something (namely, that he exists or does not exist) is added to the isolated word ("man"), then this saying becomes a κατάφασις or ἀπόφασις, an affirmation or denial.

Every proposition, as a determination of something as something, is accordingly either an affirmation or denial. These expressions are to be taken quite literally. To affirm means to assert something as belonging-to, and to deny means to reject something as not belonging-to. In his translations of Aristotelian writings and in his commentaries on the books of logic and on Porphyry, Boethius (circa 480–524) translates φάσις with *dictio*, and κατάφασις with *affirmatio*, and ἀπόφασις with *negatio*. The later positive and negative judgments correspond to this distinction. "Judgment" is the expression most frequently used today for λόγος.

We see at once how strongly Aristotle's approach is still oriented to the linguistic form of λόγος, when he presents λόγος as a connection (συμπλοκή; *nexus, connexio*) of several words having meaning in themselves. For example, the Latin *pluit*, it's raining, is rightly also a λόγος, and κατάφασις—and is nevertheless made up of only one "word." This is, to be sure, a problem all its own. What then is that about which raining is asserted; "it's raining"—what does the "it" mean?

At any rate, in the first decisive account, λόγος is conceived as a *connecting of notions*, as a conjoining of meanings, as a binding together of concepts. The elementary ingredients of λόγος are thus these individual notions, meanings, concepts; τὰ μὲν οὖν ὀνόματα αὐτὰ καὶ τὰ ῥήματα ἔοικε τῷ ἄνευ συνθέσεως καὶ διαιρέσεως νοήματι (*de interpret.* 1, 16a 13f.) [A noun or a verb by itself much resembles a concept or thought which is neither combined nor disjoined.]. And so, in clarifying λόγος, the approach suggested seems to be to start from that out of which it is made; the basic element of λόγος is the concept. Therefore the doctrine of the concept is to precede the doctrine of the λόγος (qua judgment). On the other hand, thinking then operates once again to connect and link individual propositions into particular forms of connection: A is B,

B is C, therefore A is C. This linkage of judgments is called inference.

We thus arrive at the three major divisions of logic: the doctrine of the concept, of the judgment, and of the inference. Aristotle did indeed treat all three basic ingredients—without having planned in this way to develop a discipline. That happened only later in the Scholastic elaboration of Aristotelian philosophy. From that period also came the arrangement and designation of the writings treating essentially logical problems under the title "organon" (instrument, tool). The superficially technical conception of logic is expressed in this very title. Since then, the "organon" refers to Aristotle's logic. This "organon" includes five or six different investigations of logical problems; and the traditional order results from using pedagogical viewpoints. Categories, On Interpretation, Prior Analytics (on the inference), Posterior Analytics (on the principles of demonstration and knowledge; it is more closely connected with ontology than is the Prior Analytics), Topics (probability inferences), and On Sophistical Refutation (on fallacies; usually considered part of the Topics).[4]

Now it was Aristotle's conviction that λόγος in the sense of propositional determination, λόγος in the sense of judgment, manifestly presents the basic phenomenon of logic. For, in the first place, λόγος is an original unity. Though it can be resolved into individual concepts, these dissociated elements do not, nevertheless, constitute the whole. They lack precisely their essential unity. Logos is not the sum or aggregate of two notions. But what provides unity is ultimately just what is essential in thinking, in νοεῖν and διανοεῖν. Secondly, only this unity can really be true or false. It is thus the bearer of that feature which characterizes knowledge as such.

This very same consideration has also in recent times led to seeking the core of logic in the judgment and in the doctrine of judgment. There is undoubtedly something correct in this preference for the theory of judgment (of statement)—even though the justifications given for it remain quite superficial.

Thus we also want to concentrate our initial orientation of the basic problems of logic from Leibniz upon his doctrine of judgment and from there to try to draw their main lines into the philosophical dimension of the problems mentioned: the lawfulness of the basic principles, truth, concept, ground, freedom. We come therewith to our actual theme.

---

4. Still the best separate edition, with a commentary by Theodor Waitz, *Aristotelis Organon Graece*, 2 volumes, (Leipzig, 1844 and 1846) [reprinted in Aalen in 1965].

The Metaphysical Foundations
of Logic

PRELIMINARY NOTE

The concept "metaphysics" encompasses the unity of "ontology" and "theology" in the sense already characterized. The conception itself, incidentally, is of bibliothecal origin. [Aristotle's] μετὰ τὰ φυσικά are treatises located "after" those on "physics" because they have a content of their own, namely, ontology and theology. The bibliothecal title becomes a designation of the contents: μετά, instead of "after," becomes "beyond," and φυσικά becomes beings of every kind of being. The subject-matter of metaphysics is what lies "beyond" beings—where and how it does so is not stated. It deals with a) being as such, b) beings as a whole. "Behind" the other books becomes "beyond" the others, an ordering of being and beings.

First Major Part

Dismantling Leibniz's Doctrine of Judgment Down to Basic Metaphysical Problems*

If we are now about to understand Leibniz's doctrine of judgment, this does not mean gathering some arbitrary information about what one of the previous philosophers taught regarding judgment. It is rather a concrete path of reflection on what makes thinking possible as such. We must therefore focus on how thinking is brought into view here, which basic structures it determines, how broadly these will be grounded, and what provides the ground for this characteristic of thinking.

Thinking is in each case thinking about objects, and that means about beings. As a thinking about something, thinking stands in a relationship to beings. How are thinking and beings related? Thinking is itself an activity of Dasein and is thereby a way of being—of being as a being, Dasein, toward other beings. If thinking becomes our theme, then ontological relationships become thereby thematic.

Whence shall we determine the relationship of thinking and being? Which is most proximate? For Descartes, Spinoza, and Leibniz, thinking is the nearest. Does being then follow thinking? In that case a being must thoroughly and in principle *be* in such a way that it is completely determinable by thought. According to this postulate of thorough intelligibility, the conditions of truth are

---

*This "*Destruktion*" is the same *kritischer Abbau* spoken of in the introduction (German text p. 27). The image here is not one of total demolition but of a de-construction by which the original impulses, long buried in sedimentation, are reactivated. The image of dismantling an old structure serves to translate the de-struction to which Heidegger refers.

27

the presuppositions of being. *Cum Deus calculat et cogitationem exercet, fit mundus.*[1] "When God calculates (with visible signs) and converts his thinking into deed, the world arises."[2] To determine beings as such, that is, being, one must proceed from the essence of thinking, by delineating what belongs to something thought as such, by proceeding from thought. The path goes from the essence of thinking to the essence of being, from logic to ontology.

Or, conversely, is logic founded upon ontology? It is known that the history of logic's development is largely determined by this relationship. It is a commonplace that Aristotle's logic is grounded in his metaphysics. Modern rationalism, governed as it is by the *cogito sum*, sets itself the task of freeing logic from this bond.

Assessment of the relationship of logic to metaphysics in Leibniz is controversial.[3] Yet choosing between the two main alternate views is not fruitful. The relationship between disciplines must be decided from the problems and subject-matters themselves; disciplines should not be regarded as fixed territories. It may well be the case in both disciplines that the territories are not adequately defined. We wish to present Leibniz's doctrine of judgment and its dimensions, and so we can only mention the controversy in passing.

We wish to investigate the dimensions of judgment, those connections on the basis of which anything like a judgment is possible at all. It has been indicated several times that judgment, the statement, has in itself a structure. As a predicative determination, judgment aims at knowledge, at truth. As a comportment, judgment is subject to certain principles. As a knowledge of beings, it is related to beings as such. We will accordingly outline the destructive analysis of the Leibnizian doctrine of judgment as follows:

---

1. *Die philosophischen Schriften von Gottfried Wilhelm Leibniz,* ed. C. I. Gerhardt, 7 volumes (Berlin 1875–90) [reprint, Hildesheim, 1960–61], volume 7, p. 191 note. The statement is well known: *Cum Deus calculat . . . fit mundus;* it also provides the motto for L. Couturat, *La Logique de Leibniz. D'après des documents inédits* (Paris, 1901) [reprint, Hildesheim, 1961].

2. Following D. Mahnke, *Leibnizens Synthese von Universalmathematik und Individualmetaphysik* in *Jahrbuch für Philosophie und phänomenologische Forschung,* volume 7; printed separately in Halle, 1925 [reprint, Stuttgart-Bad Cannstatt, 1964], p. 43.

3. Logic as the foundation of Leibniz's metaphysics is the thesis of Bertrand Russell's *A Critical Exposition of the Philosophy of Leibniz* (Cambridge, 1900), as well as of Louis Couturat's book, cited in note 1, which is the best known. Counterarguments to this view have not yet succeeded in refuting it.

1. Characterization of the general structure of judgment—the theory of inclusion.
2. Judgment and the idea of truth. The basic forms of truth—*veritas rationis* and *veritas facti*, *vérité de raison* and *vérité de fait*.
3. The idea of truth and the basic principles of knowledge: *principium identitatis, principium contradictionis,* and *principium rationis sufficientis.* (The *mathesis universalis* and the unity of knowledge.)
4. The idea of knowledge as such; the *intuitus*.
5. The essential determination of the being of genuine beings as possible objects of knowledge—the monad.
6. The basic notion of being as such—*essentia* and the *conatus existentiae*.
7. The theory of judgment and the notion of being—logic and ontology.[4]

§1. *Characterization of the general structure of judgment*

We are nowadays learning to see more clearly the connection modern philosophy has with medieval Scholasticism and thereby with antiquity, especially Aristotle. We can expect Leibniz's doctrine of judgment to be not completely new but rather informed by tradition, by the middle ages and antiquity. As a young man, Leibniz had in particular made a thorough study of Scholasticism,[5] especially of Francisco Suarez, the leading representative of late Scholasticism at the time of the Counterreformation. His *Disputationes metaphysicae* of 1597 systematized the traditional doctrines on metaphysics and greatly influenced Descartes and Protestant Scholasticism in the sixteenth and seventeenth centuries.

---

4. For modern developments and the contemporary state of logic see the following: *Die Logik von Port Royal: La Logique ou l'Art de Penser*, 1662, frequently reprinted and translated; Kant's *Vorlesung über Logik*, ed. Jäsche, 1800, *Akademie* edition, volume 9; C. Sigwart, *Logik*, 2 volumes, 1873, 4th edition, 1911; H. Lotze, *Logik*, 1874, 2nd edition, 1879, and 1912 edition with a valuable introduction by G. Misch, also Sigwart's smaller *Logik* of 1843; W. Schuppe, *Erkenntnistheoretische Logik*, 1878; J. Bergmann, *Reine Logik*, 1879; Husserl's *Logische Untersuchungen*, 1900–1901; A. Pfänder, *Logik, Jahrbuch für Philosophie und phänomenologische Forschung*, Volume 4, published separately in 1921, truly a handbook; otherwise, for related material, see C. Prantl, *Geschichte der Logik im Abendlande*, 4 volumes, 1855–70.

5. Cf. Leibniz's dissertation, *Disputatio Metaphysica de Principio Individui*, 1663; Gerhardt 4, 15–26.

But Leibniz also studied Aristotle directly. So we must again briefly go back to earlier things, though we have already touched on some of them.

We already said that in the wake of Aristotle, who saw λόγος as a συμπλοκή (interweaving, *nexus, connectio*) or σύνθεσις, judgment was defined as a *compositio* or *divisio*. Thomas Aquinas, in *Quaestiones disputatae de veritate*, q. XIV, a. 1, speaks of *operatio intellectus, secundum quam componit vel dividit, affirmando et negando* [the activity of the mind by which it puts together or separates, in affirming and denying]. In the broadest formal sense, judgment is a relationship between representations, a relation of concepts. These are formulations which sound alike and apparently say the same thing. Yet behind them lurks a large vagueness and disharmony in the theory. Kant says this too (in the *Critique of Pure Reason* B 140/41):

> I have never been able to accept the interpretation which logicians give of judgment in general. It is, they declare, the representation of a relation between two concepts. I do not here dispute with them as to what is defective in this interpretation. . . . I need only point out that the definition does not determine in what the asserted *relation* consists.

Attempts to explain it are still controversial today. The critical deficiency is that the conditions of the problem have not been made clear.

The relation of subject and predicate is a λέγειν τι κατά τινός: a stating something about something (*de aliquo*). That "about which" is *what underlies* , the ὑποκείμενον, the *subjectum*. The predicate is that which is said about something. The predicate *term*, therefore, is a "sign," as it were, of something said, as Aristotle says (*de interpret.* 3, 16b 10f.): ῥῆμα . . . καὶ ἀεὶ τῶν καθ' ἑτέρου λεγομένων σημεῖόν ἐστιν, οἷον τῶν καθ' ὑποκειμένου ἢ ἐν ὑποκειμένῳ. The predicate is "always a sign of that which is said about something else, i.e., about something underlying, or ⟨about something which is⟩ in what underlies." In other words, the predicate is what is stated about what underlies or is stated as being in what underlies. This [view] is first prompted by the trivial consideration that what is supposed to be able to be said of something, and said correctly, truthfully, must apply to the subject (*esse de ratione subjecti*), must be contained in the subject (ὑπάρχειν αὐτῷ).

This seemingly pellucid consideration becomes immediately vague and ambiguous when we ask; What is meant by the subject?

In the statement "the board is black," is the board itself the subject or is it the notion, the mental content, or the meaning of the word "board"? Correspondingly, there is a question concerning "black" and its being contained in the subject. Is there here a mutual containment of notions, concepts, or properties of the thing itself? Is being contained or being included in something itself thinglike, mental, or conceptual? Are there correspondences among these various relations of containment? And how is one to define these relations, as correspondence, as depiction, or as coordination?

"The board is black," "the chalk falls from the table"—how are "black" and "falling from the table" *contained* in their respective subjects? And what is meant by "being contained in"? And should anything like this be said? Or is talk of containment only a theory, an effort to explain judgment?

Whatever the case, Leibniz's conception of λόγος also moves in the direction of just such a theory of the predicate's being contained in the subject. It is a *theory of inclusion*. If the theory is not thereby characterized in a merely superficial way, then obviously a distinct conception of containment itself, of *inesse*, must be developed in it and this means a conception of *esse*, of being. In fact, with Leibniz, the inclusion theory receives a very specific expression and foundation.

First a few references to characterize Leibniz's doctrine of judgment.

(1) In the *Discours de Métaphysique* of 1686 (first published in 1846 from posthumous manuscripts), one of the main writings in the context of our study, Leibniz says in § 8 (G. IV, 432/33, Buchenau translation[6]):

> It is of course true that when a number of predicates are attributed to a single subject while this subject is not attributed to any other, it is called an individual substance. But this is not enough, and such a definition is merely nominal. We must consider, then, what it means to be truly attributed to a certain subject. Now it is certain that every true predication has some basis ⟨*quelque fondement*⟩ in the nature of things, and when a proposition is not an identity, that is to say, when the predicate is not expressly contained in ⟨*compris*⟩ the subject, it must be included in it virtually. This is what the philosophers call *in-esse* when they say that the predicate *is in* ⟨*est dans*⟩ the subject.

---

6. G.W. Leibniz, *Hauptschriften zur Grundlegung der Philosophie*, trans. A. Buchenau, revised and edited with introductions and discussions by Ernst Cassirer, 2 volumes (*Philosophische Bibliotek*, volumes 107 and 108), Leipzig 1904–6 [3rd edition, Hamburg, 1966]; volume 2, p. 143.

> So the subject term must always include the predicate term in such a way that anyone who understands perfectly the concept of the subject will also know that the predicate belongs to it. [L. 307]

The thought in this passage deals above all with the concept of "individual substance" (the monad), with Aristotle's πρώτη οὐσία (the τόδε τι). Leibniz expressly refers here to the traditional definition of substance, which was originally Aristotelian: Οὐσία δέ ἐστιν ἡ κυριώτατά τε καὶ πρώτως καὶ μάλιστα λεγομένη, ἢ μήτε καθ᾽ ὑποκειμένου τινὸς λέγεται μήτ᾽ ἐν ὑποκειμένῳ τινί ἐστιν, οἷον ὁ τὶς ἄνθρωπος ἢ ὁ τὶς ἵππος (Categoriae 5, 2a 11ff.). "Οὐσία. . . we call that which is neither named and said with respect to another underlying thing nor is understood to be something which is in some other underlying thing, for example, it is this man here, this horse here." By οὐσία (substance) Aristotle understands that which is independently present, independent presence. Regarding the meaning of ἐν ὑποκειμένῳ, Aristotle says (Ibid. 2, la 24f.): ἐν ὑποκειμένῳ δὲ λέγω, ὃ ἔν τινι μὴ ὡς μέρος ὑπάρχον ἀδύνατον χωρὶς εἶναι τοῦ ἐν ᾧ ἐστιν. [By 'in the subject' I do not mean present in it as parts are contained in a whole; I mean that it cannot exist apart from the subject referred to.] That is, it is essentially not independent. It has a similar meaning in the *Metaphysics* (Z 13, 1038 b 8ff.): ἔοικε γὰρ ἀδύνατον εἶναι οὐσίαν εἶναι ὁτιοῦν τῶν καθόλου λεγομένων. πρώτη μὲν γὰρ οὐσία ἴδιος ἑκάστῳ ἢ οὐχ ὑπάρχει ἄλλῳ, τὸ δὲ καθόλου κοινόν· τοῦτο γὰρ λέγεται καθόλου ὃ πλείοσιν ὑπάρχειν πέφυκεν. [For it seems impossible that any universal term can be substance. The first substance is peculiar to each individual and belongs to nothing else, whereas the universal is common, for by it we mean that which by nature appertains to several things.]

In the interpretation of individual substance in the passage cited from the *Discours de Métaphysique*, λέγειν was referred to in the sense that individual substance is essentially non-predicable of something underlying; it is essentially independent (and can never be predicated of something). Leibniz sees that this interpretation of substance takes its bearings from predication, and therefore a radical determination of the nature of predication, of judgment, must necessarily provide a primordial conception of substance. This concept of substance is the concept of the *subjectum*. In this passage Leibniz says that in every true statement the subject must contain the predicate in itself, whether explicitly or implicitly. Where it is contained explicitly (A is A), there is an identity; where it is not contained explicitly, we are dealing with a hidden identity. A true statement implies the predicate's being within the subject, the predicate's inclusion in the subject. Whoever then has thorough and complete insight into a subject can make all true judgments about this subject; he need only explicate them.

The passage from the *Discours* was cited first on purpose. It indicates the central problem, that of the manifold meanings of the concept of "subject" and its connection with the concept of substance. "Subject" is 1) individual substance (ὑποκείμενον), the individual independent being, the ontic subject; 2) the subject of the statement, the logical subject; not every logical subject need be a substance, and thus this concept is broader; 3) the "I" in contradistinction to the object, as the pre-eminent subject of statements and as pre-eminent individual independent being. Here in Leibniz the ontic subject, the substance, is understood from the viewpoint of the logical subject, from the subject of a statement. But the converse is also quite possible, that is, to understand the logical subject from the ontic subject: Which subject has priority, the ontic or the logical? Or neither?

(2) In the fragment *De libertate*[7] Leibniz says:

> Videbam autem commune esse omni propositioni verae affirmativae universali et singulari, necessariae vel contingenti, ut praedicatum insit subjecto, seu ut praedicati notio in notione subjecti aliqua ratione involvatur; idque esse principium infallibilitatis in omni veritatum genere, apud eum qui omnia a priori cognoscit.

> For I say that in every true affirmative proposition, whether universal or particular, necessary or contingent, the predicate inheres in [inesse] the subject, that the concept of the predicate is in some way involved in [involvatur] the concept of the subject. I saw too that this is the principle of infallibility in every kind of truth for him who knows everything a priori. [L. 263-4]

(3) Then there are two passages from Leibniz's correspondence with Antoine Arnauld occasioned by the latter's receiving the *Discours*. Arnauld was a Cartesian and a theologian of Port Royal who coauthored *The Logic of Port Royal* (1662). This correspondence is of fundamental significance for the problem of individual substance.

(a) First a thought which repeats nearly verbatim the above quotation (from June, 1686):

---

7. *Nouvelles Lettres et Opuscules inédits de Leibniz,* published by L.A. Foucher de Careil (Paris, 1857) [reprint Hildesheim 1971]; p. 179. The passage is also provided in Couturat; *La Logique de Leibniz,* p. 208, note 1.

Finally, I have given a decisive reason, which I believe has the force
of a demonstration. It is that always, in every true affirmative proposition, whether necessary or contingent, universal or particular, the
notion of the predicate is in some way included in that of the subject.
Praedicatum inest subjecto; otherwise I do not know what truth is.
[L. 337; G. II 56]

Here it is even clearer that the predicate's inclusion in the subject
is equated with being true and so defines the concept of truth as
such.

(b)
Inasmuch as I maintain the individual concept of Adam includes everything that will ever happen to him I mean to say nothing more
than what all philosophers intend when they say that *praedicatum
inesse subjecto verae propositionis* [the predicate of a true proposition is in the subject]. (June, 1686, G. II, 43)

The ontic concept of a subject is here clearly determined by the
logical subject-predicate relation taken as an *inesse.*

(4)
Omnis propositio vera probari potest, cum enim praedicatum insit
subjecto, ut loquitur Aristoteles, seu notio praedicati in notione subjecti perfecte intellecta involvatur, utique resolutione terminorum in
suos valores seu eos terminos quos continent, oportet veritatem posse
ostendi. (C. 388)[8]

Every true proposition can be demonstrated. Because the predicate
is in the subject, as Aristotle puts it, or the notion of the predicate is
implied in the perfectly understood notion of the subject, the truth
must then necessarily be able to be shown by the analysis of the
subject terms into that which they contain.

Thus Leibniz refers to Aristotle regarding his conception of the
inesse. We should note here how the being-present of the really
existing being conceived as subject gets assimilated to the concept
of subject. Proof of the truth of a statement is the result of analysis,
resolutio, breaking the subject down into its elements. The idea of
proof and its possibility rests on the structure of the proposition
taken as a relation of inclusion.

(5) Finally, a citation from the little treatise *Primae veritates,*
published by Couturat:

Semper igitur praedicatum seu consequens inest subjecto seu an-
tecedenti; et in hoc ipso consistit natura veritatis in universum seu

---

8. *Opuscules et Fragments inédits de Leibniz,* ed. L. Couturat (Paris, 1903)
[reprint, Hildesheim, 1961], p. 388.

connexio inter terminos enuntiationis, ut etiam Aristoteles observ-
avit. (C. 518-19)

The predicate or consequent therefore always inheres in the subject
or antecedent. And as Aristotle, too, observed, the essence of truth in
general or the connection between the terms of a proposition consists
in this being-in. [L. 267]

It must be kept in mind that this inclusion theory speaks of the
inclusion of the predicate concept in the subject concept, as well
as of the inclusion of the being of what is intended by the predicate term in the being of what is named by the subject term. Inclusion is as such an inclusion in λόγος, a logical inclusion; and as
intending the being itself, it is an ontic inclusion. The peculiarity
is that both of these in a certain way coincide. The reasons for this,
whether or not correct, can only be determined once we have
forged ahead to the final metaphysical foundations of this theory of
judgment.

It would be tempting to compare this general sketch of the
theory of judgment with other conceptions of judgment. Leibniz
himself makes reference to Aristotle, though with less than full
justification. Later we should be able to discuss thoroughly the
extent to which this reference is in a certain way justified and why
it is nonetheless ultimately unjustified.

Descartes seeks the essence of judgment in a wholly different
direction than did Aristotle or, later, Leibniz. According to
Descartes, judging is not a merely mental process, a connecting of
notions. Rather it is the knowing subject's assumption of a position
toward these mental contents. *Iudicare*, to judge, is *assensionem
praebere*, to give assent, to a relation between notions, *assentiri,
credere, sibi ipsi affirmare* [to assent, to believe, to affirm to
oneself]. The contrast here between affirmation and denial,
acknowledgment and rejection, does not correspond to the division of judgments into affiirming and denying, positive and negative judgments. For Descartes this conception of judgment is
connected most intimately with the way in which he lays the
foundations of first philosophy as such, with the suspension of assent, with the attitude of doubt toward previous knowledge.

Descartes' conception of judgment was taken up once again in
the nineteenth century by Franz Brentano in *Psychologie vom
empirischen Standpunkt*, 1874, and further in *Vom Ursprung
sittlicher Erkenntnis*, 1889. Brentano appeals to the threefold
classification of spiritual activities, of *cogitationes*, which Descartes provides in his *Meditationes* (III, 5): *ideae, voluntates sive
affectus* and *judicia* [ideas, volitions or affects, and judgments].

Besides these Descartes also provides a twofold division of *perceptio* and *volitio* (*Principia Philosophiae* I, 32 and 34), and here Descartes numbers acts of judgment among the acts of volition. A controversy arises because of this ambiguity. Brentano tries to show that acts of judgment constitute a class by themselves. Johann Bergmann follows him in his *Reine Logik* of 1879. Wilhelm Windelband also treats Brentano in his "Beiträge zur Lehre vom negativen Urteil" (in the *Strassburger Abhandlungen zur Philosophie. E. Zeller zu seinem 70. Geburtstage*, 1884) but Windelband maintains that the act of judgment is an act of the will. This is also the point of departure for Heinrich Rickert in *Der Gegenstand der Erkenntnis* (his Habilitationsschrift), 1892, 6th edition 1928, which is the foundation for Rickert's epistemology and even for his philosophy of values as a whole. Finally, in 1912 *Die Lehre vom Urteil* by Emil Lask was published.

Though Leibniz developed his thought in many ways by confronting Descartes and the Cartesians, their theory of judgment was unimportant for him. Their theory is based on the subject's assumption of a position and not on the content of what is stated. It was unimportant for Leibniz, and rightly too, because it moves away from central metaphysical problems.

Of wholly different value for a pertinent discussion of Leibniz's theory of judgment is Kant's presentation in the Introduction to the *Critique of Pure Reason* where he treats judgment and the division of judgments into analytic and synthetic. If the Kantian distinction is at all applicable for characterizing Leibniz's theory, then one would have to say that for Leibniz all judgments are analytic. Nevertheless, the Kantian concept of what is analytic does not coincide with what Leibniz calls the *analysis notionum*.

Were a confrontation necessary, then it would be one with Aristotle and Suarez on one side and with Kant on the other. In both cases the problem of judgment, of λόγος, of logic, would have to be decided on the basis of the problem of ontology, of metaphysics, as such. What we must do first is make visible the metaphysical perspectives of Leibniz's theory of judgment and thereby clarify the theory itself.

We recall the *inesse*, the *inclusio*, and we draw on a definition from Leibniz's *Definitiones Logicae*:

> A includere B, seu B includi A, est: de A, subjecto, universaliter affirmari B, praedicatum, veluti: sapiens includit justum, hoc est, omnis sapiens est ⟨!⟩ justus.[9]

---

9. G. W. Leibniz, *Opera philosophica quae existant latina, gallica, germanica omnia*, ed. J. E. Erdmann (Berlin, 1840) [reprint, Aalen, 1959 and 1974], p. 100a.

For A to include B, or B to be included by A, is: B, the predicate, is universally affirmed of A, the subject. Such as: The wise [man] includes the just [man], i.e., every wise man is ⟨!⟩ just. [E. 100]

Here Leibniz simply equates being affirmed and being completely included; affirmation means simply inclusion. The "is" in the sample proposition indicates the *connectio* to be a *connectio realis* (Cf. G. VII, 300f.), an inclusion of the content spoken of. It is in this sense that reality is the contrary of negation.

Can *includi* and *inesse* be further characterized? Is there a distinctive basic conception of this relation found in Leibniz, and how is the interpretation of this relation connected with the essential nature of judgment, with truth or falsity?

§2. Judgment and the idea of truth. The basic forms of truth

Traditionally, judgment is considered to be the primary and genuine vehicle of truth, and truth in general is considered the characteristic of propositions, their being true. Terminologically we can clarify this by distinguishing three meanings of "truth": 1) the idea of truth, being true as such, 2) the concretion of this idea, true propositions as "truths" which must be proved; thus Leibniz frequently refers to "basic truths," 3) truth as ideal, the totality of possible knowable truths. The first meaning is what we are, above all, considering. Truth is supposed to have its locus in statements. Insofar as a statement is true, it is itself a truth, a being that is true. Being true is the being true of propositions. The nature of the proposition must therefore have an essential connection with the nature of truth.

The concept of proposition, of judgment, must be determined by reference to the idea of truth, or else conversely. What connection, according to Leibniz, obtains between the conception of judgment (inclusion theory) and the conception of the essence of truth? In answering this question we come across a principal feature of the inclusion theory.

Leibniz answers the question about the essence of truth as follows: *Ratio autem veritatis consistit in nexu praedicati cum subjecto* [The nature of truth consists in the connection of the predicate with the subject]. (C. 11) In his correspondence with Arnauld, Leibniz says: "*Praedicatum inest subjecto,* or I do not know what truth is" (cf. 3a above). Likewise, the passage in 5 above equates the *natura veritatis in universum* [nature of truth in general] with the connection between the terms of a proposition. The nature,

the essence, of truth, and this means the interconnection of propositional terms, consists of the *inesse*. On this *inesse* the *principium infallibilitatis* is based.

To be true means to be interconnected; a determination is contained in what is being determined. Moreover, to state means
connexio, and that means to be true. Are we not moving in a circle? *Verum esse* is equated with the predicate's being in, *inesse*,
the subject. But there are multifarious statements! Now which of
them is the original and basic form of this *inesse* understood as
nexus, as *inclusio?* The basic form of being true must be manifest
in the most elementary propositions, in the simplest and most
primordial true statements, in the primary "truths."

> Primae veritates sunt quae idem de se ipso enuntiant aut oppositum
> de ipso opposito negant. Ut A est B, vel A non est non A. Si verum
> est A esse B, falsum est A non esse B vel A esse non B. Item unum-
> quodque est quale est. Unumquodque sibi ipsi simile aut aequale
> est. Nihil est majus aut minus se ipso, aliaque id genus, quae licet
> suos ipsa gradus habeant prioritatis, omnia tamen uno nomine iden-
> ticorum comprehendi possunt (C. 518)

> First truths are those which assert the same of itself or negate the
> opposite of itself. For example, A is A, or A is not non-A. If it is true
> that A is B, it is false that A is not B or that A is non-B. Likewise,
> everything is what it is; everything is similar or equal to itself; noth-
> ing is greater or less than itself. These and others truths of this kind,
> though they may have various degrees of priority, can nevertheless
> all be grouped under the one name of *identities*. [L. 267]*

The first primordial truths are *identica*, propositions in which
something is explicitly asserted as itself in its sameness to itself
and with regard to that sameness.

But there is another essential aspect of these first truths which
should be noted. *Omnes autem reliquae veritates reducuntur ad
primas ope definitionum, seu per resolutionem notionum, in qua
consistit probatio a priori, independens ab experimento (ibid.).*
[All other truths are reduced to first truths with the aid of

---

*I have changed Loemker's translation of the first sentence of these definitions.
Loemker has: "First truths are those which predicate something of itself or deny
the opposite of its opposite." In the first half of the definition Loemker omits
Leibniz's "*idem*" and so misses the meaning here. In the second half Loemker has
Leibniz defining a contradiction instead of an identity, or so, at least, it seems to
me if one construes a statement formally to be "denying the opposite of its opposite." If we recall, however, the Latin use of *nego* to express *dico non*, we can
translate the second half of the definition as "negates the opposite of itself." And
this is indeed the negative way in which identities can be stated formally, and it
also corresponds to Leibniz's examples in the passage in question.

definitions or by the analysis of notions; in this consists proof a priori, which is independent of experience.] All true statements are finally reducible to identities. Every true statement is ultimately an identity, only the identity is not necessarily explicit; but every truth is potentially an identity.

This means nothing else but that the essence of truth as such, the *inclusio* of the *nexus*, resides in identity. To be true means to be identical; *inesse* means *idem esse* [to be the same].

> Ratio autem veritatis consistit in nexu praedicati cum subjecto, seu ut praedicatum subjecto insit, vel manifeste, ut in identicis, . . . vel tecte, [C. 11]. Et in identicis quidem connexio illa atque comprehensio praedicati in subjecto est expressa, in reliquis omnibus implicita, ac per analysin notionum ostendenda, in qua demonstratio a priori sita est. (C. 519)

> The nature of truth consists in the connection of the predicate with the subject, or the predicate is in the subject either in a way that is manifest, as in identities, or hidden. . . . In identities this connection and the inclusion of the predicate in the subject are explicit; in all other propositions they are implied and must be revealed through the analysis of the notions, which constitutes a demonstration a priori.

All statements are identities. But identities in a special sense are those statements whose identity is immediately manifest *(manifeste)*. In other statements the identity is hidden *(tecte)*, and the proof of their truth consists in making explicit the underlying identity.

The essence of truth is identity, completely aside from the question of whether human knowledge can succeed at actually demonstrating all truths as identities. But truth characterizes the essence of judgment, and the nature of truth, *natura veritatis*, is equivalent to the *nexus*. The inclusion theory is therefore a theory of identity.

At this point we are not yet going to explain how Leibniz establishes this identity theory, on what assumptions it rests, how far it can be carried out for all possible judgments, or how it is possible that (AB is B)=A is A (cf. C. 369). I will anticipate only with a suggestion to make clear how with this theory of λόγος, with these logical problems, we find ourselves immediately in the most central metaphysical questions, in the ontological problematic, the question about being as such.

The link between the problem of judgment and that of "individual substance" has already been indicated in general terms. To be true means to be identical; *inesse* is *idem esse*. Identity counts as the essence of truth, and for centuries identity counted as a feature of being (cf. the ταυτότης in Plato's *Sophist*). Truth and being are interpreted in view of the same phenomenon of sameness or identity. The question of truth and the question of being are directly intertwined.

Since this theory is important for Leibniz's entire philosophy, and since its concomitant metaphysical character arises immediately, it is good to document the theory somewhat more closely:

> Nimirum ut Identicae propositiones omnium primae sunt ... atque adeo per se verae ...; ita per consequentiam verae sunt virtualiter identicae, quae scilicet per analysin terminorum ... ad identicas formales sive expressas reducuntur. Manifestumque est omnes propositiones necessarias sive aeternae veritatis esse virtualiter identicas ... Generaliter omnis propositio vera (quae identica sive per se vera non est) potest probari a priori ope Axiomatum seu propositionum per se verarum, et ope definitionum seu idearum. Quotiescunque enim praedicatum vere affirmatur de subjecto, utique censetur aliqua esse connexio realis inter praedictum et subjectum, ita ut in propositione quacunque: A est B ..., utique B insit ipsi A, seu notio ejus in notione ipsius A aliquo modo contineatur. (G. VII, 300)

> Just as identical propositions are the primary propositions of all, ... and thus true per se ...; so as a result, truths are virtually identical which can be reduced to formal or explicit identities through an analysis of their terms. ... It is obvious that all necessary propositions, or propositions which have eternal truth, are virtual identities. ... In general, every true proposition which is not identical or true in itself can be proved a priori with the help of axioms or propositions that are true in themselves and with the help of definitions or ideas. For no matter how often a predicate is truly affirmed of a subject, there must be some real connection between subject and predicate, such that in every proposition whatever, such as A is B (or B is truly predicated of A), it is true that B is contained in A, or its concept is in some way contained in the concept of A itself. [L. 226]

An *identitas expressa* [explicit identity], is a *veritas* per se. True is what is virtually identical, and virtual identities get reduced to formal identities. Generally, whether it be an original or only a possible identity, every true proposition is provable a priori. That means that all true knowledge is ultimately a priori knowledge. This claim has incredibly far-reaching implications.

The identity theory of judgment is supposed to delineate the essence of judgment and to delineate thereby the essence of every form of proposition. Now since Leibniz distinguishes two basic kinds of propositions, there being at the same time, from what was found earlier, two basic forms of "truths," the general doctrine of the essence of judgment can be tested on these two forms of truth. Precisely at this point the difficulties must become clear.

In first describing the identity character of judgments we have already seen that Leibniz distinguishes two sorts of truths, the manifest and the latent. But this distinction requires further specification, which is provided by the following reflection:

> His attentius consideratis, patuit intimum inter veritates necessarias contingentesque discrimen. Nempe omnis veritas vel originaria est, vel derivativa. Veritates originariae sunt quarum ratio reddi non potest, et tales sunt identicae sive immediatae ... Veritates derivativae rursus duorum sunt generum: aliae enim resolvendi in infinitum admittunt. Illae sunt necessariae, hae, contingentes. (F. 181)

> A careful consideration of these matters revealed a very essential difference between necessary and contingent truths. Every truth is either original or derivative. Original truths are those for which no reason can be given; such are identities or immediate truths. ... There are in turn two genera of derivative truths: for some can be reduced to primary truths; others can be reduced in an infinite progression. The former are necessary; the latter, contingent. [L. 264]

All truths are divided into original and derivative truths. This distinction is not immediately identical with that between manifest and latent truths. Original truths are those for which no justification can be given, for which no proof is possible. They are in themselves immediately evident. Derivative truths, however, are divided into necessary and contingent truths. Necessary truths are to be reduced to original truths. Not every necessary truth is an original truth, but some are capable of and require a deduction. The other derivative truths are also identities in essence, but their analysis, their proof, never comes to an end—for finite understanding. Implicit in this thesis too is the claim that all knowledge is a priori knowledge.

Truths in themselves original and truths reducible to original truths, necessary truths, were called *veritates aeternae* by the Scholastics. Clearly, this division into basic kinds of truth also has its metaphysical, ontological background. The distinction between eternal and contingent truths corresponds to a division of beings: *ens per se necessarium* and *entia contingentia, ens increatum* and *ens creatum.* Eternal truths deal "primarily" with the self-thinking of the uncreated being. They are, in the tradition of Platonism, formal truths of thought in general and of mathematics. Contingent truths relate to created beings, which exist in time, now, previously, or in the future. Eternal truths have their eternal source in the absolute reason of God, and thus Leibniz calls them also *veritates rationis (vérités de raison)*; contingent truths, related to facts, are called *veritates facti (vérités de fait)*: In the *Monadologie* (§33; G. VI, 612; B. II, 443) he puts it this way:

> There are also two kinds of truths, truths of reasoning and truths of fact. Truths of reasoning are necessary, and their opposite is impossible. Truths of fact are contingent, and their opposite is possible. [L. 646]

The foregoing relationships can be set down in a chart:

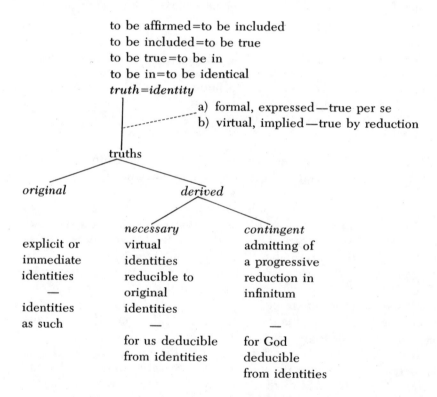

to be affirmed=to be included
to be included=to be true
to be true=to be in
to be in=to be identical
truth=identity

a) formal, expressed—true per se
b) virtual, implied—true by reduction

truths

original   *derived*

                   necessary   *contingent*

explicit or   virtual   admitting of
immediate   identities   a progressive
identities   reducible to   reduction in
                  original   infinitum
—   identities
identities   identities
as such   —   —

                   for us deducible   for God
                   from identities   deducible
                                           from identities

Contingent truths are truths about that which is not necessary, what can also not be. The basic aim of Leibniz's theory of judgment is to comprehend even these *veritates facti* as identities, as ultimately primordial, eternal truths, and thus to attribute to them as well an ideal absolute certainty and truth. There is thus the tendency in his theory to assimilate as far as possible the *veritates facti* to truths of reasoning—though this is not stated with complete accuracy, since truths of fact are supposed to retain their own quality and nonetheless have the character of identities. Truths of fact are to have the character of judgments whose entire predicates can be evolved or explicated from the very concept of the subject. To put it more accurately, *veritates facti* are not *veritates necessariae,* but they are *identicae* [truths of identity].

As odd as this tendency to assimilate *veritates facti* to *veritates rationis* may seem at first (so that even historical truth would be an a priori truth!?), it is not so completely strange if we do not lose sight of two things. 1) Leibniz's tendency as a whole is in a certain sense that of a "rationalist." He strives to conceive being from the viewpoint of *ratio* [reasoning] and conceives the *esse facti* [being of fact] from the viewpoint of *ratio;* 2) there is, furthermore, behind this tendency the *Scholastic tradition,* which precisely in this problem exerts its influence in a central way. The ideal of cognition as such is seen in the *scientia Dei* [the knowledge God has]. We will begin with the latter connections.

For Scholasticism it is the absolute intellect of God which serves as the *veritas prima,* the first truth, and as the source of all truth (Cf. Aquinas's *Quaestiones disputatae de veritate,* q. I). The original truth, the totality of all true knowledge, is absolute, and is found in the *scientia Dei.* Aquinas treats this at length in his *Summa Theologica* (I, q. XIV; also cf. *Quaest. disp. de ver.,* q. II). The basic problems of modern philosophy remain completely closed to one who has no acquaintance with and understanding of these connections. The Scholastic doctrine of God is not only the key to Leibniz's logic. Kant's *Critique of Pure Reason* as well as Hegel's *Logic* become intelligible in their authentic thrusts from the viewpoint of the Scholastic doctrine of God. This is not to say that modern philosophy modeled itself on and borrowed propositions from theology. The philosophical meaning of the orientation on the "scientia Dei" is that God's knowledge functions as the construct of an absolute cognition, on the basis of which finite, human cognition should be measured. To what extent and why such a construct belongs to the essence of philosophy, to what extent philosophical knowledge as such is a construct, cannot be discussed here.

N.B. We have to refer to metaphysical connections with Scholasticism, but certainly not for the sake of depreciating the originality of Leibniz. To ask, Where did he get that from? stems from a shopkeeper's mentality. Or, equally superficial, to ask, Which psychic complex caused that idea to occur to him? The superiority of productive work lies in its being dependent in an original and central way, as the imitator never can be because the imitator does not want to be dependent, being himself preoccupied with originality. Our orientation on the Scholastics has thus to do with something quite different. And you are not at all at a dead end if you find yourself appropriately astonished by this course on logic that treats the concept of God in Thomas Aquinas. Nevertheless, I must here forego, as really [objectively] would be required, a thorough introduction, into these problems. Only the most necessary elements can be mentioned.

The knowledge that belongs to God, who knows in an absolute way, includes what is possible as well as what is actual. With respect to both concepts a distinction is needed. "Possible" means at once *mere possibilia*, pure possibilities, what is essential in beings, the ideas of things, regardless of whether or not such an idea is ever actualized. To become actual, something must be intrinsically possible, but everything intrinsically possible need not also become actual. God has a knowledge of these pure possibilities as such (the transcendental ideal of the *omnitudo realitatis* in Kant). Or better, it belongs to God's essence simply to think the totality of what is possible. This "knowing with simple understanding," *scientia simplicis intelligentiae*, is the naturally necessary rational knowledge, *scientia necessaria naturalis*, for it belongs to the "nature" of God as absolute self-consciousness (νόησις νοήσεως). In the knowledge of his thinking, God knows what is thought in this absolute thinking, i.e., the totality of reality, the *omnitudo realitatis*, pure possibilities.

But the "possible" means, further, that which in actuality is not yet but will be, or what has been spoken out of the eternity of God before all time. That which will actualize itself out of the possible is all that which will once be a *factum* at a definite time someday, all that which is not only in general possible, but also determined. For God as absolute spirit does not first know a fact, as such, after it has occurred. Otherwise he would be in essence variable and dependent on something he is not himself, and thus finite. God has, moreover, a precognition of everything actual, a *visio*, a *scientia libera* [free knowledge], because whatever does become actual remains ultimately a matter of his willing it.

To clarify both kinds of divine knowledge, *scientia necessaria* and *libera* [necessary and free knowledge], I will briefly review the relevant article of Quaestio XIV *(De scientia Dei)* in the first part of the *Summa Theologica.*

In Article 9, *Utrum Deus habeat scientiam non entium,* Aquinas distinguishes the *non entia secundum quid* [things nonexistent in some respect] and *non entia simpliciter.* The first are those which are not now *in actu* [actual], but which are possible insofar as they have been or shall be, i.e., the not-being of this possible thing is conceived with respect to *(secundum)* what is already existent. From non-beings of this sort are to be distinguished non-beings *simpliciter,* which are pure *possibilia.* These God knows with knowledge of *simplicis intelligentiae,* the non-beings *secundum quid* in the *scientia visionis.* The *visio* is a grasping in the manner of a *praesens intuitus* [present intuition].

Praesens is understood here from the perspective of *aeternitas, quae sine successione existens totum tempus comprehendit* [which, existing without succession, comprises the totality of time]. In contradistinction to *cum successione, praesens* means that this intuition is not a series of intuitive acts, but instead realizes itself in the "Now" (Eckhart's "Nu"). The Now is not the momentary now of time, the *nunc fluens* but is the eternal now, the *nunc stans.*

Intuitus means a direct insight, a knowledge that comprehends the whole of time in a single stroke without succession. *Visio* as *praesens intuitus* is a look which must be taken to range over the whole, as present before God who has everything existing presently before him. God's present intuition reaches into the totality of time and into all things that are in any time whatsoever, as into objects present to him. *Praesens intuitus Dei fertur in totum tempus et in omnia, quae sunt in quocumque tempore, sicut in subjecta sibi praesentialiter.*

The *scientia simplicis intelligentiae* [knowledge of simple intelligence] is not a *visio,* but rather a simple understanding, since pure possibilities are not realized external to God. They are immanent in God as thought possibilities, whereas any seeing relates to the outer or external. All the past beings, and beings present and future, are viewed as present in the *praesens intuitus* of *visio.* This everlasting view includes possible and merely "arbitrary" facts actualized in a contingent way, truths of fact, the historical in the broadest sense.

It follows therefore that in this *intuitus,* God knows not only beings *in actu* but also those future things which to us are contingent. Article 13 *(Utrum scientia Dei sit futurorum contingentium)* explains more precisely how God knows future things. The contingent can come to be seen, first of all, *in se ipso*, that is, as *praesens*, as *determinatum in unum* [determined to one]. It is indeed contingent; it could also not be, but it is now factually existing, and as such I can regard it *in se ipso*. As such an actuality, it has been determined with respect to a definite possibility. It has passed into its actuality, and to that extent it is determined to one. The contingent *in se ipso* can be subject to an infallibly certain knowledge, namely, in a factual ascertainment on the basis of sensory intuition, *infallibiliter subdi potest certae cognitioni*. Such knowledge is no problem.

Secondly, the contingent can be considered as it is in its cause, *ut est in sua causa*, as futural, as not yet determined to one, as *nondum determinatum ad unum*. In this case the contingent is considered from the viewpoint of its cause, as what is yet to be actualized; it is taken as *futurum*, and as such it is still open to definite possibilities. Regarding the possible cognition of this sort of contingence, there can be no certain knowledge of it, no *certa cognitio*. For whoever regards the effect only from the cause has merely a *cognitio conjecturalis*, a conjecture; it can turn out this way or that.

According to Aquinas, God knows the *contingens futurum*, as well as the *contingens in se ipso*. He knows *contingentia non solum ut in suis causis, sed etiam prout unumquodque eorum est actu in se ipso, non tamen successive, sed simul* [contingent things not only as they are in their causes but also as each one of them is actually in itself, not however successively but simultaneously]. He knows in this way because he has already in his eternal present anticipated everything in the future. God knows in such a way, as it were, that he sees everything equally present in his presentness [Gegenwärtigkeit]; he sees *omnia prout sunt in sua praesentialitate* [all things just as they are in their presentiality]. All this is present to divine sight not only in its essential possibility but, as Thomas emphasizes, in its individual actualization. And on account of this presentness, the divine panorama is accomplished *infallibiliter*. We humans, on the contrary, according to the image in Aquinas's *responsum ad 3*, know after the manner of a person walking on a path, who does not see those coming behind him; but the person looking over the whole path from an elevated position sees everyone walking along the path.

Article 14 *(Utrum Deus cognoscat enunciabilia)* treats whether God's knowledge also includes *omnia enuntiabilia quae formari possunt* [all that can be stated propositionally]. *Enunciabilia* refer to all possible true statements, all truths possible. We already know that a proposition is a συμπλοκή, a σύνθεσις and διαίρησις, a *compositio* and *divisio*. Here Aquinas's explanation has central import for us. The question is whether God knows possible statements in the mode of composing and dividing. This is the nature of finite knowing, which happens successively: *intellectus noster de uno in aliud discurrit* [our intellect proceeds from one thing to another]. In God, however, there is no succession; it is not as if at first he might not yet have something.

If, for example, we know *quid est homo* [what man is], this means *non ex hoc intelligimus alia, quae ei insunt* [we do not from this knowledge understand other things pertaining to man]. When a human knower understands a subject, he is not in a position to extract from it all the complete predicates of the subject. Rather, because of successivity, he has to render what is known separately *(seorsum) in unum redigere per modum compositionis vel divisionis enuntiationem formando* [into a unity by way of composing or dividing in the formation of propositions]. But God, on the other hand, knows in each case the whole essence and *quaecumque eis accidere possunt* [whatever accidents can belong to it]. For he knows *per simplicem intelligentiam,* wherein all predicates belonging to a subject are all at once grasped as being in this subject, are grasped in their *inesse*. What for us is a separate and successive attribution of predicates is for God an original unity, a sameness, identity.

Article 7 *(Utrum scientia Dei sit discursiva)* again affirms that God's knowledge is in no way discursive, *nullo modo discursiva,* but according to his essence (cf. Articles 4 and 5 ·of the same *quaestio*), his knowledge is an original seeing of the whole all at once and in a single stroke: *Deus autem omnia videt in uno.*

We must keep in mind then that there is a double *scientia* in God, a *necessaria* and *libera*. But both are simply absolute and a priori. That is, God has also, in advance, a complete conception of each and every fact, and knows with absolute certainty what and how it will be. He possesses all truths about the created, and truths about the created are just as simply necessary and certain for him as truths about what is possible. In both kinds of truth it is a matter of knowing from the concept of the particular being, of a simple evolution of the determinations implied, i.e., of pure identities.

It has now become clear where the decisive motif for Leibniz resides relative to the *assimilation* of the *veritates facti* to the *veritates rationis*. What holds true of the absolute spirit of God, Leibniz takes likewise for the cognitive ideal for humans. He defines the idea and essence of human knowledge, i.e., of truth, and of the statement, from the idea of the *scientia Dei*. But, because human knowledge is finite, it has no absolute *visio libera*. For example, we do not have a priori, prior to all experience, a total concept of Julius Caesar as this definite individual subject, so that, possessing this subject concept, we could develop all the predicates from it as necessarily belonging to it.

Leibniz speaks even more clearly on the nature of contingent truths *(veritates facti)*:

> Sed in veritatibus contingentibus, etsi praedicatum insit subjecto, nunquam tamen de eo potest demonstrari, neque unquam ad aequationem seu identitatem revocari potest propositio, sed resolutio procedit in infinitum, Deo solo vidente non quidem finem resolutionis qui nullus est, sed tamen connexionem (terminorum) seu involutionem praedicati in subjecto, quia ipse videt quidquid seriei inest. *(De libertate, F. 182).*

> In contingent truths, however, though the predicate inheres in the subject, we can never demonstrate this, nor can the proposition ever be reduced to an equation or an identity, but the analysis proceeds to infinity, only God being able to see, not the end of the analysis indeed, since there is no end, but the nexus of terms or the inclusion of the predicate in the subject, since he sees everything which is in the series. [*On Freedom*, L. 265]

Though with contingent truths the predicate is also in the subject (a latent identity), no rigorous proof can ever be carried out. The relation of subject and predicate cannot be reduced to a mathematical equation, but the analysis proceeds *ad infinitum*. In such an analysis of historical truths into their identities, only God alone sees not the end of the process, for there is no end, but the whole of the predicates' containment in the subject, because he sees, and not through a step-by-step procedure, what resides in the series of predicates. (On the problem of analyzing concepts and the necessity of analysis, see also the passage cited by Couturat in *La logique de Leibniz*, p. 183, note 3: *ostenditur ad perfectas demonstrationes veritatum non requiri perfectos conceptus rerum* [it is shown that perfect concepts of things are not required for perfect demonstrations of truths].)

The truth to be distinguished has a relation to number through the concept of an infinite series (cf. *De Libertate*). Contingent truth is related to necessary truth as incommensurable magnitudes, which are not reducible to any common measure, are to commensurable magnitudes. But just as incommensurable magnitudes are also subjected to a mathematics aiming at *adaequatio*, at identity, so contingent truths are subjected to the *visio Dei*, which needs no serial discursiveness.

The distinction between truths of reasoning and truths of fact can be grasped in another way, a way also pre-shaped by the traditional ontology.

> Hinc jam discimus alias esse propositiones quae pertinent ad Essentias, alias vero quae ad Existentias rerum; Essentiales nimirum sunt quae ex resolutione Terminorum possunt demonstrari ⟨: veritates aeternae⟩ . . . Ab his vero toto genere differunt Existentiales sive contingentes, quarum veritas a sola Mente infinita a priori intelligitur. (C. 18, cf. 20)

> Hence we now learn that there are some propositions that pertain to the essences of things, and others that pertain to the existences of things. Essential propositions are, to be sure, those which can be proved through an analysis of terms ⟨veritates aeternae⟩. . . Of a wholly different kind are existential or contingent propositions whose truth is understood a priori by the infinite Mind alone.

But despite this difference *toto genere*, the nature of essential and existential truths (statements) is still the same insofar as both are identities.

The origin of these truths differs.

> Necessariae ⟨veritates⟩, quales Arithmeticae, Geometricae, Logicae fundantur in divino intellectu a voluntate independentes . . . At Veritates contingentes oriuntur a voluntate Dei non mera, sed optimi seu convenientissimi considerationibus, ab intellectu directa. (Letter to Bourget, April 11, 1710, G. III, 550)

> Necessary truths, such as the truths of arithmetic, geometry, and logic, have their foundation in the divine intellect independently of divine volition. . . . But contingent truths arise from the will of God, not simply, but from a will directed by the intellect, through considerations of what is best or most fitting.

Necessary truths dealing with pure possibilities have their foundation in the divine understanding, independently of the will of God. Leibniz adds this because Descartes taught that mathematical and logical truths also depend on God's will. But contingent truths, knowledge of what in fact happens and how it happens, and the being of what is known in this cognition, depend on God's will, not, however, on his pure willing, but on a will guided by his understanding, which is in turn guided by a consideration of what is best and most appropriate, for the actual world is the best of all worlds.

And in another passage Leibniz says: *Ut veritates necessariae solum intellectum divinum involvunt, ita contingentes voluntatis decreta* (C. 23) [As necessary truths involve the divine intellect alone, so contingent truths involve decrees of the will]. Or: *Quodsi propositio sit contingens, non est necessaria connexio, sed tempore variatur et ex suppositio divino decreto, et libera voluntate pendet* (C. 402) [If a proposition is contingent, there is no necessary connection, but it varies in time and by supposition depends on divine decree and free will]. There are, accordingly, also two kinds of impossibility: the "logical" impossibility of self-contradictions, and the imperfection of what is "morally" impossible though not self-contradictory.

Truth is identity. It is, in principle, possible to reduce all truths to identities. Derived truths divide into two classes: necessary and contingent; truths of reasoning and truths of fact, truths of essence and truths of existence. The unity of all three classes of truths takes its bearings from the *scientia Dei.*

The assimilation of truths of fact to truths of reasoning is the ideal of a knowledge of actual beings, a knowledge from sheer concepts of reason of what can be empirically experienced, a knowledge of beings from pure reason. This theory, which was behind the developing thrust of modern philosophy, was to be brought to a critique which gave the title to Kant's major work, *The Critique of Pure Reason.* This is the inner connection between Leibniz's theory of judgment and Kant's basic problem.

A twofold intention defined Leibniz's conception of truth. He tried both to reduce contingent truths to identities and, at the same time, to maintain the features peculiar to contingent truths of fact. This leads him to define the basic principles of knowledge correspondingly.

In memoriam Max Scheler

Max Scheler is dead. He was in the midst of a great and broadly based work, at the stage of a new approach for advancing toward what is ultimate and whole, at the start of a new period of teaching for which he had many hopes.

Max Scheler was, aside from the sheer scale and quality of his productivity, the strongest philosophical force in modern Germany, nay, in contemporary Europe and even in contemporary philosophy as such.

His philosophical beginnings were guided by Eucken; he began with a positive science, biology. He received decisive impetus from Husserl and the *Logical Investigations.* Scheler clearly perceived the new possibilities of phenomenology. He did not take it up superficially and use it, but furthered it essentially and unified it directly with central problems of philosophy. In particular, his critique of ethical formalism bears witness to this. His encounter with Bergson was also important for him. (But occasions, impulses, and opportunities remain inoperative unless they meet and are transformed by an already living will. The important thing is not results and progress—these are to be found only in the realm of what is at bottom irrelevant.)

Decisive for and characteristic of Scheler's nature was the totality of his questioning. Standing in the midst of the whole of beings, he had an unusual sensitivity for all the new possibilities and forces opening up. He had a peculiar irrepressible drive always to think out and interpret things as a whole.

And so it is no accident that Scheler, who was raised a Catholic, in an age of collapse took his philosophical path again in the direction of what is "catholic" as a universal-historical world power, not in the sense of the Church. Augustine and Pascal acquired new meaning—new as answers to and against Nietzsche.

But this new possibility broke down again too for Max Scheler. Once again the question, What is man? moved to the center of his work. This question he asked again within the whole of philosophy, in the sense of Aristotle's theology. With enormous boldness he saw the idea of the weak God, one who cannot be God without man, so that man himself is thought of as "God's co-worker." All this was far removed from a smug theism or a vague pantheism. Scheler's scheme moved toward a philosophical anthropology, an attempt to work out the special position of man.

Were his changing views a sign of a lack of substance, of inner emptiness? But one recognizes here—something which of course only a few could directly experience in day-and-night-long conversations and arguments with him—an obsession with philosophy, which he himself was unable to master and after which he had to follow, something which in the brokenness of contemporary existence often drove him to powerlessness and despair. But this obsession was his substance. And with every change he remained loyal to this inner direction of his nature in always new approaches and endeavors. And this loyalty must have been the source from which sprang the childlike kindness he showed on occasion.

There is no one among today's serious philosophers who is not essentially indebted to him, no one who could replace the living possibility for philosophy which passed away with him. This irreplaceability, however, is the sign of his greatness.

The greatness of such an existence can only be measured by the

standards it must itself give. The greatness of Scheler's philosophical existence lay in a relentless encounter with what time only
dimly lets come upon us, an encounter with what permits of no
easy reckoning into what has come down to us, an encounter with
mankind that allows for no appeasement and leveling through a
sterile humanism that returns to the ancients. What Dilthey and
Max Weber encountered, each in his own way, was in Scheler
powerful in a completely original way and with the strongest
philosophical force.

Max Scheler is dead. We bow before his fate. Once again a path
of philosophy falls back into darkness.

§3. *The idea of truth and the principles of knowledge*

The essence of truth as such resides in the identity of subject and
predicate. Knowledge of truths is accordingly a grasp of identities.
There are then different signs and criteria for the truth of cognition, depending on whether the identities are either manifest or
must first be proved, and proved in the double sense of necessary
and contingent truths.

The usual conception of the principles of knowledge in Leibniz
depends on the idea that a parallel distinction between two basic
principles is to be added to the distinction between truths of reasoning and truths of fact. Truths of reasoning follow the law of
non-contradiction, and truths of fact follow the principle of
sufficient reason (Cf. *Monadologie*, n. 31ff.). The Leibnizians
Wolff and Baumgarten *(Metaphysica,* section 19ff.) went so far as
to prove even the latter principle from the former and to place all
knowledge ultimately under the principle of non-contradiction.
Taken as negative expression of the principle of identity, the
principle of non-contradiction is then the basic principle of all
cognition, of all truths as identities. There is some justification for
this interpretive trend, a trend which nonetheless goes counter to
Leibniz and especially to the problems themselves, as should become clear immediately.

We shall begin with the first class of truths. Express identities,
primary truths, wear their identity character for all to see. What
indicates their truth is just this manifest identity itself (A is A). If
we make this criterion for the truth of primary truths into a principle, the principle would itself be: A is A, *the principle of identity.* The principle of the knowledge of primary truths is nothing
other than the most elementary of primary truths. That is essential.

The criterion, identity, is itself the first truth and the source of truth. Accordingly, we should note that this principle does not remain extrinsic to those cognitive statements for which it is the guiding principle. Rather, it itself belongs to the statements as their first statement.

These truths are those *quarum ratio reddi non potest*, for which no reason can be given (cf. the passage in *De Libertate* cited above on p. 41). This does not mean they are groundless, but, on the contrary, they are themselves ground, so that they are in no need of a grounding, of a deduction. They are precisely *veritates originariae*. The usual truths, necessary and contingent, are in need of grounding. They fall under the *principium rationis*, or better, under the *principium reddendae rationis*, the *principle of demonstrating grounds*, i.e., the *resolutio* (the principle of the need for proof). It is therefore not only the class of derivative truths, contingent truths, that come under the principle of reasoning, but each derivative truth in its very essence is under this *principium rationis*. Nevertheless, the *veritates necessariae* are referred to a special principle: the *principium contradictionis*.

The second class of truths includes necessary truths, those directly reducible to identities. *Absolute necessaria propositio est quae resolvi potest in identicas, seu cujus oppositum implicat contradictionem... Quod vero implicat contradictionem, seu cujus oppositum est necessarium, id impossible appellatur* (C. 17) [An absolutely necessary proposition is one which can be reduced to identities or one whose opposite implies a contradiction. ... For whatever implies a contradiction, or whatever has an opposite that is necessary, is called an impossibility]. Criterion of necessary truths is, in accord with their essence, reducibility to identities. Reducibility to identities, however, denotes an accordance with identities. What is not in accord but in discord with identities "speaks against" (contra-dicts) identities and contains a contradiction. Reducibility to identities denotes *non-contradiction*. Whatever contains a contradiction is what cannot at all be, since *esse* denotes *inesse* and this denotes *idem esse*. What basically cannot be is impossible.

Yet insofar as these necessary truths are subject to the principle of non-contradiction as principle of their reducibility, i.e., of their demonstrability, the *principium reddendae rationis* pertains to them also. Indeed, one could and must say, conversely, that the latter principle is more primordial than the principle of non-contradiction.

To be sure, Leibniz also says:

Absolute autem et in se illa demum propositio est vera, quae vel est identica, vel ad identicas potest reduci, hoc est quae potest demonstrari a priori seu cujus praedicati cum subjecto connexio explicari potest, ita ut semper appareat ratio. Et quidem nihil omnino fit sine aliqua ratione, seu nulla est propositio praeter identicas in qua connexio inter praedicatum et subjectum non possit distincte explicari, nam in identicis praedicatum et subjectum coincidunt aut in idem redeunt. Et hoc est inter prima principia omnis ratiocinationis humanae, et post principium contradictionis maximum habet usum in omnibus scientiis. (C. 513 f.)

But that proposition is absolutely and in itself true which either is an identity or can be reduced to an identity, i.e., which can be demonstrated a priori or whose connection of the predicate with the subject can be made explicit such that its reason always may appear. And indeed nothing at all can come about without some reason, or, except identities, there is no proposition in which a connection between predicate and subject cannot be made distinctly explicit, for in identities the predicate and subject terms coincide or can be reduced to the same. This is among the first principles of human ratiocination and it has, after the principle of all non-contradiction, the greatest use in all sciences.

Here the ontological position of the *principium rationis* remains unclarified, only the "use" of the principle is discussed. But the *principium rationis* is the principle for unfolding the identity that is to be revealed.

On the other hand again, since the principle of noncontradiction is at bottom the principle of identity, it cannot be restricted to a class of identities, but it must be related to all identities, and therefore also to contingent truths. In proving contingent truths we make no real use of the principle because it is impossible for us to carry out the reduction to identities.

Two things thus result: 1) The relationship between both these principles, or among the three principles, is not directly clear, even in Leibniz himself. 2) Even when Leibniz himself often related explicitly both principles to the two classes of necessary and contingent truths, he nevertheless says, in important passages of three major works, that both principles obtain in both classes, namely, hold true for all derivative truths.

N.B. Compare, first, in the appendix to the *Theodizee* (1710), in the section treating controversies over the book by King, section 14, "On the Origin of Evil":

Absolute necessaria propositio est quae resolvi potest in identicas, seu cujus oppositum implicat contradictionem. ... Quod vero implicat contradictionem, seu cujus oppositum est necessarium, id impossible appellatur. (cf. G. VI, 414)

The one principle and the other has its validity not only in the field of necessary truths but also in the field of contingent truths. . . . For one can in a certain sense say that these principles are included in the definition of true and false.

In the treatise on *Primae veritates* Leibniz says, after he has shown identity to be the essence of truth:

Ex his propter nimiam facilitatem suam non satis consideratis multa consequuntur magni momenti. Statim enim hinc nascitur axioma receptum: nihil esse sine ratione, seu: nullum effectum esse absque causa. Alioqui veritas daretur, quae non posset, probari a priori, seu quae non resolveretur in identicas, quod est contra naturam veritatis, quae semper vel expresse vel implicite identica est. (C. 519)

These matters have not been adequately considered, because they are too easy, but there follows from them many things of great importance. At once they give rise to the accepted axiom that there is nothing without a reason, or no effect without a cause. Otherwise there would be truth which could not be proved a priori or resolved into identities—contrary to the nature of truth, which is always either expressly or implicitly identical. [L. 268]

This means: from what was explained about identity and truth, which on account of its self-evidence is not investigated sufficiently, much follows of great importance. From the definition of truth follows the principle of sufficient reason. Were the principle of ground not an original principle of that truth, then there would be no a priori proof, no reduction to identity, which is contrary to the essence of truth as such. Finally, in the *Monadologie* (1714), in section 36, he says: "Yet the sufficient reason must also be such that it can be found in contingent truths or truths of fact, that is to say, in the reciprocal connectedness of all created things." Leibniz here refers to section 33, where he suggested that with necessary truths one can "find the ground through analysis" and through it arrive at identities (cf. G. VI, 612).

This summary of the principles of knowledge shows their connection with identity as the essence of truth. Identity is, however, the basic feature of the being of all beings. The principle of reason holds first rank, albeit unclearly, among the principles. A connection emerges between reason, or ground, and truth and being, with reference to identity. The fundamental meaning of the principle of reason first becomes clear, however, when one realizes that the main principles of Leibnizian metaphysics are based on it and that Leibniz even deduces his metaphysical principles from it (cf. *Primae veritates*). There thus arises a far-reaching ambiguity in this *principium rationis:* principles of harmony, constancy, fittingness or *melius* (the better), existence, the identity of indiscernibles, are all connected or identical with the *principium rationis.*

As a whole it becomes clear that the tendency to assimilate both basic forms of truth *(veritas rationis* and *veritas facti),* and accordingly the connection between both basic principles, though still unclear, takes its bearings from the *scientia Dei,* the idea of absolute knowledge. Then the question is whether and how Leibniz defines the idea of knowledge in general, where he sees the nature of cognition as such. Since truth is an essential characteristic of knowledge—false knowledge is not knowledge—the essence of truth, hitherto defined as identity, must become clear with the clarification of the idea of knowledge. But to be true coincides with being included and being identical. Accordingly, by clarifying the idea of knowledge, we should be able to gain sharper insight into the basic connections in which we are now moving. The question is: How, according to their essential structure, do the following fit together: judgment, truth, identity, knowledge, being, and the basic principles of knowledge?

N.B. It is good to notice that we are continually moving about in the same dimension of basic phenomena with such terms, without our yet being in a position to recognize an unambiguous order of interdependence. Indeed, perhaps there is no order in the sense that one would be "linearly" deducible from the other. And in fact none of these basic phenomena is more primordial than the other. They are equiprimordial. But precisely on that account there is a central problem concerning: 1) the inner constitution of this equiprimordiality, and 2) the ground which makes it possible. The question concerns the nature of the integrity (non-decomposability) of this equiprimordial dimension of the transcendental.

Summary

We are searching for a philosophical logic and therewith an introduction to philosophizing. We are trying to grasp the foundations of the logic that is traditionally explained in a superficial, technical way. We are trying to understand the elemental grounds of what logic usually treats. These grounds and foundations are attained only by metaphysics; thus our title: "The Metaphysical Foundations of Logic." In the introduction we showed how the main phenomena of what is discussed in logic refer back to metaphysics. Truth refers to transcendence, ground to freedom, concept to schema, the copula to being. Because this connection is essential, it had to reassert itself repeatedly in previous philosophy, though there was a trend, which arises today more than ever, to isolate logic and base logic upon itself alone.

If we, on the contrary, wish to ground logic metaphysically, we need communication with the history of philosophy, because metaphysics itself must be grounded anew. For we are not in possession of a finished metaphysics so as to be able to build logic into it, but the dismantling of logic is itself part of the grounding of metaphysics. But this is nothing else than a confrontation about principles with the whole previous tradition.

We seek, then, first to press ahead on historical paths into the dimension of the metaphysical foundations of logic. We choose no arbitrary orientation, but take our bearings, for the reasons given, from Leibniz. This major section is therefore entitled: "Dismantling the Leibnizian Doctrine of Judgment Down to Basic Metaphysical Problems." The task is divided into seven headings, three of which we have already treated: 1) characterization of the general structure of judgement—the theory of inclusion, 2) the idea of truth, the theory of identity, and the basic forms of truth (*veritas rationis, veritas facti*), 3) the idea of truth and the principles of knowledge (*principium contradictionis, principium rationis sufficientis*). By this time the presupposition of an idea of absolute truth has become clear. Knowledge is projected toward a definite ideal.

All historical orientation is only living when we learn to see that what is ultimately essential is due to our own interpreting in the free re-thinking by which we gain detachment from all erudition.

§4. *The idea of knowledge as such*

In characterizing the *scientia Dei* we came to the following conclusions: it is an *intuitus praesens omnia subjecta sibi praesentialiter* [a present intuition to which all things are subject in their presentness]. Intuition is immediate seeing, looking, and *praesens* refers to "present," in contradistinction to *cum successione*. God's knowledge is not achieved in a succession of acts intuiting individual things but it occurs without succession, all at once in a moment. But it is a moment that lasts not momentarily but remains the same for eternity. Thus it has *aeternitas*. It is the *nunc stans*, the abiding and remaining Now, the ever-lasting present. This present intuition, constantly present in God, has for its part everything "present" [gegenwärtig] before it. That is, this constantly present intuition has its intuited object—the whole of what actually has been, is now, and will be—lying before it as present [anwesend]. Knowledge is *intuitus, visio,* immediate constant seeing of everything in its presentness [Anwesenheit].

This idea of knowledge, however, follows from the eternity of God. Eternal is what is always all at once, *totum simul.* Eternity is the *mensura temporis* [the measure of time]. But eternity is itself inferred from *immutabilitas,* from *simplicitas.* The reconstructed inference is therefore as follows: *simplicitas→immutabilitas→aeternitas→intuitus praesens.* What by its nature is unchangeable cannot be altered by the addition of new knowledge. What is unchangeable is eternal, and as eternal it must possess everything at once free of change. Therefore the mode of knowledge of such an absolute being must have the character of *intuitus praesens (omnia sibi praesentialiter subjiciens)* [bringing everything before itself in its presentness].

Leibniz answered the question about the idea, about the essence of knowledge as such, in a small treatise, *Meditationes de Cognitione, Veritate et Ideis,* published by himself, an unusual circumstance with him, (November, 1684, in *Acta Eruditorum Lipsiensium* pp. 537–42, two years before the *Discours;* G. IV, 422-26) [L. 291]. Following Descartes, the Cartesians dealt with the theme frequently at that time. The questions entered a new phase through a polemic published against Malebranche by the aforementioned Antoine Arnauld, *Traité des vraies et des fausses idées.* It is a fundamental confrontation with Descartes and his principles of knowledge, and an important stage on the way from Descartes to Kant regarding the problem of "categories." Leibniz begins his treatise by taking a position toward those controversies:

> Quoniam hodie inter Viros egregios de veris et falsis ideis controversiae agitantur, eaque res magni ad veritatem cognoscendam momenti est, in qua nec ipse Cartesius usquequaque satisfecit, placet quid mihi de discriminibus atque criteriis idearum et cognitionum statuendum videatur, explicare paucis. (op. cit., 422)

> Since distinguished men are today engaged in controversies about true and false ideas, a matter of great importance for understanding the truth and one to which even Descartes did not entirely do justice, I should like briefly to explain what I think may be established about the different kinds and the criteria of ideas and of knowledge. [L. 291]

Then follows the sentence which, in a condensed form, anticipates the contents of the subsequent treatise.

> Est ergo cognitio vel obscura vel clara, et clara rursus vel confusa vel distincta, et distincta vel inadaequata vel adaequata, item vel symbolica vel intuitiva: et quidem si simul adaequata et intuitiva sit, perfectissima est. (Ibid.)

> Knowledge is either obscure or clear; clear knowledge is either confused or distinct; distinct knowledge is either inadequate or adequate, and also either symbolic or intuitive. The most perfect knowledge is that which is both adequate and intuitive.

Leibniz progressively designates two contraries characteristic of knowledge; he always further divides the emerging positive characteristic, and then concludes with the idea of the most perfect knowledge. The most perfect knowledge is *adaequata, intuitiva,* direct intuition. Schematically the progression is:

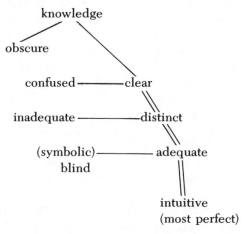

We will try to interpret briefly the characteristics of knowledge mentioned.

A *notio* is *obscura, quae non sufficit ad rem repraesentatam agnoscendam* [A notion is obscure which does not suffice for recognizing the thing represented]. Knowledge of or acquaintance with something is confused when the knowledge is insufficient for recognizing what the being itself, as such, is, in the event one comes across it. For example, I have knowledge of a certain animal I saw previously. In the event I come across this animal again, but do not recognize it on the basis of my knowledge, mistaking it instead for another animal, then my knowledge is confused. Confused cognitions are those which lead to the conflation of things in themselves different. There are also confused terms in philosophy, such as Aristotle's too little explicated concept of *entelecheia,* or also the concept of *causa. Unde propositio quo que obscura fit, quam notio talis ingreditur* [Therefore a proposition too becomes obscure insofar as such a notion is an ingredient in it]. *Clara ergo cognitio est, cum habeo unde rem repraesentatam agnoscere possim.* That knowledge is *clear* which makes it possible for me to recognize a being I encounter as the same being I saw previously, to grasp it as the same, to "identify" it.

Now it can be that I truly have a clear notion and can thus with certainty distinguish, every time, a hawk from a buzzard, but am not able to provide in detail those features on the basis of which both animals can be adequately distinguished. The *notio clara* can still be *confusa.*

Knowledge is *confusa,* confused, or, more exactly, "flowing to-gether," *cum scilicet non possum notas ad rem ab aliis discernen-dam sufficientes separatim enumerare, licet res illa tales notas atque requisita revera habeat, in quae notio ejus resolvi possit,* when I cannot enumerate one by one the marks which are sufficient to distinguish this clearly known thing from others, even though the thing may have such marks and *requisita* [constituents] into which its concept can be analyzed.

The concept of *nota,* "marks" or denotations contained in a term, means essential attribute and individual feature. *Requisita,* "constituents," are the moments into which knowledge of a thing is analyzable. (Cf., in what follows, the double determination of *cognitio distincta.* For the relationship between *notae* and *re-quisita,* see the difference between implicit and express identity in § II.)

Leibniz gives the following examples of ideas that are *clarae* but *confusae:* colors are distinguishable from odors and flavors *satis clare* [with sufficient clarity], *sed simplici sensuum testimonio, non vero notis enuntiabilibus* [but only by the simple evidence of the senses and not by marks that can be expressed]. To the blind, red is not to be explained by definition but only *eos in rem praesentem ducendo* [by bringing them into the presence of the thing]. Artists know with absolute clarity *quid recte, quid vitiose factum sit* [what is done well and what poorly], but when asked how or in what way, they can only say there is something missing, *nescio quid* [something, I know not what].

A "clear" knowledge, on the other hand, is *distincta* (distinct, articulate) when we have *notae et examina sufficientia ad rem ab aliis ... similibus discernendam* [sufficient marks and characteristics to distinguish the thing from other similar things]. We have such distinct knowledge, for example, of what is common to several senses (Aristotle's τὰ κοινά): number, magnitude, and figure. According to the *Nouveaux Essais sur l'Entendement* (II,5; G. V 116), these notions stem from the mind itself, and are ideas of the pure understanding (cf. Kant, *De mundi sensibilis atque intelligibilis forma et principiis*, 1770). We also have distinct knowledge of affects such as fear and hope.

Of what is distinct we have a *definitio nominalis* (G. IV, 423), *quae nihil aliud est, quam enumeratio notarum sufficientium* [nominal definition, which is nothing but the enumeration of sufficient marks]. We have *cognito distincta* of (a) that which has a nominal definition, but also of (b) a *notio indefinibilis, quando ea est primitiva sive nota sui ipsius, hoc est, cum est irresolubilis ac non nisi per se intelligitur, atque adeo caret requisitis* (cf. below concerning *intuitiva*) [indefinable concept, when this concept is primitive or is the mark of itself, that is, when it is irreducible and is understood only through itself, and when it therefore lacks requisite marks]. It is important here that the concept of nominal definition does not mean a simple verbal definition, but rather a knowledge of what is intended and named in the naming, and a knowledge sufficient for distinguishing the named from other things. By "nominal definition" Leibniz does not mean a word clarification or providing a word with meaning, but he means a knowledge with content, though not the really primary knowledge. For what characterizes the nominal definition is that in it the marks [*notae*] are only "enumerated" (*enumeratio*). It is important to keep nominal definition, as mere enumeration of distinguishing marks, separate from "real" definition, which we will describe subsequently.

A *cognitio distincta* is one in which the object named as such is not only clearly distinguished from another, but in which also the marks of its difference are expressly enumerable. Let us stay with *notiones compositae* (in contradistinction to *notiones primitivae*). In this case it can be that individual marks are indeed enumerable, separate from one another, that the marks as well stand in a relationship of clarity to one another, but that each mark is still confused when taken by itself: *rursus notae singulae componentes clare quidem, sed tamen confuse* [The single component marks are indeed sometimes known clearly but nevertheless confusedly]. What is clear can still be confused! Such clear knowledge where the marks too are clear, but still no more than clear, Leibniz terms *cognitio inadequata*, inadequate knowledge. What is thus contained in clear (distinct) knowledge is still restricted and therefore admits of further clarification. Confused, unclear marks can each be again reduced to clear moments of the marks.

Cum vero id omne quod notitiam distinctam ingreditur, rursus distincte cognitum est, seu cum analysis ad finem usque producta habetur, cognitio est adaequata [When every ingredient that makes up a distinct concept is itself known distinctly, or when analysis is carried out to the end, knowledge is *adequate*]. An adequate knowledge is thoroughly clear knowledge where confusion is no longer possible, where the reduction into marks and moments of marks *(requisita)* can be managed to the end. Of course, Leibniz immediately adds regarding *cognitio adaequata: cujus exemplum perfectum nescio an homines dare possint; valde tamen ad eam accedit notitiam numerorum* [I am not sure that a perfect example of this can be given by man, but our notion of numbers approximates it]. Here too the primary interest lies in construing the ideal of an adequate knowledge, aside from the question of whether or not it can in fact be realized by the human being as a finite knower. At the same time, the mathematical ideal of knowledge appears again in connection with this idea of knowledge.

The whole content of knowledge is supposed to be maintained with complete clarity in the *cognitio adaequata,* is supposed to be—according to the ideal. If it were in fact to exist, then we would have the kind of knowledge described as *totum simul, omnia sibi praesentialiter* [all at once, everything before it in its presentness]. But the case in fact is that we *non totam simul naturam rei intuemur* [do not intuit the entire nature of the thing at once], but *rerum loco signis utimur* [in place of things we use signs]. Instead of maintaining ourselves in the total intuition of things, we use signs. For example, when we think of a chiliagon, a polygon of a thousand equal sides, we are incapable not only of appropriately intuiting such a thing ideally, but also we do not always simultaneously conceive along with it the "nature" (essence) of side, of equality, of the number one-thousand, etc. Rather, we use the words for the thing itself named, with the accompanying awareness that we know the essence of this definite thing and can at anytime put it before us. Those "natures" then also belong to the *notae,* namely as *requisita.* This implies that the marks are not only and primarily individual properties (cf. below concerning *possibilitas*).

Adequate thinking operates by using substitutional, referential signs, *symbola.* Thus this *cognitio adaequata* is called *symbolica* or *caeca,* blind, for we do not attain a view of the totality of clear "marks" individually and as a whole. We are acquainted with them, to be sure, know of them, can move among them, but we do not see them.

> Et certe cum notio valde composita est, non possumus omnes in-gredientes eam notiones simul cogitare: ubi tamen hoc licet, ... cognitionem voco *intuitivam.*

> When a notion is very complex, we certainly cannot think simulta-neously all the notions composing it. But when this is possible ⟨!⟩ I call the knowledge intuitive.

And the latter is the most perfect knowledge, *cognitio perfectis-sima!*

What Leibniz calls *cognitio caeca,* blind knowledge, is essen-tially different from obscure knowledge (*obscura*) and confused knowledge (*confusa*), since in order for knowledge to be blind, we must have adequate knowledge. Adequate knowledge is com-pletely clear, clear relative to a *notio composita* [complex idea], and only such adequate knowledge can be, in principle, blind. Thus for it to be blind, there must be superior knowledge, the highest stage of the progression of knowledge. It follows that both the characteristics mentioned last by Leibniz: the *caeca* (*sym-bolica*) and the *intuitiva,* arise from another consideration than that of the previously mentioned characteristics. Those mentioned earlier (*obscura—clara, confusa—distincta, inadaequata—adaequata*) each refers to a stage of analysis, a step in making ex-plicit marks and moments of marks (*requisita*). With the last dis-tinction, however, we are dealing with a possible double way of appropriating and possessing the adequate, the completely analyzed as such.

It is not that intuitive knowledge is no longer ranked higher, as a new degree of a still further developed analysis, than adequate knowledge. Rather, intuitive knowledge expresses the special mode in which the content already fully analyzed is appropriated. This can be inferred from the fact that intuitive knowledge is al-ready possible at a stage prior and subordinate to *cognitio adaequata,* i.e., at the stage of *cognitio distincta,* namely, when the *notio est primitiva et caret requisitis* [idea is primitive and lacks the moments of marks]. A simple notion is no longer reduci-ble; it is totally analysed and adequate, already at the highest possible stage of analysis. Thus: *Notiones distinctae primitivae non alia datur cognitio, quam intuitiva, ut compositarum plerumque cogitatio non nisi symbolica est* [There is no knowl-edge of a distinct primitive notion other than intuitive knowledge, while for the most part we have only symbolic knowledge of composite notions].

Knowledge can be either blind or seeing (*intuitiva*). Intuition is not a still higher degree of analysis, but a mode of appropriating the highest stage of analysis, i.e., of its result, of *cognitio adaequata*. In Leibniz's sense, *intuitus* presupposes *adaequatio*, the latter residing in the concept of the former. *Intuitus* is not simply "intuition," but adequate intuition. *Totum distinctum simul intueri; in totum praesens ducere* [to in-tuit, look into, the distinct totality simultaneously; to bring to complete presence].

It becomes then quite clear that Leibniz's concept of *intuitus* is not merely a general term for some vague intuition and seeing, but he intends by it a way of seeing, a way of possessing a simply appropriate knowledge. In other words, this concept of *intuitus* implies the orientation to the ideal described earlier as God's way of knowing, the knowledge of the simplest being, *ens simplicissimum. Intuitus* is therefore: 1) direct grasp, 2) grasp of what is not further analyzable in its wholeness.

Nor should the notion of *cognitio adaequata* be superficially conceived, as usually happens when one speaks simply of stages and degrees of knowledge and pays no attention to the manner in which the gradations are made. While in *cognitio distincta* the marks are only clear, in *cognitio adaequata* the marks are clear and distinct, so that no confusion remains. This looks as if there were only some greater clarity in adequate knowledge compared to merely clear knowledge, as though adequate knowledge were clear regarding the sum of all marks. But adequate knowledge contains not merely "quantitatively more" clarity, but something essentially different. We learned how in adequate knowledge the analysis proceeds *ad finem usque producta* [carried out to the end]. All marks are present in clarity, and among them "natures" as well, *essential determinations,* i.e., what makes the thing itself *possible.* In this analysis the clear connection of the "marks" which are clear in themselves is shown to be possible. With Leibniz the distinction between *essentia* and *existentia* is again fluid.

Et quidem quandocunque habetur cognitio adaequata, habetur et cognitio possibilitatis a priori; perducta enim analysi ad finem, si nulla apparet contradictio, ubique notio possibilis est [Whenever our knowledge is adequate, we have a priori knowledge of a possibility, for if we have carried out the analysis to the end and no contradiction has appeared, the concept is obviously possible]. In adequate knowledge we grasp what the thing is, its content, or, as Leibniz expressly says in this essay, the *realitas notionum*, that to which the concepts refer in its what-it-is, its essence. *Possibilitas* is the inherent possibility of the thing. Adequate knowledge as knowledge of essence is a priori knowledge of what makes the known itself possible, for it is the clear grasp of thorough compatibility, *compatibilitas*. We know a notion a priori: *cum notionem resolvimus in sua requisita, seu in alias notiones cognitae possibilitatis, nihilque in illis incompatibile esse scimus* [when we resolve it into its necessary elements, *requisita*, or into other notions whose possibility is known, and we know that there is nothing incompatible in them].

Enumeratio, as we learned above, is the enumeration of marks sufficient to distinguish the thing from another, and it corresponds to merely distinct but not yet adequate knowledge. The enumeration does not itself attain clarity of individual marks; only a succession of marks is manifest, not the inner structure, the inherent compatibility of marks and their possible connection. For the latter, adequate knowledge is required, insight into the *realitas notionum*. Thus the *real definition* corresponds to adequate knowledge, *definitiones reales, ex quibus constat rem esse possibilem* [real definitions from which the thing is established as possible]. Merely clear knowledge is insufficient for real definition. So there is an intrinsic difference in principle between *cognitio distincta* and *cognitio adaequata*, between nominal and real definition.

Kant makes exactly the same distinction almost verbatim in his "Logik" lecture §106. It is crucial for understanding the Kantian concept of reality. Simple uncertainty about those connections misled the entire neo-Kantian interpretation of the *Critique of Pure Reason* into a misguided search for an epistemology in Kant. But under the heading, "the objective reality of the categories," Kant tries to understand the essence of categories in such a way that categories can be real determinations of objects (of appearances) without having to be empirical properties (of appearances). If determinations of being are not ontic properties of the things that are, in what way do they still belong to *realitas*, to the what-content of objects? Their reality, their belonging to essential content, is a transcendental reality, a finite, horizonal-ecstatic reality. (Compare Kant's distinction between empirical reality and the transcendental ideality of space and time.)

As we said, Leibniz sees the ideal of knowledge in the *intuitus*. Intuitive knowledge is necessarily *adequate* insofar as it pertains to composite notions, or it is *distinct* insofar as it deals with primitive notions which require no process for making them adequate. But, as frequently emphasized earlier, this ideal construct is not the assertion of its factual or even possible actualization. That would mean we as finite beings would be put on a par with God who knows absolutely, i.e., we would be in a position to know the same thing in the same way God knows, namely, absolutely. We would also be able to know absolutely God himself in a direct way. In any case, Leibniz does not risk deciding the question of whether such knowledge, presumably a cognition of the first essential possibilities of all beings as such, is possible for us. Thus he says:

> an vero unquam ab hominibus perfecta institui possit analysis notionum, sive an ad prima possibilia ac notiones irresolubiles, sive (quod eodem redit) ipsa absoluta Attributa Dei, nempe causas primas atque ultimam rerum rationem, cogitationes suas reducere possint, nunc quidem definire non ausim. Plerumque contenti sumus, notionum quarundam realitatem experientia didicisse, unde postea alias componimus ad exemplum naturae.

> Whether men will ever be able to carry out a perfect analysis of notions, that is, to reduce their thoughts to the first possibles or to irreducible concepts, or (what is the same thing) to the absolute attributes of God themselves, that is, the first causes and the final end of things, I shall now venture to decide. For the most part we are content to learn the reality of certain notions by experience and then to compose other concepts from them after the pattern of nature [L. 293]

We are usually satisfied if we can extract the content of our knowledge from experience and, with that as guide, construct for ourselves other concepts.

It also becomes clear, moreover, to what extent Leibniz hits the Cartesian doctrine full center with his critique and conceives the problem of ideas more radically. Leibniz agrees with Descartes, and that means with the entire metaphysical tradition, that grasping "ideas," knowledge of essence, is presupposed, consciously or not, for the knowledge of beings. But Leibniz disagrees with Descartes that the ideas themselves can be sufficiently known according to the epistemological principle expressed by Descartes as a "general rule" (*Meditationes* III, 2): *ac proinde jam videor pro regula generali posse statuere, illud omne esse verum quod valde clare et distincte percipio* [it seems to me that already I can establish as a general rule that all things which I perceive very clearly and very distinctly are true]. (Cf. Descartes' *Principia Philosophiae* I, 45 ff.: *quid sit perceptio clara, quid distincta* [what clear and distinct perceptions are]; the *regula* itself: *Principia* I, 43.) Leibniz provides not only more rigorous concepts of clarity and obscurity, distinctness and confusion, but he shows there is an essentially higher stage above them, where we first attain knowledge of essence, since here the totality of the necessary marks of realities are first revealed. The general rule is not a criterion for knowledge of essence and ideas, but it remains beneath them.

To be sure, this critique by Leibniz does not become central. Only Kant, who attacks Leibniz himself, has a more radical grasp of the problem of the possibility of ontological knowledge of the intrinsic content of essence. Kant inquires anew into the conditions for the possibility of objects and grounds ontological knowledge in the transcendental imagination. *Intuitus* gains a constitutive character. Today phenomenology speaks of the "vision" of essence, *Wesens-"schau."* The purport of this frequent but misleading term can only be clarified by radicalizing this entire problematic.

So Leibniz says of Descartes' principle:

> Nec minus abuti video nostri temporis homines jactato illo principio: quicquid clare et distincte de re aliqua percipio, id est verum seu de ea enuntiabile. Saepe enim clara et distincta videntur hominibus temere judicantibus, quae obscura et confusa sunt. Inutile ergo axioma est, nisi clari et distincti criteria adhibeantur, quae tradidimus, et nisi constet de veritate idearum.

> Nor is it less deceptive, I think, when men today advance the famous principle that whatever I perceive clearly and distinctly in some thing is true, or may be predicated of it. For what seems clear and distinct to men when they judge rashly is frequently obscure and confused. This axiom is thus useless unless the criteria of clearness and distinctness which we have proposed are applied and unless the truth of the ideas is established. [L. 293]

By this he means unless the principle is maintained in its function as criterion for the truth of ideas. (Ibid; the Buchenau translation, volume I p. 27 f., has "if the truth of ideas is not demonstrated," which does not make sense.) In another passage Leibniz compares the abuse of the Cartesian principle with the arbitrary appeal theologians make to the inner testimony of the Holy Spirit.

What can we extract from this whole discussion for our main problem? We learned that truth is equivalent to identity and that to be true is to be identical. Now Leibniz says against Descartes, in effect, if not in so many words, that to be true is not the same as to be perceived clearly and distinctly. Instead he says that to be true is equivalent to being adequately perceived by intuition. At first truth was defined in relation to the statement (*enuntiatio*), namely, as being identical. Now truth is defined in relation to the idea of knowledge as such. How is the earlier definition of truth, *verum* is equivalent to *idem esse,* connected with the present definition, *verum* is equivalent to *adaequate intuitive perceptum esse* [being adequately perceived intuitively]? More precisely, how does *idem esse* [being identical] have the slightest thing to do with *adaequate intuitive perceptum esse?* There seems to be an insoluble difficulty here. Identity and being perceived with adequate intuition cannot be joined in the definition of one and the same concept, the concept of truth. What does identity mean anyway? *Idem* means "the same." Does it mean that several things are the same?

If we try to see more sharply what we have already said, then we find that not only is this difficulty soluble but we find ourselves now in a position to grasp more clearly what Leibniz means by "identity," without his having expressly explained it himself.

In adequate knowledge that which is known is the *totum* of the *requisita,* i.e., that which, as a whole, constitutes the reality of a thing. This thing known is the true, the *verum;* the totality of the *requisita* is the *possibilitas,* that which makes possible the thingness of the thing. This content of the *res* [thing] is compatible with itself, for only by being compatible can it make possible. Incompatibility as conflict breaks apart, as it were, the essence of a thing; it falls apart and "can" not "be." What is known in adequate knowledge is the coherent connection of the thing's mutually compatible determinations. In fact, the thing, if adequately known, is known precisely with regard to the compatibility of its realities. Adequate knowledge is the total grasp of the harmony of multiplicity.

But we previously came to the conclusion that judgment is a *connectio,* and specifically a *connectio realis.* This connection is grasped as *identitas.* And this implies that what is in the *nexus,* what is grasped in the *connectio* does not fall apart, does not clash with itself, but all is in itself unified and, as determination, relates to one and the same, to what the thing is, to the identical in its identity.

Identity does not then basically refer to an empty uniformity stripped of difference. On the contrary, it means the entire richness of real determinations in their compatibility without conflict. Identity is not the negative concept of the absence of all differentiation. It is, conversely, the idea of the uni-sonous unity of what is different.

One must nevertheless keep in mind, and this is essential for Leibniz, that he also uses identity in the empty, formal sense of A=A. He uses it interchangeably with real identity, or he tries to deduce identity in the sense of the harmonious and mutual coherence of the different from formal identity in the sense of empty sameness with itself. Only in the ideal of the *simplicitas Dei* [simplicity of God] is this in a sense, possible, for in it the *totum* of *omnitudo realitatis* [all reality] is joined with absolute simplicity.

If the unity of identity means the compatible harmony of what belongs together, then it is clear that both characterizations of the essence of truth, true as being the same and true as being adequately perceived, surely go together and mean the same thing.

For Kant, both concepts, that of identity and of truth, are linked together in the primordial unity of the synthesis of transcendental apperception. [In Kant] identity is traced back, with the help of the truth of judgment, to the condition of the possibility of the execution of every cognitive act. The "I" is that subject whose predicates consist in all representations, everything in any way contributing to knowledge.

Only now it becomes fully clear how this concept of knowledge is connected with the idea of what simply is and its being. *Intuitus* and *identitas*, as essential characteristics of truth and knowledge, the "logical" in the broadest sense, are derived from the *simplicitas Dei* as guiding ideal of what, in the genuine sense, is. Because the identity theory of judgment refers back to these metaphysical connections, to the construal of being mentioned, and because all judgment and knowledge is knowledge of beings, we must now also make clear how Leibniz orients the interpretation of being on the same ideal. Even the exemplary being, God, still appears in the light of a definite construal of being as such.

Because the concept of subject and predicate, namely the logical concept of subject, refers directly to the ontological-metaphysical subject (cf. *Discours de Métaphysique*, §8), and because the metaphysical concept of subject, namely that of the individual substance, must in turn express genuine being, we must find a connection between the interpretation of being and the theory of judgment.

§5. *The essential determination of the being*
of genuine beings

a) **The monad as drive**

Genuine knowledge is adequate knowledge, knowledge contain-
ing with complete clarity all the determinations cohering in a being. Adequate knowledge is the complete or perfect notion, *notio*
completa seu perfecta. In it, all the predicates that determine the
subjectum are available. This *subjectum* of the statement is, however, also the *subjectum* as the underlying being itself, the individual substance. Thus Leibniz declares in *Primae Veritates:*
Notio completa seu perfecta substantiae singularis involvit omnia
ejus praedicata praeterita, praesentia ac futura (C. 520) [The
complete or perfect concept of an individual substance involves
all its predicates, past, present, and future, L. 268].

> Si qua notio sit completa, seu talis ut ex ea ratio ⟨reddi⟩ possit om-
> nium praedicatorum ejusdem subjecti cui tribui potest haec notio,
> erit notio Substantiae individualis; et contra. Nam substantia indi-
> vidualis est subjectum quod alteri subjecto non inest, alia autem in-
> sunt ipsi, itaque praedicata omnia ejusdem subjecti sunt omnia
> praedicata ejusdem substantiae individualis. (C. 403)

> If any concept is complete, or if it be such a concept that from it
> reason can be given for all predicates of the same subject to which
> this notion is attributed, it will be the concept of an individual sub-
> stance; and the contrary holds. For substantial individuality is a sub-
> ject which is not in [*inest*] another subject, but others are in it, and
> thus all predicates of that subject are all the predicates of the same
> substantial individual.

There is here a clear identification of the subject of true statements with the individual substance as genuine being. But up
until now the being of this being, the *substantiality* of this substance, remained vague. And we must further ask what sort of
connection obtains between the metaphysical characteristic of the
substantiality of individual substance and the logical identity
theory of judgment, or, what then the word "logical" means here.

The doctrine of the substantiality of the individual substances is
set down in Leibniz's monadology, which constitutes the core of
his whole metaphysics. The main metaphysical claim we have to
elucidate is that individual substance is monad. Leibniz's interpretation of being is monadological.

The main texts on monadology are: 1) *Discours de*

Métaphysique, 1686 (G. IV 427–63) [L. 303]; 2) The correspondence with Arnauld, 1686 ff. (G. II, 47–138) [L. 331]; 3) *De
primae Philosophiae Emendatione, et de Notione Substantiae,* in
the *Acta Eruditorum Lipsiensium* of 1694 (G. IV 468–70) [L. 432];
4) *Système nouveau de la Nature et de la communication des substances* . . . in the *Journal des Savants,* 1695 (G. IV 477–87) [L.
453]; 5) *Principes de la Nature et de la Grace, fondés en Raison,*
1714 (G. VI 598–606) [L. 636]; 6) *Monadologie,* 1714 (G. VI 607–
23) [L. 643]. This last writing was composed by Leibniz in French
during his last stay in Vienna two years before his death. It too
was not published during his lifetime. In 1721 a Latin translation
of it appeared in the *Acta Eruditorum,* under the title *Principia
Philosophiae.* In 1840 it was first published in its original form by
J. E. Erdmann, under the title *La Monadologie.*

Here we can present only some features of the monadology important for us, not all its interwoven themes. Leibniz himself only
suggested the essentials and did not work it out thoroughly and
systematically.[10] Here, as in his other teachings, much remains in
the phase of initial conception just as it originated, usually in some
polemical exchange. While we do have a publication explicitly on
the subject, the *Monadologie,* it characteristically contains ninety
theses listed one after another.

The monadological metaphysics is therefore subject to the most
diverse interpretations, any of which can appeal to Leibniz in one
or another of his theses. But this is true for all authentic philosophy. Agreement prevails only about pseudo-philosophy, but it is
the agreement of the mob. Thus it would be a totally misguided
conception of the essence of philosophy were one to believe he
could finally distill *the* Kant and *the* Plato by cleverly calculating
and balancing off all Kant interpretations or all Plato interpretations. This makes just as little sense with Leibniz. What would
result would be something dead. "Kant as he is in himself," *Kant
an sich,* is an idea running counter to the nature of history and
most certainly to philosophical history. This historical Kant is always only the Kant that becomes manifest in an original
possibility of philosophizing, manifest only in part, if you will, but
in an authentic part that carries in it the impact of the whole.

The actuality of the historical, especially the past, does not

---

10. Cf. the summary on Leibniz's monadology in the lecture *Einleitung in die
Philosophie, Winter-Semester 1928/29* [planned as volume 27 of the *Gesamtausgabe*]; the monadology is also dealt with in the seminar in winter semester 1929/30
on truth and certainty in Descartes and Leibniz.

emerge in the most complete account of "the way it happened." Rather, the actuality of what has been resides in its possibility. The possibility becomes in each case manifest as the answer to a living question that sets before itself a futural present in the sense of "what can we do?" The objectivity of the historical resides in the inexhaustibility of possibilities, and not in the fixed rigidity of a result.

We want to keep this in mind for the following interpretation of the monadology. Our interpretation must risk proceeding beyond Leibniz, or, better, going back more originally to Leibniz—even with the danger of departing far from what he in fact said.

Two things must first be emphasized: 1) The monadology as an interpretation of the substantiality of substance defines the being of genuine beings. It is ontology, metaphysics. And it is general metaphysics, for a concept of being is sought that applies to every genuine being, whether physical nature, living beings (plants, animals), beings existing the way humans exist, God. At the same time the concept of being must make it possible to establish differences among the various beings in the unity of a general concept. 2) The very nature of ontological knowledge, and its explicit development by Leibniz, is still, by and large, obscure and groping. Thus his monadological interpretation of substance, wherever it follows up the more radical impulses, grows muddy and adulterated by the admixture of other things. Leibniz's thought is only a preparation for the eventual separation of metaphysical from nonmetaphysical knowledge. The separation emerges with Kant, and then it is again completely buried.

I want to recall again the guiding context of the problem. On the basis of the monadology, we want to know about the being of beings (of substance). We learned previously, however, that being, the subject about which judgment is made, is defined by the whole of mutually compatible marks, by their coherence, by identity as the unity of this multiplicity. Is there a connection, and what sort of connection, between the interpretation of being as *identity* and the interpretation of being as *monad*? Does discovery of this connection give us insight into what we seek: the metaphysical foundations of Leibniz's logic—and with it a paradigmatic insight into the deep roots logic has in metaphysics?

The expression Leibniz chose to designate the substantiality of substance is already indicative: "monad." The Greek word μονάς means the simple, unity, the one. But it means also: the individual, the solitary. Leibniz uses this term only later, after he had developed his metaphysics of substance, after 1696. He took the term from Giordano Bruno via Francis Mercury van Helmont. All the Greek meanings are contained, as it were, in what Leibniz intends by the term. The essence of substance resides in its being a monad. Genuine being has the character of the simple "unit" of the individual, of what stands by itself. To anticipate, the monad is that which simply originally unifies and which individuates in advance.

The direction in which Leibniz attempts to conceive the nature of substance anew, and more primordially and universally, becomes clear if we recall the immediately preceding attempts by Descartes and Spinoza. In *Principia Philosophiae* Descartes says (I, 51): *Per substantiam nihil aliud intelligere possumus quam rem quae ita existit, ut nulla alia re indigeat ad existendum* [By substance, we can understand nothing else than the thing which so exists that it needs no other thing in order to exist]. The characteristic of substance is seen in its needing nothing else. Spinoza has (*Ethica* I, def. 3): *Per substantiam intelligo id, quod in se est, et per se concipitur: hoc est id, cujus conceptus non indiget conceptu alterius rei, a quo formari debeat* [By substance I mean that which is in itself and is conceived by itself: this is that of which the concept does not require the concept of another thing from which it needs to be formed]. According to this definition, substance is what remains in itself. But here too the essential is defined negatively.

"To reside in itself, to be irreducibly at the basis of," belonged to the conception of substance since ancient times, as the designation ὑποκείμενον indicates. What Descartes and Spinoza add to this is essentially negative, or rather, relates to the manner in which substance is conceived. Leibniz, on the contrary, desires a positive definition of the substantiality of substance. To what extent does describing substance as monad, as "unit," achieve such a positive interpretation, and what is meant here by "unit"?

We said monadology is general metaphysics. Precisely because of this, it must be oriented to all beings. Thus the burning problem in Leibniz's era, the problem of the being of nature, of the physical-inorganic as well as the organic, becomes then a guiding clue for the development of the monadology—not, to be sure, the only and ultimately decisive clue.

Descartes had attempted to see the being of physical nature, the *res corporea*, in *extensio*. Extendedness is the primary attribute, and all properties of the physical thing are supposed to be reducible to it. Now all features of natural happenings are, as such, related to change, to motion. All motion is *motio localis*, change of place, and only as such is movement supposed to be considered scientifically. In this way motion becomes accessible to the supposedly most rigorous conception, that of mathematical-geometrical theory. The Cartesians applied this theory particularly to organic nature, to plants and animals. The latter were also regarded as a network of mere alterations of place; they were studied purely mechanically—animals as machines. The mere reference to this domain of beings could place limits on the Cartesian ontology of nature. But it is inadequate even within inorganic nature. Descartes had tried explicitly to exclude the concept of force from physics: *ac de vi qua ⟨motus localis⟩ excitatur ... non inquiramus (Principia Philosophiae* I, 65) [we shall best understand motion if we inquire only about locomotion, without taking into account the force that produces it]. More precisely, Descartes did not yet have a concept of physically determinate force, but under the term *vis*, force, he thought of the "occult qualities" of the Scholastic philosophy of nature.

Leibniz, on the contrary, intends dynamics to be the basic site for mathematical physics. But this observation does not touch on his authentic philosophical intention. His metaphysical-ontological purpose always accompanies the physical-ontic intent without a clear division of domains, without difference in kind of problem and proof. If one wishes to minimize the implications of the move toward dynamics in physics, regarding its metaphysical significance and intention, then something else must be considered, namely, that which requires also the monadological structure of physical nature.

If we assume Descartes' ontological premise according to which the essence of the physical object lies in its extendedness, then every extended thing can be finally reduced to the ultimate elements of what is extended, mathematical points. In a certain sense they are "unities." But in what sense? Only as limits. That points are limits means two things: 1) they are themselves divisible ad infinitum; that is, they never lose their character as limits, *limes*; 2) the point is no longer a cube, a surface, a line, but only the limit of these. Such a unit is defined purely negatively. That is what, for example, emerges later in the Hegelian metaphysics of space, when Hegel says that the point is a simple negation. It is none of the rest of the spatial figures there are in space, and, as this primary "none of the rest," every point is at the same time the negation of the rest. The point is a unity only in the sense of what is still left. But in its very notion, it is the further reducible, limit-like remainder of a total fragmentation of the whole.

The basic element of *extensio* has merely the character of limit and negation. As negative remainder, it cannot have the property of unifying a whole. It can only enter into a unification and itself is in need of a unification. If *extensio* is to constitute the ontological essence of the natural thing, then what is primordial in this essence, the mathematical point, can never make intelligible and ground the ontological unity of a being which is for itself. It is decisive for the ontological considerations of the essence of things that, if *extensio* metaphysically constitute the corporeal thing [*res corporea*], and if *omne ens unum* [every being is one], then the basic element of *extensio,* the mathematical point, must constitute the unity of a *res corporea.* Is that possible? No. If not, then *extensio* is not the essence, then a new definition of substance is required, along with a new determination of what "unity" means here.

Leibniz also maintained against Descartes that what remains invariable and constant is not the quantity of motion but the magnitude of force. This magnitude is not, however, determined by the formula $m \times v$ (the product of mass and velocity) but rather by $m \times v^2$ *(the product of mass and the square of velocity).* From this, Leibniz concluded that something belongs to body which goes beyond mass and locomotion, and thus beyond *extensio.*

Thus Leibniz says in the *Système nouveau* (G. IV, 478f.):

> At first, after freeing myself from bondage to Aristotle, I accepted the void and the atoms, for it is these that best satisfy the imagination. But in turning back to them after much thought, I perceived that it is impossible to find the principles of a true unity in matter alone or in what is merely passive, since everything in it is but a collection or aggregation of parts to infinity.[L. 454]

What is negative and passive, itself in need of unification, cannot be the principle of unity, cannot be what truly unifies. The principle of unity is thus to be sought in what is itself positively unifying and thereby active. Multiplicity is by its nature, its *realitas,* only possible on the basis of a true unity. Leibniz continues (Ibid.):

> Now a multiplicity can derive its reality only from true unities which have some other origin and are entirely different from mathematical points, these being merely the limits of what is extended, and modifications of which it is certain the continuum cannot be composed. To find the real unities ⟨*unités réelles*⟩, therefore, I was forced to have recourse to a real and animated point, so to speak, or a substantial atom which must include something formal ⟨forming⟩ or active to

make a complete being. I was thus compelled to call back substantial forms, so attacked nowadays, and to bring them again into a place of honor.

But here Leibniz remarks explicitly that these substantial forms may not and can not serve to "explain particular problems of nature." They have no ontic function in problems of positive natural science. They are, however, "necessary for ascertaining true general principles" (Ibid.). The "animated points" are supposed to deal with an ontological-metaphysical problem. These points are unities, but animated unities, monads. The "formal atom" is precisely not some remainder of ὕλη, "materia," something to be determined, but it is determining.

Were one to take this doctrine superficially and not with a purely metaphysical intent—an intent not consistently sustained by Leibniz himself throughout his work—were one to understand the monadology popularly, as it were, naively, then it would be making a claim for something like animism: Everything down to the atomic bodies is alive and full of little souls and minds. Leibniz himself refers to "little gods." One can then recount the standard routine of favorite clichés: With Leibniz we have a dynamic instead of a mechanistic world-view; he "advocates" spiritualism instead of materialism, his explanation of the world is teleological instead of one-sidedly causal—and all the other nursery stories one finds in the usual histories of philosophy.

We, on the contrary, must suppose, and with good reason, that this monadological interpretation of beings was initiated with an authentically philosophical intention. In our effort to bring out this intention, the problem of the substantiality of substance is authoritative as a metaphysical-ontological problem for our interpretation, even though Leibniz himself is not everywhere clear in this regard, because the very concept of metaphysics itself is still confused. Our methodological maxim must be: First clarity about our guiding intention, and then clarity about what Leibniz himself says about the monadological interpretation of nature. We must try to expose the authentic philosophical core of the monadology. Only then can and may we retrospectively assess the extent to which Leibniz's intention was possible and was carried out, how and why it was necessarily distorted. The distortion did not occur accidently, because every philosophy, as a human thing, intrinsically fails; and God needs no philosophy. But for a philosophy to be even capable of failing, a vigorous effort must be made to have it succeed!

In first characterizing monads, the "animated" and animating points, we purposely began with *extensio,* to make it clear that the monadological problem becomes pressing even where beings as such do not have the same mode of being as living things.

What then is especially to be kept in mind regarding the idea of monads? Three things: 1) The units, points, are not themselves in need of unification but they are that which gives unity. They make something possible. 2) The units that confer unity are themselves primordially unifying, in a certain sense active. Therefore Leibniz designates these points *vis primitiva, force primitive,* primordially simple force. 3) This conception of the monad has metaphysical-ontological intent. Thus Leibniz also calls the points *points metaphysiques (op. cit.* 482), "metaphysical points," and not mathematical points. They are further called "formal atoms," not material atoms. That is, they are not ultimate, elemental pieces of ὕλη, of *materia,* but they are the primordial indivisible principle of formation, the *forma,* the εἶδος.

Every independent being is constituted as monad, that is, *ipsum persistens . . . primitivam vim habet* [what itself persists . . . has originary force] (Letter to de Volder, January 21, 1704; L. 533). What does it mean to say that every independent being is endowed with force? Understanding the metaphysical meaning of the doctrine of monads depends on correctly understanding the concept of *vis primitiva.*

The problem of the substantiality of substance should be solved positively, and for Leibniz the problem is the "unity" of the monad. Everything said about "force" and its metaphysical function must be understood from the perspective of the problem of defining the unity of substance in a positive way. The nature of "force" must be understood by way of the problem of unity as it is inherent in substantiality.

We are only today rediscovering the basic meaning of the problems of general metaphysics, along with their difficulties. The helplessness about metaphysical problems can only be explained by the total break contemporary philosophy has made with the great ancient tradition. This is the sole reason why there has not been an effort to grasp Leibnizian monadology radically in its essential intent, despite the fact that Leibniz unequivocally explained the general metaphysical sense and significance of the monadological problem of substance. He did this in the previously mentioned little article *De primae Philosophiae Emendatione, et de Notionc Substantiae.* It deals with the improvement of first philosophy, of general metaphysics (ontology), by clarifying the concept of substance, by a monadological interpretation of substantiality.

The concise article takes up just one page in the Erdmann edition (121/22; G. IV, 468–70) [L. 432–33]. Whether we push through to the ontological significance of the monadology or remain stuck in the vapidity of popular philosophy depends on whether we understand this article or not. The theme is the *natura substantiae in universum*, the nature of substance in general, substantiality as such.

> Notio substantiae, quam ego assigno, tam foecunda est, ut inde veritates primariae, etiam circa Deum et mentes, et naturam corporum, eaeque partim cognitae, sed parum demonstratae, partim hactenus ignotae, sed maximi per ceteras scientias usus futurae, consequantur. (G. IV, 469)

> The concept of substance as I offer it is so fruitful that from it follow primary and primordial truths, truths in fact about God and souls and the nature of bodies ⟨that is, about all beings and their domains⟩, truths in part known but little proved, in part heretofore unknown but nonetheless of the greatest significance for the other (nonphilosophical) sciences. [L. 433]

Leibniz prefaces his brief discussion of substance as the basic ontological concept with a general reflection on the need to refine metaphysical concepts, the attendant difficulties, and the previous attempts. It is, typically, mathematics with its definitions that stands as the paradigm of clarity and distinctness, even though Leibniz sees to some extent here that refining and justifying basic metaphysical concepts is a different sort of procedure.

> Video pleroque, qui Mathematicis doctrinis delectantur, a Metaphysicis abhorrere, quod in illis lucem, in his tenebras animadvertant. Cujus rei potissimam causam esse arbitror, quod notiones generales, et quae maxime omnibus notae creduntur, humana negligentia atque inconstantia cogitandi ambiguae atque obscurae sunt factae; et quae vulgo afferuntur definitiones, ne nominales sunt quidem, adeo nihil explicant.... Nec vero substantiae tantum, sed et causae, et actionis, et relationis, et similitudinis, et plerorumque aliorum terminorum generalium notiones veras et foecundas vulgo latere manifestum est. Unde nemo mirari debet, scientiam illam principem, quae Primae Philosophiae nomine venit. .., adhuc inter quaerenda mansisse. (G. IV, 468–69)

> I find that most people who take an interest in the mathematical sciences are disinclined toward metaphysics because they perceive light in the former but darkness in the latter. The main reason for this

is, I believe, that the general notions everyone takes for granted have become ambiguous and obscure through carelessness and the changeableness of human thinking; the definitions commonly given for these basic concepts are not even nominal definitions and thereby provide not the least light. .. It is obvious that true and fruitful concepts, not only of substance, but of cause, action, relation, similarity, and many other general terms as well, are commonly hidden. So no one should be surprised if that main science, which arose under the name of first philosophy, has hitherto still remained among that which has yet to be found. ... Yet it seems to me that light and certainty are more needed in metaphysics than in mathematics itself, because mathematical matters carry their own tests and verifications with them, this being the strongest reason for the success of mathematics. But in metaphysics we lack this advantage. And so a certain distinctive order of procedure is necessary, like the thread in the labyrinth, ... with no less clarity preserved than anyone would want to allow in everyday speech. [L. 433]

According to Leibniz, metaphysics requires a mode of assertion and explanation which differs from what proved useful for the advance of mathematics. This clarity is to be striven for, but that does not mean making concessions to popular talk and to "general intelligibility."

Assessing general metaphysics by comparing it with mathematics occurred in a certain sense already with Plato, and it continues as a general principle since Descartes, so that even for Kant it was necessary to state this relationship explicitly, (cf. *Critique of Pure Reason,* "Transcendental Doctrine of Method," chapter 1, section 1: "The Discipline of Pure Reason in its Dogmatic Employment, A 712–38, B 740–66). He says: "Philosophical knowledge is the knowledge gained by reason from concepts; mathematical knowledge is the knowledge gained by reason from the construction of concepts" (A 713, B 741). In this particular methodological reflection Kant does not attain the level of clarity reached by his actual philosophical interpretation in the chapter on schematism.

Cujus rei ut aliquem gustum dem, dicam interim, notionem virium seu virtutis (quam Germani vocant Krafft, Galli la force) cui ego explicandae peculiarem Dynamices scientiam destinavi, plurimum lucis afferre ad veram notionem substantiae intelligendam. (G. IV, 469)

To provide a foretaste, I will say for the present that the concept of forces or power, which the Germans call *Kraft* and the French *la force,* and for whose explanation I have set up a distinct science of dynamics, brings the strongest light to bear upon our understanding of the true concept of substance. [L. 433]

Here Leibniz at first only asserts that the concept of force is constitutive for the interpretation of the substantiality of substance. But he does not bring to light the inherent connection between the characteristics of force and the unity of substance. He restricts himself to a preliminary task,—that of making clear what he understands by force. He does this by distinguishing it from the Scholastic metaphysical concepts of *potentia nuda (passiva)*, *potentia activa*, and *"actio,"* which in turn go back to Aristotle's discussion of δύναμις, ἐνέργεια, and ἐντελέχεια.

The theory of *potentia passiva* [passive power] and *potentia activa* [active power] is a large and important part of the doctrine of Aristotelian Scholasticism. We cannot go into it deeply here. This distinction is the subdivision of a more general distinction we have to some extent considered in another direction under the term *essentia* or *realitas*, namely, possibility in the sense of that which constitutes the essence of a thing, enabling the thing in its essential constitution aside from whether or not this possibility is ever actualized. The Scholastics called this *possibility* also *potentia objectiva* or *metaphysica;* "objective" in the old sense (as *realitas objectiva* is still for Descartes): *ob-jectum*, what stands opposite to oneself—for the mere thinking to oneself and construing for oneself pure possibilities, the essence of a thing. Besides this *potentia objectiva (possibilitas, essentia)* there is a *potentia subjectiva; subjectum* not in the modern sense but in the ancient sense of the term: what lies at the basis, is present by itself; and so it is also called *potentia physica*, physical power. It is the *power*, the ontological *capacitas rei ad aliquam perfectionem seu ad aliquem actum* [capacity of the thing for some completion or for some act].

This *potentia subjectiva (physica)* is divided into *activa* and *passiva*. Thomas Aquinas, in *Questiones disputatae de potentia* (q. I, a. 1, resp.), says:

> Duplex est potentia, una activa, cui respondet actus, qui est operatio; et huic primo nomen potentiae videtur fuisse attributum; alia est potentia passiva, cui respondet actus primus, qui est forma, ad quam similiter videtur secundario nomen potentiae devolutum.

> Power is twofold: one is active, to which corresponds the act which is activity [functioning, *operatio*]; the second is passive power, and to it corresponds primary act which is form, to which the term "power" seems to be applied secondarily.

The term "power" has a twofold meaning. It designates first the *power to accomplish,* the achieving itself, *actus* in the sense of *actio.* The designation "power" seems to be attributed in the first place to this phenomenon, to the ability to accomplish. The primary occasion for developing the concept of possibility evidently stems from this phenomenon of power. Power in the second sense is the capacity to undergo, to allow something to be made out of itself. Power in this sense is an *inclination towards,* an aptitude. Its correlative term is *actus* in the sense of *forma,* actuality. "Power" as designating that which allows itself to be actualized as something seems to be a derivative meaning of the term.

The twofold concept of *potentia,* power, clearly corresponds to the twofold concept of *actus.* Thomas says in the same passage: *Actus autem est duplex: scilicet primus, qui est forma; et secundus, qui est operatio* [Act, however, is twofold: first act, of course, is form; and second act is activity]. The concept of act is twofold. "First" act denotes enactedness, or better, the actuality of something, *forma.* "Second" act denotes act as acting—by something already actual. The numerical order thereby reflects the order of the matter itself.

Potentia passiva corresponds to *actus qua forma,* and *potentia activa* corresponds to *actus qua actio.* But the sort of correspondence in both pairs of concepts differs. On this Thomas says in the *Summa theologica* I, q. xxv, a. 1, ad 1:

> Potentia activa non dividitur contra actum, sed fundatur in eo; nam unumquodque agit secundum quod est in actu. Potentia vero passiva dividitur contra actum; nam unumquodque patitur, secundum quod est in potentia.

> Active power is not contrary to act, but is founded upon it, for everything acts inasmuch as it is actual; but passive power is contrary to act, for a thing is passive inasmuch as it is potential.

The power to accomplish is not distinguished here from *actus* qua activity. That is, power to accomplish is not something independent, but a thing can only actively accomplish when it is itself in actuality. Something can not be what it is if it is not *actual.* Power, on the contrary, as power to become something, to allow something to happen with itself, is distinct from actuality, for in this case something which becomes actual is particularly dependent on the disposition of that which allows something to happen to itself. The aptitude is distinct from that which is and can come to be on the basis of the aptitude. The aptitude itself requires no actualization.

These are important distinctions for general ontology, and they have long been inadequately interpreted and assimilated. It is important to see beyond the Scholastic form of a mere list of distinctions.

Leibniz delineates his concept of active force [*vis activa*] against this distinction between active and passive power. More exactly, he delineates it against active power. *Vis activa* and active power [*potentia activa*] seem literally to say the same. But:

> Differt enim vis activa a potentia nuda vulgo scholis cognita, quod potentia activa Scholasticorum, seu facultas, nihil aliud est quam propinqua agendi possibilitas, quae tamen aliena excitatione et velut stimulo indiget, ut in actum transferatur. (G. IV, 469)

> Active force differs from the mere power familiar to the Schools, for the active power or faculty of the Scholastics is nothing but an approximate possibility of acting, which needs an external excitation or stimulus, as it were, to be transferred into action. [L. 433]

The *potentia activa* of the Scholastics is merely a disposition to act, a disposition which is about to act but does not yet act. It is an existing capability in something existing, a capability which has not yet come into play.

> Sed vis activa actum quendum sive entelecheia continet, atque inter facultatem agendi actionemque ipsam media est, et conatum involvit. (Ibid.; see also below for *nisus*, inclination.)

> But active force contains a certain act or ἐντελέχεια and is thus midway between the faculty of acting and the act itself and involves a conatus. [L. 433]

The *vis activa* is then a certain activity and, nevertheless, not activity in its real accomplishment. It is a capability, but not a capability at rest. We call what Leibniz means here "to tend towards . . ." or, better yet, in order to bring out the specific, already somewhat actual moment of activity: to press or drive towards, *drive*. Neither a disposition nor a process is meant, rather a "taking it on," namely, a "taking it upon oneself." What he means is a setting-itself-upon, as in the idiom "he is set on it," a taking-it-on-oneself.

Of itself, drive characteristically leads into activity, not just occasionally but essentially. This leading into requires no prior external stimulus. Drive is the impulse that in its very essence is self-propulsive. The phenomenon of drive not only brings along with it, as it were, the cause, in the sense of release, but drive is as such already released. It is triggered, however, in such a way that it is still always charged, still tensed. Drive correspondingly can be hindered in its thrust, but it is not in that case the same as a merely static capability for acting. Removing the hindrance can nevertheless allow the thrust to become free. Drive, accordingly, needs no additional cause from outside, but, on the contrary, needs only the removal of some existing impediment, or, to use Max Scheler's felicitous expression, it needs "de-hindrance." In the same article Leibniz says (ibid.): *Atque ita per se ipsam in operationem fertur; nec auxiliis indiget, sed sola sublatione impedimenti* [it is thus carried into action by itself and needs no help but only the removal of an impediment]. A bent bow illustrates his meaning.

After this clarification of *vis activa* as drive—the translation "force" is misleading because it easily leads to the notion of a static property—Leibniz arrives at the essential definition: *Et hanc agendi virtutem omni substantiae inesse ajo, semperque aliquam ex ea actionem nasci;* "I say that this power of acting inheres in every substance ⟨constitutes its substantiality⟩ and that some action always arises from it." It is drive and is productive. *Producere* means: "to lead forth," to come out of itself and maintain the outcome in itself. This definition as drive applies also to corporeal substances. When bodies impact on one another, the drive only becomes variously limited and restricted. The Cartesians overlooked this *qui essentiam ejus ⟨substantiae corporeae⟩ in sola extensione . . . collocaverunt* (ibid.) [who located the essence ⟨of corporeal substance⟩ in extension alone].

Every being has this character of drive and is defined, in its being, as having drive. This is the monad's basic metaphysical feature, though the structure of drive has not yet been explicitly determined.

Implied here is a metaphysical statement of the greatest importance, which we must now anticipate. For, as universal, this interpretation of genuine being must also explain the possibility of beings as a whole. What does the basic claim of the monadology imply about the way the various beings exist together in the whole universe? If each being, each monad, has its own impulse, that means it brings along with it the essentials of its being, the goal and manner of its drive. The all being present together, or better, thrusting together of the other monads, is essentially *negative* in its possible relation to each individual monad. No substance can confer its drive, which is its essential being, on other substances. It can merely impede or not impede, and even this function it can exercise only indirectly. The relation one substance has to another is solely restrictive and hence negative in nature. Leibniz is very clear on this point:

Apparebit etiam ex nostris meditationibus, substantiam creatam ab alia substantia creata non ipsam vim agendi, sed praeexistentis jam nisus sui, sive virtutis agendi, limites tantummodo ac determinationem accipere. (*Ibid.*)

It will be apparent from our meditations that one created substance receives from another created substance, not the force of acting itself, but only the limits and the determination of its own pre-existent striving or power of action. [L. 433]

This *nisus praeexistens* is important. Leibniz concludes the article by saying: *Ut alia nunc taceam ad solvendum illud problema difficile, de substantiarum operatione in se invicem, profutura* [Not to speak now of other matters, I shall leave the solution of the difficult problem of the mutual action of substances upon each other for the future].

N.B. Leibniz describes *vis activa* also as ἐντελέχεια, [entelechy] with reference to Aristotle, in, for instance, the *Système nouveau* and the *Monadologie* (§18; G. VI, 609) [L. 453, 643, respectively], and he adds the explanation: *car elles ont en elles une certaine perfection* (ἔχουσι τὸ ἐντελές); "for they have in them a certain *perfectio* or completeness." They are complete insofar as each monad (as will be shown later) brings its positive content already with it, and brings it in such a way that the content is potentially the universe itself. This construal of ἐντελέχεια does not conform to Aristotle's real intention. On the other hand, by giving it new meaning, Leibniz claims this very term for his monadology. Already in the Renaissance ἐντελέχεια was translated in the Leibnizian sense with *perfectihabia*; the *Monadologie*, in §48, names Hermolaus Barbarus the translator of the term. In the Renaissance, Hermolaus Barbarus (1454–93) translated and commented on Aristotle and on the commentary of Themistios, and he did so in order to restore the Greek Aristotle against medieval Scholasticism. Naturally his task harbored considerable difficulties. The story goes that, compelled by his perplexity over the philosophical meaning of the term ἐντελέχεια, he invoked the Devil to provide him with instruction. (Today we are in the same situation.)

At this point we have explained, in general, the concept of *vis activa:* 1) *vis activa* means drive; 2) this drive is supposed to be inherent in every substance as substance; 3) some accomplishing or carrying out continually arises from drive.

But now we are just coming to the real metaphysical problem of substantiality, to the question about the *unity* of substance as primary being. Leibniz calls that which is not substance a "phenomenon," something derivative, a surplus. Regarding the problem of

unity we read passages in Leibniz criticizing Descartes' conception of reality as extension, the *res extensa*. The critique claims a
"unity" is not the result of an accumulation, a subsequent addition, but the unity is to be found in that which confers unity in
advance. Unity as the conferral of unity is active, *vis activa*, drive.
It is the *primum constitutivum*, of the unity of substance (Letter to
de Volder, June 30, 1704, (G. II, 267) [L. 535]. Here is the central
problem of the monadology, the problem of *drive* and of
substantiality.

The basic character of this activity has now come into view, but
it remains to be seen how something like drive should itself be
unity-conferring. The further important question is: On the basis
of this self-unifying monad, how does the entirety of the universe
constitute itself in its interconnectedness? We need first interpose
another consideration.

b) Intermediate reflections to find the guiding clue
for the interpretation of being

We emphasized several times that we can find the metaphysical
meaning of the monadology only when we risk constructing essential connections and perspectives, and when we do so by following that which directed Leibniz himself in projecting the
monadology. The monadology tries to clarify the being of beings.
Hence a paradigmatic idea of being must be obtained somewhere,
and it must be found where something like being manifests itself
immediately to the one asking philosophical questions.

We relate to beings, become involved with and lose ourselves in
them. We are overwhelmed and spellbound by beings. Yet not
only do we relate in this way to beings, but we are likewise ourselves beings—this we each *are*. And we are so, not indifferently,
but in such a way that our very own being is a concern for us.
Aside from other reasons, one's own being is therefore in a certain
way always the guiding clue. So also with the monadology. What
is implied by this function of guiding clue, and what is thereby
evisioned (ex-istence), remain uninvestigated ontologically.

Constant reference to one's own Dasein, to the being-structure
and being-mode of one's own "I," provides Leibniz with the
model of the "unity" he attributes to every being. Beings are interpreted by analogy with the soul, life, the spirit. This becomes
clear in many passages. Clarity about this guiding clue is crucial
for understanding Leibniz's interpretation of beings, which has
grave consequences.

By means of regarding the "soul" or the "form" there results the idea of a true unity corresponding to what in us is called the "I"; such a unity could not occur in artificial machines or in a simple mass of matter . . . it can be compared to an army or a herd, or to a pond full of fish, or a watch made of springs and wheels. (*Système nouveau*; G. IV, 482) [L. 546]

I regard substance itself, if it has then original drive, as an indivisible and perfect monad—comparable to our ego. (Letter to the Cartesian de Volder at the University of Leyden, June 20, 1703; G. II, 251) [L. 530]

It can be further suggested that this principle of activity ⟨drive⟩ is intelligible to us in the highest degree because it forms to some extent an analogue to what is intrinsic to ourselves, namely, representing and striving. (Letter to de Volder, June 30, 1704, G. II, 270)

Here it is evident that the definition of substance follows, first of all, by analogy with the "I" and, secondly, that on account of this origin it possesses the highest degree of intelligibility.

I, on the contrary, presuppose everywhere only that which all of us have to admit happens frequently enough in our soul, that is, intrinsic self-activated changes, and with this single presupposition of thought I exhaust the entire sum of things. (Letter to de Volder, 1705, G. II, 276)

So the only presupposition, the real content of the metaphysical project, is the idea of being taken from the experience of the self, from the self-activated change perceptible in the ego, from drive.

"If we conceive substantial forms ⟨vis primitiva⟩ as something analogous to souls, then one may doubt whether they have been repudiated rightfully" (Letter to John Bernoulli, July 29, 1698 *Math. Schr.*[11] III 12, 522, transl. from Bk. II, 366). This does not mean substantial forms are simply souls, that they are new things and small particles, but they rather correspond to "souls." The latter merely serves as incentive for projecting the basic structure of the monad.

It is thus, as we think of ourselves, that we think of being, of substance, of the simple and the compound, of the immaterial, and of God himself, conceiving of that which is limited in us as being without limits in him. (*Monadologie*, §30; G. VI, 612.) [L. 646]

---

11. *Leibnizens Mathematische Schriften*, ed. C.I. Gerhardt, 7 volumes (in 8) (Berlin and Halle, 1849–63) [reprint, Hildesheim, 1962].

For the entire problem, in general, concerning the guiding clue of self-reflection and self-consciousness there is a helpful letter to Queen Sophia Charlotte of Prussia, which we must draw on here, "On What is Independent of Sense and Matter," (1702, G. VI, 499–508) [L. 547]. Here we read:

This thought of myself, who perceive sensible objects, and of my own action which results from it, adds something to the objects of sense. To think of some color and to consider that I think of it—these two thoughts are very different, just as much as color itself differs from the ego who thinks of it. And since I conceive that there are other beings who also have the right to say "I," or for whom this can be said, it is by this that I conceive what is called substance in general. It is the consideration of myself which provides me also with other metaphysical concepts, such as that of cause, effect, action, similarity, etc., and even with those of logic and ethics.

And finally, in that letter:

Being itself and truth are not understood completely through the senses. . . . This conception of being and of truth is thus found in the ego and in the understanding rather than in the external senses and the perception of exterior objects. (G. VI, 502/3)

What is the upshot of all this? First, though he has many differences with Descartes, Leibniz maintains with Descartes the primacy of the ego's self-certainty. Like Descartes, he sees in the "I," in the *ego cogito*, the dimension from which all basic metaphysical concepts must be drawn. Yet the guiding function of the *ego* still remains ambiguous in several ways. First, the subject which poses for itself the problem of being can put itself into question. The subject can then take itself as paradigmatic inasmuch as it provides, as itself a being with its being, the idea of being as such. The subject can further consider itself as that which understands being. As a being of special structure, the subject has in its being an understanding of being; in which case being refers not merely to the existence of Dasein.

Regarding knowledge of being as such, Leibniz says: *Et je voudrois bien savoir, comment nous pourrions avoir l'idee de l'estre, si nous n'estions des Estres nous mêmes, et ne trouvions ainsi l'estre en nous. (Nouveaux Essais* I, 1, §23; G. V, 71; cf. also §21 and *Discours,* §27, and *Monadologie,* §30)[12] [And I would like to

---

12. Compare with D. Mahnke, *Leibnizen Synthese von Universalmathematik und Individualmetaphysik,* p. 104, and further passages in note 125. Here, also, being and subjectivity are linked–through a misunderstanding, however.

know how we could have the idea of being if we were not ourselves beings and did not thus find being in ourselves]. Here
Leibniz expressly questions the idea of being and answers, following Descartes, that we would not have the idea unless we were
ourselves beings and found being within us. Leibniz means also
that, in order to have this idea, we must of course be. But he
means more. It is, to speak metaphysically, our very nature that we
cannot be what we are without the idea of being. That is, the understanding of being is constitutive for Dasein.

But from this it does not follow that we obtain the idea of being
by recourse to ourselves as beings. Rather, the proximate origin of
the idea is indifferent—the undifferentiated presence of the world
and ourselves. (Incidentally, the "mana" concept is to be explained by this non-differentiation and being delivered over to
[world].) We ourselves are the source of the idea of being, but this
source is to be understood as the primal transcendence of Dasein.
This is what is meant by drawing the idea of being from the "subject." An understanding of being belongs to the subject only insofar as the subject is something that transcends. Various articulations of being arise, then, from transcendence. The idea of being
as such is, however, a difficult and ultimate problem.

In the multifaceted function as guiding clue of the *ego*, the subject itself remains altogether unclarified ontologically. Leibniz
poses and solves the problem of being, the basic problem of
metaphysics, by recourse to the subject. Despite its highlighting
genuine ontic phenomena, this recourse to the ego, with Leibniz
as well as with his predecessors and successors, remains ambiguous precisely because the "I" itself is not understood in its essential structures and its specific way of being.

This is why, with Leibniz, the impression must arise that the
monadological interpretation of beings is simply anthropomorphism, some universal animism by analogy with the "I." But Leibniz
is not to be taken so superficially and arbitrarily, aside from the
fact that he tries to justify this analogical consideration metaphysically: "For since the nature of things is uniform, our nature cannot
differ infinitely from the other simple substances of which the
whole universe consists" (Letter to de Volder, June 30, 1704; G.
II, 270) [L. 537]. Of course the justification he gives here is a general ontological principle, which is itself in need of proof.

Instead of assuming a direct and crude claim of an anthropomorphism, we must ask conversely: Which structures of our
own Dasein are supposed to become relevant for the interpretation of the being of substance? How are these structures modified

so as to have the prerogative of making intelligible all levels of being monadologically? To raise again the central problem: How does the drive of substance confer unity, how must the drive itself be defined?

c) The structure of drive

If drive, or what is defined as that which is as drive, is supposed to confer unity insofar as it is as drive, then it must itself be simple. It must have no parts in the sense of an aggregate, a collection. The *primum constitutivum* must be an indivisible unity.

> Quae res in plura (actu jam existentia) dividi potest, ex pluribus est aggregata, et res quae ex pluribus aggregata, et res quae ex pluribus aggregata est, non est unum nisi mente nec habet realitatem nisi a contentis mutuatam. Hinc jam inferebam, ergo dantur in rebus unitates indivisibiles, quia alioqui nulla erit in rebus unitas vera, nec realitas non mutuata. Quod est absurdum. (Letter to de Volder, June 30, 1704; G. II, 267)

> Whatever can be divided into many (actually existing) is an aggregate of many, and something that is an aggregate of many is not one, except mentally, nor does it have reality except by borrowing it from its contents (it borrows only its essential content). From this I now inferred that there are indivisible unities in things because otherwise there will be no true unity in things nor a reality that is not borrowed. And that is absurd.

And in §1 of the *Monadologie* Leibniz says: "The monad we are to discuss here is nothing but a simple substance which enters into compounds. It is simple, i.e., it has no parts" (G. VI, 607).

Now, however, if substance is simply unifying, there must already be something *manifold* which it unifies, for otherwise the entire problem of unification would be senseless and superfluous. What unifies and that whose essence is to unify must therefore essentially have a relation to the manifold. This means that there must be a manifold right in the monad as simply unifying; the monad as simple and unifying must as such predelineate the possible manifold.

Inasmuch as what simply unifies is *drive* [Drang] and only as executing drive at the same time carries within itself the manifold, and is manifold, the manifold must have the character of drive, must have movement as such. But the manifold in motion is the changeable and that which changes. The manifold within drive must have the characteristic of being compressed [Gedrängte]. What is compressed is something pressed upon [Be-drängte]. But in drive it is drive itself which is pressed on. There is thus in drive itself a self-surpassing; there is change, alteration, movement. This means that drive is what itself changes in driving on; drive is what is pressed onward [Ge-drängte].

Drive, as *primum constitutivum* of substance, should be simply unifying and both origin and mode of being of the changeable. The meaning of "simply unifying" needs further definition. Unity should not be the subsequent assembling of a collection, but the original organizing unification. This means the constitutive principle of unification must then be prior to that which is subject to possible unification. What unifies must anticipate by reaching beforehand toward something from which every manifold has already received its unity. The simply unifying must be originally a *reaching out* and, as reaching out, must be *gripping in advance* in such a way that the entire manifold is already made manifold in the encircling reach.

What unifies in this sense antecedently surpasses that which it unifies in its own developing. It is *substantia prae-eminens* (Letter to de Volder, June 20, 1703; G. II, 252) [L. 530]. The *"prae"* of pre-eminence does not mean an existence that precedes chronologically, but a structurally antecedent reaching and gripping.

It is accordingly necessary that *vis primitiva*, namely, drive as *primum constitutivum* of original unification, be a reaching out and gripping. Leibniz expresses it by saying that the monad is in its essence basically "pre-hensive" [re-präsentierend].*

The deepest metaphysical motive for the monad's characteristic prehension [Vorstellungscharakter] is the ontologically unifying function of drive. This motive remained hidden from Leibniz himself. But it can be, according to the very nature of the matter, the only reason for the characteristic of prehending [Repräsentationscharakter]. It is not because the monad is, as force, something living, and living things have a soul, and the soul, in turn, has apprehension [Vorstellen]. That would be a truly superficial applica-

---

*In translations of German philosophy the customary rendering of *"Vorstellung"* is "(mental) representation," though sometimes "notion" or "idea" is also used. In discussing the monad's mode of apprehension, however, Heidegger plays on the temporal, out-stretching meaning of *"vor-stellend"* and thus suggests the necessity of a different English translation. To "pre-hend" does not share the same root meaning as *"stellen"* (to place) but derives from the Latin *prendere* (to grasp, reach). "Prehension" is nevertheless connected with "apprehension" and has enjoyed a felicitous usage in the English-language philosophy influenced by Leibniz, namely in the speculative thought of Alfred North Whitehead.

tion of the psychic to being in general and in this form would be metaphysically unjustified.

Because drive is supposed to be what originally simply unifies, it must be reaching out and gripping; it must be *"pre-hensive"* [vor-stellend]. Pre-hension [vor-stellen] is to be understood here quite broadly, structurally, and not as a particular faculty of the soul. Thus, in its metaphysical essence, the monad is not soul, but, conversely, the soul is one possible modification of the monad. Essentially, prehensive drive is therefore not a process which occasionally also prehends or even produces prehensions, but the structure of the drive process is itself reaching out, is ek-static. In this sense drive is a pre-hending. This prehending is not, however, to be understood as a mere staring, but as apprehension, *perceptio*, that is, as a pre-unifying of the manifold in the simple, *dans le simple (Principes de la Nature . . . §2; G. IV, 598)* [L. 636]. Leibniz defines *perceptio* as *nihil aliud, quam multorum in uno expressio* [nothing other than the expression of many in one]. And later he writes: *Nunquam versatur perceptio circa objectum, in quo non sit aliqua varietas seu multitudo* (Letter to des Bosses, September 20, 1706, G. 11, 311) [Perception never turns to an object in which there is not some variety or multiplicity].

Along with "apprehension" there is also a "striving" that belongs to the structure of drive. This juxtaposition refers back to νόησις and ὄρεξις, thought and desire, the basic faculties of all living things according to Aristotle. Next to *perceptio (repraesentatio)*, Leibniz expressly mentions a second faculty, *appetitus*. He has to give special emphasis to appetition only because he has not himself immediately grasped the essence of *vis activa* with sufficient radicality—despite his clearly contrasting it with *potentia activa* and *actio*. Force apparently remains itself still something substantial, a core which is then endowed with perceiving and striving, whereas in fact drive is in itself already a perceptive striving or a striving perception. To be sure, the characteristic of appetition has, nevertheless, a special meaning and does not mean the same as drive. *Appetitio*, moreover, refers to a particular, essential, constitutive moment of drive, as does *perceptio*.

Inasmuch as drive primordially unifies, it must already anticipate every possible multiplicity, must be able to deal with every multiplicity in its possibility. That is, drive must have already surpassed and overcome multiplicity. Drive must therefore bear multiplicity in itself and allow it to be born in the driving. This is its "world" character. It is important to see the essential source of multiplicity in drive as such.

Let us remember that drive, as surpassing in advance, is the primordially unifying unity, and in this way the monad is conceived as *substantia*. *Substantiae non tota sunt* ⟨not such "wholes"⟩ *quae contineant partes formaliter, sed res totales quae partiales continent eminenter* (Letter to de Volder, January 24, 1704; G. II, 263) [Substances are not such wholes that contain parts formally but they are total realities that contain particulars eminently]. Drive is the "nature," the essence, of substance. Substance as drive is in a certain way active, but as active it is always primordially prehensive (*Principes de la Nature. . .*, §2) [L. 636].

In the letter to de Volder cited above, Leibniz continues:

> Si nihil sua natura activum est, nihil omnino activum erit; quae enim tandem ratio actionis si non in natura rei? Limitationem tamen adjicis, ut res sua natura activa esse possit, si actio semper se habeat eodem modo. Sed cum omnis actio mutationem contineat, ergo habemus quae negare videbaris, tendentiam ad mutationem internam, et temporale sequens ex rei natura.

> If nothing is active by its own nature, there will be nothing active at all, for what reason for activity can there be if not in the nature of a thing? Yet you add the restriction that "a thing can be active by its own nature, if its action always maintains itself in the same mode." But since every action contains change, we must have in it precisely what you would seem to deny it, namely, a tendency toward internal change and a temporal succession following internal change, and a temporal succession following from the nature of the thing. [L. 534]

Here it is stated very clearly that the activity of the monad as drive is *eo ipso* drive toward change. Drive, of its very nature, presses out to something; there is a self-surpassing in it. This means that multiplicity arises in the driving thing itself, as driving. Substance is given over to *successioni obnoxia*, successiveness (same letter). Drive delivers itself, as drive, to manifold succession—not as if to something other than itself, for it is that which itself as drive seeks to press. Drive submits itself to temporal succession, not as if to something alien to it, but it is this manifold itself. From drive itself arises time.

In drive resides a trend toward transition, a tendency to overcome any momentary stage. And this *trend toward transition* is what Leibniz means by *appetitus*. But it must be kept in mind that *perceptio*, in the sense characterized, is an equiprimordial feature of the monad. The tendency is itself pre-hending, and that means it unifies from a unity which overtakes in advance. What it unifies thereby is nothing other than the transitions from prehension to pre-hension [von Vorstellen zu Vor-stellen], transitions which are pressed on in the drive and which press themselves on.

Regarding the final definition of monads Leibniz writes to de Volder:

> Imo rem accurate considerando dicendum est nihil in rebus esse nisi substantias simplices et in his perceptionem atque appetitum . . . . Revera igitur ⟨principium mutationis⟩ est internum omnibus substantiis simplicibus, cum ratio non sit cur uni magis quam alteri, consistitque in progressu perceptionum Monadis cujusque, nec quicquam ultra habet tota rerum natura. (June 30, 1704; G. II, 270f.)

> Indeed, considering the matter carefully, it may be said that there is nothing in the world except simple substances and, in them, perception and appetite. . . . ⟨The principle of change⟩ is therefore truly internal to all simple substances, since there is no reason why it should be in one rather than in another, and it consists in the progress of the perceptions of each monad, the entire nature of things containing nothing besides. [L. 538]

The *progressus perceptionum* is what is primordial in the monad; it is the pre-hending transition tendency, the drive.

> Porro ultra haec progredi et quaerere cur sit in substantiis simplicibus perceptio et appetitus, est quaerere aliquid ultramundanum ut ita dicam, et Deum ad rationes vocare cur aliquid eorum esse voluerit quae a nobis concipiuntur. (Ibid.)

> To go beyond these principles and ask why there is perception and appetite in simple substances is to inquire about something ultramundane, so to speak, and to demand reasons of God why he has willed things to be such as we conceive them to be.

The following passage from the first draft of the letter of January 19, 1706, to de Volder is illuminating on the genesis of the doctrine of drive and the transition tendency:

> Mihi tamen sufficit sumere quod concedi solet, esse quandam vim in percipiente sibi formandi ex prioribus novas perceptiones, quod idem est ac si dicas, ex priore aliqua perceptione sequi interdum novam. Hoc quod agnosci solet alicubi a philosophis veteribus et recentioribus, nempe in voluntariis animae operationibus, id ego semper et ubique locum habere censeo, et omnibus phaenomenis sufficere, magna et uniformitate rerum et simplicitate. (G. II, 282)

> But it is enough for me to accept what is usually granted, that there is a certain force in the percipient's forming for itself new perceptions from previous ones, which is the same if you were also to say that a new perception at times follows from some previous perception. What is usually recognized by philosophers everywhere, both ancient and more recent, in the voluntary activities of the soul, I judge to have always and everywhere a place and to be sufficient for all phenomena in both the great regularity and simplicity of things.

The answer to the question, To what extent is drive as drive unifying? demanded penetration into the essential structure of drive: 1) Drive is *primordially unifying*: it is not unifying thanks to that which it unifies. It is not a conglomeration of what is unified. It is a reaching out and grasping, apprehension, *perceptio*. 2) But this *percipere* [Latin, to take, grasp] comprises and is oriented toward a manifold which is itself already involved in drive and originates from it. Drive is self-surpassing, *pressing on*. It is a multiplicity of phases which are themselves always pre-hending. 3) Drive is a *progressus perceptionum*. As pressing, self-surpassing, drive is *appetitus*, a *transition tendency*, a *tendentia interna ad mutationem* [internal tendency to change].

Let us quickly recall what was said about the sustantiality of substance. Substance is that which constitutes the unity of a being. What unifies is drive, and drive taken in the precise sense we have just now elaborated, as pre-hension and the transition tendency. That is, drive develops the manifold in itself.

As what unifies, drive is the nature of a being. At the same time, every monad has its *propre consitution originale*. The latter is given along with the creation. What then makes each monad ultimately just this particular monad? How is this *individuation* itself constituted? Recourse to the creation is of course only the dogmatic explanation of the origin of what is individuated, not the clarification of individuation itself. What makes up the latter? The answer to this question must explicate the essence of the monad even further.

Obviously individuation must also take place, as it were, in that which basically constitutes the essence of the monad, in the drive. Where can and must the ground of the peculiar uniqueness of the monad reside? What essential character in the structure of drive makes a particular individuation possible? To what extent is the primordially unifying self-individuating in its unifying?

When we previously put aside the connection with the creation, we did so only inasmuch as it is a dogmatic explanation. Nevertheless, the metaphysical sense expressed in describing the monad as created, is its finitude.

Considered formally, finitude means restrictedness. To what extent can drive be restricted? If finitude as restrictedness belongs to the essence of drive, then finitude must be defined within the basic metaphysical feature of drive. But this basic feature is unification, and unification as pre-hending, as surpassing in advance. In prehensive unifying there is a *possession of unity in advance* to which drive *looks*, as prehending and tending toward transition. In drive as prehending appetition there is a "point," as it were, upon which attention is directed in advance. This point is the unity itself from which drive unifies. This attention point or point of view, view-point, is constitutive for drive. What is in advance apprehended in this viewpoint is also that which regulates in advance the entire drive itself. Insofar as drive as prehensive motion is always what is pre-hended in advance in the motion's free moving, the drive is not pushed extrinsically. *Perceptio* and *appetitus* are therefore determined in their drive primarily from the viewpoint.

But here is something which has not yet been conceived explicitly, something which, like drive, is in itself a reaching out, and it reaches so that it is and maintains itself in this reaching out, something having in itself the possibility of grasping itself. In driving towards, that which has drive always traverses a dimension. That is, what has drive traverses itself and is in this way open to itself. And it is open by its very essence. Because of this dimensional *self-openness*, what has drive can therefore grasp its own self, can thus, in addition to perceiving, present itself at the same time along with perception. It can perceive itself concomitantly; it can *apperceive*. In *Principes de la Nature et de la Grace. . .*, §4, Leibniz says:

Ainsi il est bon de faire distinction entre la Perception qui est l'état interieur de la Monade representant les choses externes, et l'Apperception qui est la Conscience, ou la connoissance reflexive de cet état interieur, laquelle n'est point donnée à toutes les Ames, ny toujours à la même Ame. (G. VI, 600; cf. *Monadologie* §21 ff.)

So it is well to make a distinction between perception, which is the inner state of the monad representing external things, and *apperception*, which is consciousness or the reflective knowledge of this inner state itself ⟨i.e., awareness, being awake⟩ and which is not given to all souls nor to the same soul all the time. [L. 637]

In this viewpoint the whole universe is in each case held in view, as it were, in a definite perspective of beings and of the possible. But the view is refracted in a definite way, namely, in each case according to the monad's stage of drive. That is, it is refracted in each case according to the monad's possibility for unifying itself in its multiplicity. This "itself' in the latter "unifying itself" expresses the fact that a certain co-presentation of itself is found in the monad as prehensive drive. Now this revealment of self can have various degrees, from full transparency to insensibility and captivated distraction. No monad lacks *perceptio* and *appetitus* and thus a certain accompanying openness to itself, though this need not be full self-apprehension. Every monad is open to itself, be it at the lowest degree of openness possible. Accordingly, the particular viewpoint, and the correlative possibility of unification, its unity, constitutes the uniqueness of each monad.

Inasmuch as it unifies—and that is its essence—the monad individuates itself. The inherent possibility of individuation is based on its essence as drive. Yet, in individuation, in the drive from its own particular perspective, the monad unifies the universe prehended in advance, only according to the possibility of the perspective. Each monad is thus in itself a *mundus concentratus* (Letter to de Volder, June 20, 1703, G. II, 252) [L. 530]. Every drive concentrates in itself, in its driving, the world in each case after its own fashion.

But because each monad is, in a way of its own, the "world," every drive is *in consensus* with the universe, insofar as it presents the world. Because of the consonance every prehensive drive has with the universe, the monads themselves are also interconnected with one another. The idea of the monad as prehensive drive tending toward transition implies that the world belongs in each case to the monad in a perspectival refraction, that all monads as units of drive are oriented in advance toward a pre-disposed harmony, the *harmonia praestabilita* of the totality of beings. In every monad the whole universe is potentially present.

As the structure of the actual world, the *actualia*, however, pre-established harmony is what, as pressed upon, stands opposite the central monad, God. God's drive is his will. But the correlate of divine will is the *optimum*.

> Distinguendum inter ea, quae Deus potest, et quae vult: potest omnia, vult optima.—Actualia nihil alium sunt, quam possibilium (omnibus comparatis) optima.—Possibilia sunt quae non implicant contradictionem. (Letter to John Bernoulli, February 21, 1699; Math. Schr. III/2, 574)

> We must distinguish between the things which God can do and those which he wills to do; he can do all things, but he wills the best.— Actual things are nothing but the best of possibles, all things considered.—Possible things are those which do not imply a contradiction. [L. 513]

The individuation which takes place in drive as unifying is always the individuating of a being that belongs to the world. Monads are not isolated pieces producing the world by their addition, but each monad, as drive, is, in its own way, the universe itself. Each presents the world from a viewpoint. Talk about the monad as a "little world," as microcosm, does not touch the essential, inasmuch as each in driving apprehends the whole world in its unity, though the monad never comprehends it totally. Each monad is, according to its particular level of awareness, a world-history making the world present. So the universe is, in a certain sense, multiplied by as many times as there are monads, just as the same city is variously represented by each of the various situations of individual observers (*Discours,* §9).

From what has been said we can now elucidate the image Leibniz uses preferably and frequently to describe the total nature of the monads, the monad is a living mirror of the universe. One of the most important passages is contained in the Letter to de Volder from June 20, 1703:

> Entelechias differre necesse est, seu non esse penitus similes inter se, imo principia esse diversitatis, nam aliae aliter exprimunt universum ad suum quaeque spectandi modum, idque ipsarum officium est ut sint totidem specula vitalia rerum seu totidem Mundi concentrati. (G. II, 251/52)

> It is necessary that entelechies ⟨monads⟩ differ from one another or not be completely similar to each other; in fact, they are the principles of diversity, for each differently expresses the universe from its own way of seeing ⟨pre-hending⟩. And precisely this is their peculiar task, that they should be so many living mirrors or so many concentrated worlds. [L. 530]

This statement contains a multiplicity of things: 1) The differentiation of monads is necessary. It belongs to their nature that, as unifying, each unifies from its own viewpoint, and thus they individuate themselves. 2) On account of their perceptive-appetitive way of seeing, monads are themselves the origin of their particular diversity. 3) This unifying presentation of the universe in each individuation is precisely what concerns each monad in its being, its drive. 4) Monads are each the universe in concentrated form, *concentrationes universi* (Letter to de Volder, 1705; G. II, 278) [L. 530]. The center of concentration is drive determined from a particular viewpoint. 5) The monad is a *speculum vitale* [living mirror] (cf. *Principes de la Nature et de la Grace.*, §3; *Mondalogie,* §63 and 77; Letter to Remond from July, 1714) [L. 637, 649, 651, 656, respectively]. The monad is a *miroir actif indivisible,* an active, indivisible, simple mirroring. Mirror, *speculum* (the same root as the Latin *spectare, species*), means a making visible. But the monad makes visible as drive. That is, it mirrors as pre-hending, and only in this activity does the particular manifestation of the world come about. Mirroring is not a fixed copying, but drives as such to ever new predelineated possibilities of itself. The mirror is simple because of the prior possession of the one universe from a viewpoint from which the manifold itself first becomes visible.

Now we can grasp more sharply the essence of finite substance from an aspect we have not considered. Leibniz says in one place (in the Letter to de Volder of June 20, 1703; G. II, 249): *Omnis substantia est activa, et omnis substantia finita est passiva, passioni autem connexa resistentia est* [Every finite substance is active and every finite substance is passive as well, and connected with this passivity is resistance, L. 528]. What is this supposed to mean? Substance is active, is drive. In every finite drive occurring in a particular perspective, there is always and necessarily something resistant which opposes the drive. For, driving out of a particular viewpoint toward the whole universe, there are so many things which the drive is not. It is modified by the viewpoint. Because drive can be the whole universe potentially but in fact is not, drive is for this reason related to resistance in its driving. Insofar as the monad is always the whole from a viewpoint, it is finite precisely insofar as it is ordered to the universe. That is, the monad relates to resistance, to something it is not but could well be. This passivity, in the sense of what the drive does not drive, belongs to the finitude of drive.

This negative aspect, purely as a structural moment of finite drive, characterizes the nature of what Leibniz understands by *materia prima*.

> Materia prima cuilibet Entelechiae est essentialis, neque unquam ab ea separatur, cum eam compleat et sit ipsa potentia passiva totius substantiae completae. Neque enim materia prima in mole seu impenetrabilitate et extensione consistit. (Letter to des Bosses, October 16, 1706; G. II, 324)

> Prime matter is essential for any entelechy, nor can it ever be separated from it since it completes the entelechy and is the passive power itself of the total complete substance. For prime matter does not consist in mass nor in impenetrability and extension.

Because of this essential primordial passivity, the monad has the intrinsic possibility of *nexus* with *materia secunda,* i.e. with *massa,* with definite resistance in the sense of material mass and weight. (Cf. on this Leibniz's correspondence with the mathematician John Bernoulli and with the Jesuit des Bosses, professor of philosophy and theology at the Jesuit college in Hildesheim.) This structural moment provides Leibniz with the foundation for making metaphysically intelligible the *nexus* of the monad with a material body (*materia secunda, massa*) and for demonstrating positively why *extensio* cannot constitute the essence of substance. We cannot pursue this here nor can we go into the further development of the monadology and the metaphysical principles connected with it.

Our guiding problem is the way logic is rooted in metaphysics, the way the doctrine of judgment is rooted in the doctrine of substance, and the identity theory in the monadology. The monadology defines the substantiality of substance, the unity of a being as a being. Unity is thereby conceived as primordially unifying. That is, "*monas*" proves to be drive. The latter is a prehensive tendency toward transition. How does drive unify, and how is it individuated in the unification? Drive unifies as a foregrasping grip. Hence it unifies with a glance toward unity, within a point of view. A viewpoint is in each case guiding, and the whole is in each case apprehended from this viewpoint. Thus each monad is a perspective of the universe or a *mundus concentratus,* and it is, insofar as it is a monad, in consensus with the other monads. Therefore monads have "no windows," because they need none (*Monadologie,* §7, G. VI, 607) [L. 643]. There is no influx, not because it would be inexplicable, but because it would be superfluous.

Summarizing, Leibniz writes:

> Non credo systema esse possibile, in quo Monades in se invicem agent, quia non videtur possibilis explicandi modus. Addo, et superfluum esse influxum, cur enim det monas monadi quod jam habet? Nempe haec ipsa natura substantiae est, ut praesens sit gravidum futuro et ut ex uno intelligi possint omnia, saltem ni Deus miraculo intercedat. (Letter to des Bosses, August 19, 1715; G. II, 503)

> I do not believe a system is possible in which the monads act upon each other mutually, for there seems to be no possible way to explain such action. I add that influence is superfluous, for why should one monad give another what it already possesses? It is the very nature of substance that the present is great with the future and the everything can be understood out of one, at least if God does not intervene with a miracle. [L. 613]

It was necessary to interpret the monadology in order to expose the genuinely metaphysical foundation of Leibniz's logic. We reached this foundation in the monadological constitution of *ens qua substantia* [being as substance]. At the same time our result needs a still deeper basis: the problem of ens qua essentia and *existentia* being as essence and existence, of being as something possible which is as such a possible actuality. But with a regard for the economy of the whole lecture series, we must omit §6, "The basic structure of being in general—*essentia* [essence] and the *conatus existentiae*." Confer the discussions of "Essence and existence: the basic articulations of being" in the lectures from summer semester 1927.[13] The discussion of Leibniz's conception of essence and existence, which was to be carried out in § 6, required relatively far-reaching considerations and a thorough textual exegesis, especially since Leibniz speaks to these problems in only very few passages.

[§6 was not delivered in the lecture course]

§7. Theory of judgment and the conception of being. Logic and ontology

In describing Leibniz's logic, we began with his doctrine of judgment. In doing so we followed up a connection established in philosophy since ancient times, namely, judgment as the real vehicle and locus of truth. More precisely, the proposition is that which has the alternative of being either true or false insofar as something is said about something. On the other hand, merely presenting something in a simple direct intuition, say a perception, is supposed to be neither true nor false; something is either intuited or not. If, in contradistinction to the judgment "the board is black," I simply perceive: board—black, I do not "assert" anything, and thus do not state what is "true" or "false." Now, since the distinctive characteristic of knowledge as such is truth—false knowledge not being a knowledge of something—and since truth, however, resides in the proposition, in the judgment, knowing is equated with judging. Contemporary epistemology is logic. Inquiry into the essence of truth shifts to the theory of judgment.

The question arises as to how such a doctrine of the essence of judgment should itself be organized and approached. What does it mean to explain "judgment" in its essence? Judging is an activity of humans. As a judging about beings, judging-about is in itself

---

13. [Published as volume 24 of the *Gesamtausgabe: Die Grundprobleme der Phänomenologie*, ed. F.-W. von Herrmann (Frankfurt a.M., 1975)] [*The Basic Problems of Phenomenology*, translation, introduction and lexicon by Albert Hofstadter (Bloomington: Indiana University Press, 1982).]

related to beings. We call this relationship to beings "intentionality." Judging about is in itself intentional. Yet even merely looking at something, perceiving the wall, for example, is being related to something. What then first characterizes the intentionality of judgment? Judging about, making statements about, is in itself a determining, and a determining wherein that which is judged is determined in the judging. In the judgment about the blackboard as black, black is set in relation to board. Thus there is still another relation. And this relation now determines that about which the judgment is made. Not only is there a relationship that the judging Dasein has to that about which judgment is made, but the latter is in itself articulated relationally, articulated by a relation. Thus the intentional relation of making statements is in itself a *relating relationship*. To be intentionally related effects, as intentional, an additional relating, in the sense of determining something as something. The intentional relation the proposition has to that about which judgment is made is in itself bifurcated. This can be, crudely and inadequately, represented in the following way:

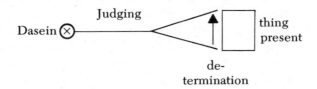

The statement possesses a referential intentionality. It is an originally single bifurcated relation (the unity of synthesis and diairesis) and not two or more unbifurcated relations next to or after one another. I do not first perceive board and then black and subsequently conjoin both perceptions. In the "is" of the judgment "A *is* B," there is both the "is" of the relation to a being and the bifurcation.

The question about the essence of truth, truth understood as located in judgment, became the question about the essence of judgment. Judgment then first showed the structures of intentionality and bifurcation, and both of these as structures of judging Dasein. What is Dasein and how is it that it can make statements and must make them in the manner of a bifurcated intentionality? Wherein is the intrinsic possibility of judgment grounded as the characterized mode of Dasein's activity? We need then to illuminate the being structure of Dasein, first in this one definite aspect, then ultimately with regard to an ontology, a metaphysics of Dasein.

But let us now go further into the question concerning the relation of judgment to truth. What does it mean to say that truth has its locus in the proposition? Is truth a "property" of judgment, as color is the property of a material thing? This too can only be decided after we have clarified the way truth is related to judging Dasein and to Dasein as such. Only insofar as the intrinsic possibility of truth becomes clear will the possibility of knowledge, and therefore of judgment and thinking, become intelligible, and not conversely!

The implication of this for the concept of logic is that the task for logic is, put quite generally, to clarify the essence of truth. If, however, clarifying the essence of truth can only be carried out as a metaphysics, as an ontology, then logic must be conceived as *the metaphysics of truth*.

We have therefore traced features of Leibniz's doctrine of judgment down a route on which we came across the character of "truth." Judgment is *connectio*, more exactly, *inclusio;* the main feature of the subject-predicate relation is identity, but being true is itself, for Leibniz, nothing more than being identical. The justification, clarification, and certification of being true is accomplished by reduction to identities and is made possible by the mutual coherence of the determinations as compatible in the unity of that about which judgment is made, in the unity of the *subjectum.* But we have to keep in mind that the conception of judgment and truth refers here not only to essential truths but to existential truths as well. And this means that all possible propositions that define a certain individual being must be ideally reducible to a connection of pure identities. In this way they are determinations of what belongs together.

The multiplicity of what belongs together, in order to be able to be a possible coherent whole, requires a unity of belonging together. This must be, however, a unity in advance, for only in such a way can it function as a standard for the coherence of things or for the incoherence of what was presumably coherent. The coherence of a multiplicity, as belonging appropriately together, requires a unity that regulates in advance. Reduction to identity, as a whole of mutually compatible and coherent determinations, is, as a mode of judging about beings, only possible metaphysically if the being itself is constituted by an original unity. Leibniz sees this unity in the monadic structure of substance. Thus the monadic structure of beings is the metaphysical foundation for the theory of judgment and for the identity theory of truth. Our dismantling of Leibniz's doctrine of judgment down to basic metaphysical problems is hereby accomplished. We must especially keep in mind that every monad is a mirror, is potentially the universe. It is therefore ideally coordinated with the universe as the object of absolute divine knowledge. In this way we obtained the metaphysical basis for the idea of knowledge as *intuitus* [intuition] for the ideal of knowledge as *cognito adaequata intuitiva* [adequate intuitive knowledge], as absolute clarity, the monad's pure and simple awareness.

Leibniz's logic of truth is consequently possible only on the basis of the monadological metaphysics of substance. This logic has essentially metaphysical foundations. It is indeed, as radical consideration can demonstrate, nothing other than the metaphysics of truth.

True, Leibniz himself nowhere explicitly elaborated on the problem of the metaphysical foundations of logic. On the contrary, his inclination to develop logic out of itself and metaphysics, as it were, out of logic repeatedly comes through. And in this endeavor the concepts of metaphysics and logic are preserved in their basic features, despite all the transformations of their specific problems. Our orientation to Leibniz's logic and its connection with metaphysics has the task of making a horizon of possible problems in this field visible in the first place, so as to remove some of the strangeness from the purely systematic discussions that are to follow. But more especially, we have tried to destroy the assumption that logic is something free-floating, something ensconced within itself.

There is of course an argument frequently enlisted by those who believe the primacy of logic over metaphysics can be conclusively proved. This argument has the additional advantage of being capable of deciding the problem of their relationship on the basis of quite general notions of logic and metaphysics, without having to go into the specific problems belonging to the content of either logic or metaphysics. While our thesis is that, a) logic is grounded in metaphysics, and b) logic is nothing other than the metaphysics of truth; the other argument is based on, 1) the assumption that logic is free-floating, something ultimate, "thinking" as it were, and 2) the general argument that logic has primacy over all the sciences, an argument rooted in the first assumption.

This argument has the advantage of a) being maintained in general, formally, without going into the content of the disciplines of metaphysics and logic, and b) being immediately intelligible on the level of common sense. It suggests that metaphysics is, as a science, knowing, and so it is a thinking; as thinking, it presupposes the science of thinking, and consequently presupposes logic. Logic is, concludes the argument, the presupposition of metaphysics, for without it even metaphysics cannot be justified or carried out. Now because this argument has validity for every science, for all knowing and thinking, therefore "logic" presupposes logic! A consistently drawn conclusion such as this naturally gives one pause, especially as to whether the argument decides anything about the relation logic has to metaphysics. For the argument applies equally to both logic and metaphysics. If such is the case, then this argument must finally be tested by its implications.

The argument says that metaphysics, as philosophical knowledge and as knowing, is a thinking. Thinking presupposes logic, and before one can lay the foundations of metaphysics, logic must be therefore established as the foundation for metaphysics, and not conversely. It is easy to see that this argument can be applied to every science, with the conclusion that logic must provide the presupposition for all sciences. But in the end it is precisely the applicability of this argumentation to any science whatsoever which argues against the claim that logic is the presupposition of all the sciences, and thus in particular of metaphysics. For what is meant here by "presupposition"?

Every science, including metaphysics, and every form of prescientific thinking uses, as thinking, the formal rules of thought. Using the rules of thought in the thinking process is inevitable. Let us for the moment leave open why this is so. But does it follow from the inevitability of using rules in the thought process that science has its basis in logic? Not at all. For the inescapability of rule usage does not in itself immediately imply the inescapability of logic. Using rules does not necessarily require a science of the rules of thought and certainly not a reasoned knowledge of these rules in the sense of traditional logic. For otherwise the thoughtful justification of logic itself would be intrinsically impossible, or superfluous. A fully developed logic would have to exist then already insofar as there was thought.

Even if one wished to concede that the inevitability of using rules in scientific thought implies the inevitability of logic for science and for metaphysics, this would not in turn mean logic is the foundation of science as such. The procedure of thinking and the use of rules are, among others, requirements which flow from the essence of science, but the essence of science does not have its intrinsic possibility in the procedure of thinking and the use of rules. Moreover, the converse is true. The unavoidability of rule usage can be established only from the intrinsic essential possibility of science, can only be justified metaphysically. Not only rule usage, but the rules themselves, need metaphysics for their justification. One could, however, bring the rejoinder that this metaphysical justification of the rules of logic again presupposes scientific thinking, presupposes the rules themselves and necessarily uses them.

So the primacy of the rules of thought is thus, for all that, not to be dismissed, however one might twist and turn. In fact, this argument cannot be evaded. But it is especially impossible to evade the question whether the conditions necessary for the operations of thinking are foreordained prior to the essence of thinking and of that wherein thinking as an activity of Dasein is grounded, or whether, conversely, the essence of Dasein and thinking first makes possible the operational conditions of thinking and the way in which they must necessarily be employed. Thinking and rule usage may be inevitable for the operation of all thinking, and thus also for establishing metaphysics as well, but it does not follow from this that the foundation consists in the use of rules. On the contrary, it merely follows that rule usage is itself in need of justification. And it further follows that this apparently plausible argument is not in any position to establish a foundation at all. The argument from the inevitability of using rules can make its appeal solely on this fact, the fact of its inevitability, but it is not even in a position to make this fact, in its intrinsic possibility, into a problem, much less solve it.

Therefore: 1) Logic is not even the operational condition for thinking but only a science of the rules as such preserved in a tradition. 2) But if it is a science of rules, then obviously logic, in its traditional form, can neither clarify nor justify these very rules in their essence. 3) Insofar as the intrinsic possibility of something that provides a foundation must be prior in order to the actual operation and the conditions of thinking, the explication of the intrinsic possibility of thinking, as such, is the presupposition of "logic" as a science of the rules of thinking. 4) The entire problem of the possible precedence of metaphysics over logic or logic over metaphysics cannot be posed, discussed, and solved by logic, unless logic is conceived as the metaphysics of truth. If it is possible to discuss these issues according to the manner of metaphysics, then the usage of logical rules is, to be sure, one condition among others for its operation.

Let what has been said suffice for the favorite argument proving the primacy of logic. This is a classic argument—for all *sophistry*. It arouses the illusion, and can do so at any time, that it is pushing

onto an ultimate foundation and is not resting with any penulti-
mate grounds. It has every thoughtful justification refuted by the
fact that it, as justification, even thinks. Although, in this illusion,
it appeals to something for which it can give no justification,
nevertheless—and here is what is sophistical—it creates the
semblance that this formal argumentation is the most rigorous and
that all justification is only satisfactory in the mode of formal
argument.

It would be erroneous to believe that, because it is formal and
empty, this argument can be refuted in the same way, formally.
The refutation, rather, consists solely in showing why this argument is possible and why it is even necessary under certain
presuppositions. In first producing the justification for the argument, it becomes evident that the argument lives and feeds on
something, something which the argument itself not only cannot
produce but which it even believes it must deny!

This argument is not arbitrary. It has metaphysical roots and so
crops up recurrently, especially wherever a radical foundation is
supposedly sought. And so Leibniz time and again comes close to
founding metaphysics on logic, probably most clearly and emphat-
ically in the treatise mentioned many times already, *Primae veritates* (C. 581-23) [L. 267]. Contemporary logic shows a new distortion of the problem. Not only is metaphysics reduced to logic, but
logic is itself reduced to mathematics. Contemporary logic is symbolic, mathematical logic, and thus a logic which follows the
mathematical method.

Even if, through the previous reflections on Leibniz, we could
employ the terms "metaphysics" and "logic" with a more definite
content, we are still not able to resolve the problem of the relation
of metaphysics to logic through such general discussions. This is
especially so because we do not have before us two secure, stable
disciplines which can be simply set against one another. Rather, it
is important to put forth a central problem of logic on the background of the previous, primarily historically oriented reflections
and clarify the problem in a way that shows concretely how logic
is only possible as the metaphysics of truth. As in all philosophical
tasks of laying foundations, it is of prime importance to observe
that laying the foundation does not mean shoving another fundament under a finished discipline. Laying the foundation implies
always a new draft of the blueprints. Every foundation for philosophy must transform philosophy itself, but transformation is only
possible in seizing and maintaining what is essential.

In concluding the first major half of the lecture series, we recall that our aim is, as a whole, a philosophical logic. That is, we are seeking the metaphysical foundations of logic. As concrete introduction to basic metaphysical problem, we used the dismantling of the Leibnizian logic—this would be in principle also possible with Plato or Aristotle. The connection between the identity theory and the monadology then became evident. The connection justified our claim that logic is founded upon metaphysics and is nothing other than the metaphysics of truth. A critical preliminary discussion was devoted to the usual objection which maintains the primacy of logic. A necessary condition for doing something is not to be identified with the reason for the intrinsic possibility of what can be done. Reference to this necessary condition produces no foundation; it rather curtails the question and obstructs the path of inquiry. The characteristic blindness of the argument is indicated by the fact that it arises recurrently. And with this we arrive at the second major part of the lectures.

Second Major Part

The Metaphysics of the Principle of Reason as the Foundational Problem of Logic

We must first sketch out the context of the problem so that our discussions will be organized properly. Leibniz is generally regarded as the discoverer of the principle of reason. We learned earlier that Leibniz considers the two basic principles of truth and knowledge to be the *principium contradictionis* and the *principium rationis sufficientis seu determinationis* [principle of sufficient reason or of determination]. But this central portion of the Leibnizian doctrine on logic and metaphysics is the most obscure. 1) It is not unambiguously clear how the *principium rationis sufficientis* is related to the *principium contradictionis*. 2) It is not clear, or even open to a rough guess, where the *principium rationis sufficientis* receives its foundational justification. 3) The connection of the principle with the metaphysical basis in the monadology is doubtful. 4) The meaning of *principium*, the nature of principle, in the principle of reason is highly problematic. 5) Furthermore, is this *principium* primarily a part of the doctrine of judgment and logical truth, or does it have other roots? The last question asks about how the concept of a metaphysical principle can be properly understood as a "logical" principle.

In order to ask these questions more clearly and pose them as problems, we need a more radical approach to metaphysics than is available in Leibniz.

Relying on the preceding inquiry, we want first to try, in our orientation from Leibniz, to concentrate on approaching the problem of the metaphysics of the principle of reason. And it is important to see that, in Leibniz, the principle of reason functions with completely diverse meanings. We are not dealing here with the historical question of whether these [diverse] formulations can be consolidated within the Leibnizian system and shown to be interdependent.

The most general formulation of the *"principium rationis"* is the commonplace, *nihil est sine ratione*, "Nothing is without reason"; to formulate it positively: "Everything has its reason [or ground]." *"Ratio"* [reason] is connected with *reor* [Latin], "to consider something as." *Ratio* is that with regard to which I consider something as something, that because of which I take something to be such-and-such. Here then *ratio* means ground, in the sense of the foundation for a true assertion. "Ground" in this sense is relative to knowledge, is an *epistemological ground*. Aristotle says: Ἐπίστασθαι δὲ οἰόμεθ' ἕκαστον ἁπλῶς..., ὅταν τήν τ' αἰτίαν οἰώμεθα γινώσκειν δι' ἣν τὸ πρᾶγμά ἐστιν, ὅτι ἐκείνου αἰτία ἐστί, καὶ μὴ ἐνδέχεσθαι τοῦτ' ἄλλως ἔχειν (*Posterior Analytics* A2, 71 b9ff.). "We believe we understand something unqualifiedly when we believe we know that this reason is the ground, the cause, of the thing and that the latter can accordingly not be otherwise than it in fact is." Here "to understand" means to know the grounds for something, and this implies knowing how and in what respect it grounds. To understand or know means to have grasped the explanatory ground in its grounding.

Αἰτία is usually translated by *"cause,"* and cause [Ur-sache, primary or original thing] taken as ground for the actual occurrence of something. A brick, for example, falls from the roof, caused by a bad storm that damaged the roof. But that this particular something falls at all has its ground in its being a material thing determined by gravity. That is its *essential ground*, its *possibilitas*. This is the sense of ground Aristotle had clearly in view in another definition of true knowledge: καὶ εἰδέναι τότ' οἰόμεθα ἕκαστον μάλιστα, ὅταν τί ἐστιν ὁ ἄνθρωπος γνῶμεν ἢ τὸ πῦρ, μᾶλλον ἢ τὸ ποιὸν ἢ τὸ ποσὸν ἢ τὸ πού, ἐπεὶ καὶ αὐτῶν τούτων τότε ἕκαστον ἴσμεν, ὅταν τί ἐστι ποσὸν ἢ τὸ ποιὸν γνῶμεν (*Metaphysics* 21, 1028a 36ff.). "And we assume we know each particular thing most truly when we know *what* 'man' or 'fire' is—rather than know its quality or quantity or position; because we know each of these things too when we know *what* the quantity or quality is." Here "ground" is that to which explanation refers back, that wherein explanation terminates as in something irreducible or from which explanation proceeds, as from something first and originary. Here ground means ἀρχή, beginning and departure, the first from which explanatory knowledge proceeds, upon which it primarily relies.

But this notion of ground as ἀρχή can be conceived still more broadly so that it encompasses both primal cause [Ur-sache] and essential ground: the first from which a being, insofar as it is this being, takes its essence, and also the first from which a being, insofar as it is actualized in such a way, begins in its actualization, in its emergence. Understood in this way, ground is the τὸ τί ἐστιν, what a thing is, its λόγος. *Ratio* also has this meaning of ground as essence, and in this sense *causa* is equated by Christian Wolff with a definite mode of *ratio;* this *ratio* is not primarily related to knowledge (or nevertheless to ontological knowledge?!).

Aristotle conjoins all three main notions of ground as ἀρχή, according to which αἴτιον [cause] is also an ἀρχή, in *Metaphysics* Δ1 (1013 a17ff): πασῶν μὲν οὖν χοινὸν τῶν ἀρχῶν τὸ πρῶτον εἶναι ὅθεν ἢ ἔστιν ἢ γίγνεται ἢ γιγνώσκεται. "It is a common property then of all 'beginnings' to be the first thing from which something either exists or comes into being or becomes known." Ἀρχή is the ground for whatness [Wassein]; it is *essence.* Ἀρχή is ground for something to exist, that it is [Vorhandensein (Dass-sein)]; it is *cause.* Ἀρχή is ground for being true; it is *argument,* justifying a proposition. And if we add Dasein (human existence) and its activity, as essentially belonging with whatness, actual existence, and being true, then we have the grounds for acting: the *intention* (the οὐ ἕνεκα in the *Nicomachean Ethics*).

We can already roughly see four concepts of ground, four variations on what we can mean by "ground" and, correspondingly, four possible ways of grounding, explaining, and giving grounds: essence, cause, argument (in the sense of a "truth"), and intention. The general-formal character of ground is "the first from which." But this neither exhausts the idea of ground nor are the four concepts of ground grasped in their interconnection with sufficient radicality and clarity, since their origin and order remain obscure.

But one thing has been attained. We have defined the range that the common formulation of the *principium rationis* in its generality can and usually does have. *Nihil est sine ratione. Nihil,* nothing—be it whatness, existence [Vorhandensein], being true, and action—nothing is as this being [Sein] without its ground. Each mode of being always has its ground. This is something new and essential: the conjunction of the idea of being as such with the idea of ground as such. *Ground pertains to being.*

It is easy to see that this claim itself, the *principium rationis* in the broadest sense, requires grounds or proof, and that this proof can obviously be given only when the essence of being as such is clarified. Inasmuch as this question is the basic question of metaphysics, the principle of reason emerges as a basic problem of metaphysics, which includes logic, the metaphysics of truth.

In proceeding first to clarify the general formulation of the *principium rationis,* we have already brought out the connection the problem of ground has with the problem of being. We must nevertheless be on guard at this point against assuming the common formulation of the principle as our exclusive clue; we must maintain a critical caution, because the sort of generality in the commonly formulated principle is completely obscure. This vagueness is connected with the complete lack of clarity about the sense of "principle" in this principle, something which has never, since antiquity, posed a problem. It is easy to see that the nature of principle as a problem refers to *principium,* to ἀρχή—thus to ground! The nature of the principle in this principle is itself to be attained only by clarifying the essence of ground as such.

Schopenhauer was the first to attempt a presentation of the principle of sufficient reason, relating all previous formulations of the problem. This remains a service, especially the effort in his doctoral dissertation, "Über die vierfache Wurzel des Satzes vom zureichenden Grunde" ["On the Fourfold Root of the Principle of Sufficient Reason"] of 1813. The second edition was edited by Schopenhauer in 1847, and in 1864 the third edition was done by J. Frauenstädt, with additions by Schopenhauer from his manuscripts, though the passages with the wildest outbursts were deleted. The second edition is questionable in that it is neither philosophically more radical nor more rigorous in argumentation, but it is bristling with tasteless outbursts against Hegel, Schelling, and philosophy as taught in the universities. The essay can always be used as a first orientation, as well as an attempt to unfold the problem in a relatively unified way. But it is totally inadequate with regard to general scientific solidity, historical presentation, as well as philosophical argumentation. In the latter it is trivially Kantian and simply superficial. It is more resentment than philosophical inability that blinded Schopenhauer and entangled him in an astonishing lack of freedom. Since the problem of ground as such has found a place neither in logic nor in metaphysics, and since in addition little attention is paid to Schopenhauer, this little piece is easy to obtain, particularly in later editions—assuming that it does not become philosophically fashionable overnight to work on the principle of sufficient reason.

In the second chapter of his dissertation Schopenhauer gives "A Survey of the Main Points that have been hitherto taught concerning the Principle of Sufficient Reason." His main purpose there is

to show how the concept of ground became gradually differentiated first into the cause [Sachgrund] of something *(causa)* and
the reason for something known *(ratio)*. In section 9, "Leibniz,"
he says: "Leibniz is the first to have a clear conception of that
distinction. In the *Principiis Philosophiae* he definitely distinguishes the *ratio cognoscendi* [reason of cognition] from the *causa
efficiens* [efficient cause], and he presents them as two variations
of the *principium rationis sufficientis* which he formally defines
here as a main principle of all knowledge."[1] We can appropriately
overlook the extreme brevity of his description of the Leibnizian
doctrine of the *principium rationis* and the fact that it is not solid
on the essentials. It may be adequate for a survey of the history of
a problem in a dissertation.

But the way the sixty-year-old Schopenhauer thought it necessary to correct the twenty-five-year-old dissertation author is more
dubious and indicative of Schopenhauer's sort of philosophizing
and perhaps of post-Hegelian philosophy in general. In the second
edition, 1847, the same passage is reformulated in section 9 (p.
16/17; Deussen volume III, p. 125 or 749): "Leibniz was the first
to formally present the principle of ground as a main principle of
all knowledge and science. In doing so he refers to the distinction
in the two main meanings of the principle, but he did not expressly emphasize them nor discuss them clearly anywhere else.
The main passage is in his *Principiis Philosophiae* §32, and a little
better in the French version of that treatise, entitled
Monadologie." What is still acceptable in this completely superficial report comes from the earlier period and is due to its having
originated in his philosophical milieu. Schopenhauer contributes
nothing to the subject on the basis of his own philosophy, except
the irritated manner. This manner took quite different forms
against Schelling and Hegel and was used later by others as well;
the tone cannot hide the endless superficiality with which these
blustering epigones of the nineteenth century believed they had
surpassed great and genuine philosophy from Plato to Hegel.

Schopenhauer's kind of historical orientation to the problem,
especially regarding Leibniz, led to his formulating the problem of
the principle of ground in a very superficial way, that did not in
fact grasp the root at all. This is most evident in §5 (p. 7; Deussen
volume III, p.7), where Schopenhauer formulates the principle in
general and in so doing stops with Wolff's formulation, which goes

---

1. Original edition, Rudolstadt, 1813, pp. 13-14; *Arthur Schopenhauers
sämtliche Werke*, ed. P. Deussen, volume 3 (Munich, 1912), p. 11.

back to Leibniz: *Nihil est sine ratione cur potius sit quam non sit.*
Schopenhauer translates this simply as "Nothing is without a reason why it is." And so it remained in subsequent editions. But this
formula contains something quite different. It does not say *nihil
est sine ratione cur sit* [nothing is without a reason why it is]. The
potius quam was ignored by Schopenhauer. This is, of course, no
mere error in translation, and it would not be worthwhile to fault
Schopenhauer for a mere lack of philological exactitude. But this
omission of the *potius* indicates that Schopenhauer followed the
old route in which the problem was superficially thrown together
but not understood. For this *potius quam*, μᾶλλον ἤ, "rather than,"
is precisely the central problem of the *principium rationis*. This
can be seen, nevertheless, only when the effort is made to root
Leibniz's logic in his metaphysics and to understand in turn this
metaphysics in a philosophical way that goes beyond the customary schemata of the histories of philosophy.

The shortened common formula for the principle of reason is as
general as it is vague. Now Leibniz nowhere set down an
adequate, unambiguous formulation of the principle, which en-
compassed all possible variants of it and its applications. Nevertheless, three formulations can be set up schematically to clarify
somewhat the problem behind the real formulation of the *principium rationis:* 1) *Ratio 'est' cur aliquid potius existit quam nihil*
[There "is" a reason why anything exists rather than nothing]; 2)
Ratio 'est' cur hoc potius existit quam aliud [There "is" a reason
why this exists rather than anything]; 3) *Ratio 'est' cur sic potius
existit quam aliter* [There "is" a reason why it exists in such a way
rather than in another way]. The *principium rationis* is *the principle of "rather than,"* the principle of the primacy of something
over nothing, of this thing over that, of in this way over another
way. Right away it is becoming clear that the emphasis in this
principle lies on the factually existing beings, on factuality in the
broadest sense, and that a definite choice, as it were, is made in
what is factual in contrast to what is still possible. In this conception, then, the principle depends upon the connection of
possibility and actuality. Leibniz says this in the treatise *De rerum
originatione radicali* ["On the Radical Origination of Things"],
1697:

Hinc vero manifestissime intelligitur ex infinitis possibilium com-
binationibus seriebusque possibilibus existere eam, per quam
plurimum essentiae seu possibilitatis perducitur ad existendum.
Semper scilicet est in rebus principium determinationis quod a
Maximo Minimove petendum est, ut nempe maximus praestetur ef-

fectus, minimo ut sic dicam sumtu. (first published by Erdmann; G. VII, 302-8, 303)

> Hence it is very clearly understood that out of the infinite combinations and series of possible things, one exists through which the greatest amount of essence or possibility is brought into existence. There is always a principle of determination in nature which must be sought by maxima and minima; namely, that a maximum effect should be achieved with a minimum outlay, so to speak. [L. 487]

This means that, from the endless possible combinations and series, those things become actual through which the greatest amount of essentiality, i.e., possibility, is brought into existence; that which we find factual is the best realization of all that is possible.

The whole treatise shows that the idea of being created is the background and center, and that the *ultima ratio rerum* is *unum dominans extramundanum* [The ultimate reason for things is one, ruling, and extramundane]. *Nam non tantum in nullo singulorum, sed nec in toto aggregato serieque rerum inveniri potest sufficiens ratio existendi* (ibid., 302) [For neither in any individual particular, nor in the whole aggregate or series, can there be a sufficient reason for existence]. Now there is not much gained by merely suggesting Christian dogmatic theology lurks somehow behind the conception of the principle of sufficient reason. On the contrary, that would just circumvent the real contents of the problem itself. (This is always the case when one believes he has solved a problem by figuring with psychological probability what impulses might have been involved in posing and solving the problem. One can pacify himself with the satisfactions of such world-view psychological curiosity, but it must remain clear that hunting for instinctual motivations in the history of the mind would have neither a possible object to study, nor any justification whatever, nor the possibility of accomplishing anything, if the problems were identical with the psychological motivations that play a part in mastering problems.)

The *principium rationis sufficientis* as the principle of the *potius* remains, even if the specifically theological reference is not taken into account. It is easy to show briefly that there is a central problem of metaphysics as such hidden here. We have already seen that the idea of ground (as essence, cause, truth or argument, intention) is originally and closely connected with being. Now a seemingly totally different sort of connection emerges, a connection between ground, *ratio*, and precedence, *potius*, between justification and pre-ference [Vor-ziehen], freedom of choice, (ultimately, *propensio in bonum*, the propensity toward the good), hence the connection between *ground and freedom*. The concept of *potius*, "rather than," μᾶλλον, contains a moment of preference. We know possibilities of preference only in areas where there are decisions about value or lack of value, higher or lower value. Of course reference to the dimension of value as a possible horizon for preference, assessment, and disapprobation does not provide a solution to the problem, since the idea of value is as òbscure in its metaphysical genesis as is the good, the ἀγαθόν or *bonum*. Nevertheless, the connection between the good or ἀγαθόν and being or ὄν emerged already in ancient philosophy.

The intrinsic connection between the problem of being and the problem of preference is especially apparent in Plato where in the *Republic* he teaches that "beyond being," ἐπέκεινα τῆς οὐσίας there is still the idea of the good, ἰδέα ἀγαθοῦ: 1) Ἡ ἀγαθοῦ ἰδέα ἐν τῷ γνωστῷ τελευταία (*Rep.* VII, 517b8f.) [The last thing in the realm of the knowable is the idea of the good]. But it is last in such a way that the idea of the good completes everything; it is that which embraces all beings as beings. Being has an inner relation to the ἀγαθόν. This idea of the good is μόγις ὁρᾶσθαι, difficult to see. 2) Πάντων αὕτη ὀρθῶν τε καὶ καλῶν αἰτία (517c2), it is the cause of all things right and fine. The idea of the good is the basic determination of all order, all that belongs together. Insofar as belonging together, κοινωνία, is the essential determination of being, Plato is saying that the idea of the good is the primary bearer of this coherence, κοινωνία. 3) Ἔν τε ὁρατῷ φῶς καὶ τὸν τούτον κύριον τεκοῦσα (517 c 3) [In the realm of the visible, the idea of the good bears the light and its master]. The idea of the good brings the light, in the realm of the visible, and at the same time the master of this light, i.e., the sun. Here would be the place for a thorough interpretation of the myth of the cave. Light is the prerequisite for vision. The sight of the understanding also requires light, and what originally provides light for knowing beings, i.e., for understanding being, is the idea of the ἀγαθόν. 4) Ἔν τε νοητῷ αὐτὴ κυρία (517c 3/4) [The idea of the good dominates in the realm of reason]. It is directly dominant in the realm of what is graspable by human reason, so that it provides truth and reason. The intrinsic possibility of truth and reason is based on the idea of the good. 5) Ἡ τοῦ παντὸς ἀρχή (511 b 7) [It is the origin of all]. It is beginning, ground, cause of all. 6) The idea of the good is ἔτι ἐπέκεινα τῆς οὐσίας (509 b a) [even beyond being], transcending even beings and their being. What then does the idea of the good

mean? We must be satisfied here with a reference to its close conjunction with the idea of being in general, with the idea of ground,
(in its manifold meaning) and with the idea of preference, of the
most preferred, of the ἀγαθόν (cf. more broadly, §11b, pp. 218 ff.).[2]

So far several things are clear: there is a common general formulation of the principle of ground; this formulation, however, conceals the multi-layered nature of the problem; this problem of
ground seems, however, intrinsically related to the problem of
being as such. At the same time, we maintain the problem of
ground is the central problem of logic. We shall therefore try to
treat the whole problem we described in three sections: I. Exposition of the dimension of the problem, II. the problem of ground
itself, III. the principle of reason and the basic problems of logic
as the metaphysics of truth (cf. §14).

We must bear in mind, however, that we are not trying to take
up the principle of reason in any of its formulations and prove it.
We are rather concerned first with shedding light on what the
principle means and can mean. By clarifying what the principle
means, the general nature of its being a principle must become
clear; from there we can first envision what possibilities there are
for proving this principle and what sort of proof it requires. It
would be not only unmethodical but pointless to discuss whether
the principle is immediately evident or is entailed by the nature of
reason, whether it rests on experience or provides a practical postulate, before clarifying the meaning of the principle. Perhaps
none of those conceptions is relevant to the essence of the principle. The principle is much too rich to be forced into these commonplace distinctions.

FIRST SECTION:
EXPOSITION OF THE DIMENSIONS OF THE PROBLEM

We want to concentrate here on the understanding of the idea of
ground as it was first developed and remained prevalent, even
though the whole problem has already begun to emerge. It is no
accident that the idea of ground first emerges as "cause" and as

---

2. Cf. also the lecture course from the summer semester of 1926, *Grundbegriffe
der antiken Philosophie* [planned as volume 22 of the *Gesamtausgabe*].

"argument" (as the grounds for maintaining an assertion, the grounds of proof), and both are designated by "αἰτία." Why is this not accidental? First, because the idea of cause and causation emerge immediately and urgently, on account of our being engaged in the world in producing one being from another, i.e., in the know-how related to producing, in τέχνη. Another reason is that beings show themselves at once as that which speech is about, i.e., as emerging in λόγος, in the ἐπιστήμη concerned with "truth." Understood in this way, λόγος with its τί ἐστιν [what it is] is related to ἰδέα, to εἴδη. We are then referred at once from τέχνη, through αἴτιον [cause] as ἀρχή [reason, origin] to εἶδος [specific form].

Λόγος and τέχνη are, taken in a broad sense, those comportments in which beings as such are manifest, and manifest in such a way that the idea of being first develops in this horizon. But we already learned that the problem of ground is intimately connected with the problem of being as such. Thus it is clear why the exposition of the problem of ground moves also in the same dimension as the basic problem of metaphysics as such. Formulated differently, the problem of ground also belongs to the basic problem of metaphysics.

We must obtain the dimension of the problem of ground, and this means to open a field of vision in which we can begin to see the phenomenon of ground, in which we can come to an understanding of what ground as such means and whence this idea arises. It is of the essence of philosophy that none of its problem areas is directly i.e., immediately, to be found in the line of vision of the common everyday understanding. Entrance into the specific field of a problem requires its own proper pathway. We shall not now discuss the peculiarity of that path, though we are here necessarily giving some previews of what can really be seen only in retrospect; we are instead going some length on that path ourselves. We shall proceed from the common opinion, or from the closest formulation that approximates the common opinion, because such opinions have each their own hidden and perhaps distorted truth.

In traditional logic the principle of ground also appears, in some inconspicuous passage next to and under several other principles. It is numbered, among the laws of thought, after the principle of identity, the principle of non-contradiction, and the principle of excluded middle. To start with, we select the commonest and crudest possible formulation, so we can move on from there to a new statement of the problem and at the same time show how many diverse meanings this principle can take on and how it does so because it has never been seriously posed as a problem.

§8.   *The principle of ground as a rule of thought*

We must make clear what the [logical] formulation of the principle of ground as a rule of thinking means, and whether this formulation expresses the original meaning of the *principium rationis,* and whether the idea of ground is clarified by it at all. If the latter is not the case, then this basic principle of logic is a poor candidate for the principle of a presumably fundamental science. We will use Sigwart's formulation as he states it in §32 of his *Logik.*[3]

It states in general terms: "The fourth of the so-called laws of thought ... asserts the quite general property of all judging as such, that in believing in the validity of a judgment, there is at the same time a belief in its necessity" (Ibid. p. 257). The common interpretation of the principle of ground says a human being cannot make a judgment without having grounds for his assertion. Or, as Sigwart says, "there is no judgment expressed without psychological grounds for its certainty" (Ibid. p. 256). What does he mean by this? Why does he speak here of the grounds for certainty? "Certainty" is apparently to be distinguished from that characteristic of the proposition which we discussed earlier, i.e., truth. But for being-true we have already mentioned a kind of ground, the "argumentative grounds," the "cognitive grounds." Now we are hearing about a ground for certainty. How are the ground of truth and the ground of certainty related to one another? What does certainty mean, as distinguished from truth?

The certainty of a piece of knowledge consists in my being sure of the truth of a proposition. Certainty therefore always presupposes truth! And being certain of truth depends upon something on the basis of which that certainty holds the relevant truth to be a legitimate cognitive possession. But what creates the legitimacy for the possession of knowledge? Obviously the insight that what is so possessed is truth, which in turn means that this truth is justified or grounded. What is the upshot of this? Are not then the ground of truth and the ground of certainty one and the same? Being certain of a truth is plainly insight or the completed insight into the grounds of truth. The ground of certainty is accord-

---

3. C. Sigwart, *Logik,* volume 1, 4th edition (revised by H. Maier) (Tübingen, 1911).

ingly the ground of truth, and as such a ground, as grounding a truth, it is a ground that is seen. The ground of certainty is the ground of truth become insight. The ground of certainty and the ground of truth are materially the same and only formally different by the moments of being acquainted with and thoroughly grasping something [Erkanntheit and Erfasstsein]. The grounds of certainty are the grounds of truth made evident.

One thing follows immediately from this consideration. Holding a true statement to be true, accepting a truth, must ultimately be supported by grounds of truth in order to be sure of itself. Certainty, as a mode of holding something to be true, as a way of possessing truth, is codetermined by that which is appropriated, by the truth. And the truth has itself "grounds." Certainty and its certification is dependent on the grounds of truth.

Is this essential connection formulated in the statement from Sigwart cited above? Or is something else meant by the statement that no judgment is asserted without psychological grounds for its certainty? Obviously! Because this statement says nothing about essential connections, but is a statement of facts. In positive form the statement says that in all asserting and making judgments there are psychological grounds for certainty. But this cannot mean that every judgment is evident, i.e., is made with an insight into the reason for its being true. For many judgments do occur and are taken to be certain while involving no insight. Of course a lack of insight into the legitimating grounds of truth does not exclude the fact that making judgments and holding something to be true has its motivating ground. The ground that motivates one's being certain and maintaining something, the motivating grounds for conviction, is not simply identical with evidential grounds. If these judgments therefore lack the grounds for certitude, they do not then necessarily lack motivating grounds for our conviction of their truth. And so the above claim [by Sigwart] can mean at best that in every judgment made there are motivating grounds for its being held to be true. This does not mean, however, that a ground belongs to the essence of truth and accordingly also to the possession of truth qua certainty.

In fact even our last interpretation of the above claim can be made dubious. Has every judgment a motivating ground for holding something to be true? Insufficiently grounded and even completely ungrounded propositions are also asserted and adhered to as true—without one being able to say that this particular adherence has no ground motivating it. There can be assertions without such grounds, unmotivated and unjustified assertions, but even these are still not completely groundless, insofar as even unmotivated, unjustified assertions can still have their "causes."

What does the statement cited mean then? Solely that in making judgments people usually have motivating reasons. The statement is thus a claim about what in fact the average man usually does in making his judgments. Yet it says nothing about the essence of grounds, be it the ground of truth or the ground of certainty. It only characterizes the usual way and manner of relating to the grounds motivating judgment.

If the claim be taken for what it is, there would, to be sure, be nothing to say against it, except that it has nothing to offer philosophically. Nevertheless, this assertion not only usurps the principle of reason, but one believes he has the right with the statement mentioned to say even more, inasmuch as he introduces it into logic as a science of the rules of thinking. The statement of factual normality in the usual process of judging is considered the foundation for a statement of a wholly different sort, namely, for the requirement that all thinking, all judging should have grounds. Because it is commonly the custom to have a psychological ground in judging, therefore judgment should in every case consider a legitimating ground. Thinking should ground and be grounded. This normative statement is based on the former assertion of fact, and the statement expressing the norm is taken to be the genuine formulation of the principle of reason. Yes, one goes even further and identifies the normative statement with the statement that every assertion needs a proof, that all statements be simply provable and need to be proved.

We shall disregard the fact that this is an attempt to justify a general norm for thought on the basis of a reference to facts of experience, that this is an attempt to give empirical grounds for an a priori statement. Husserl's critique of psychologism in Volume I of the *Logical Investigations* shows the absurdity of such an attempt. His argument there is of course only relatively conclusive and only negative. For the question still remains: What are a priori statements, and are such normative statements then a priori statements and in what sense?

It is far more important to ask in what way the normative statement, "all thinking should give reasons," is connected with the general *principium rationis*. At first it is easy to conclude that this statement is only a special case of the general statement that all human comportment, as free, has its motivating grounds; thus also human comportment qua thinking. (Correctly understood, the statement is an essential proposition about comportment as such

and not about how humans commonly on the average try to act.)
More is, nevertheless, intended by the normative statement than
that a grounding is required in holding something to be true, because the attempt to satisfy this requirement leads to the demonstration of grounds for the truth to be held. We again come across
the connection of the grounds for truth and the grounds for certainty, and we can conceive the connection more clearly now by
reference to the statements we are examining. We are asking: Why
should every possession of truth, every holding something to be
true, have its ground? Only because it is one comportment among
others? Or also and precisely because holding something to be
true as such, the true statement itself, and as a true statement, has
a relation to something like grounds?

But does truth then have as such a relationship to ground? In
what sense? And what is meant here by "ground"? And if ground
belongs to the essence of truth, is this essential connection then
itself the ground for the possibility of the demand for the groundedness of a true judgment? And does this requirement for the
groundedness of true statements first then imply the postulation of
a ground for certainty? And what does it mean to say that the essence of truth implies a demand?

Our discussion of one particular formulation of the principle of
reason led us to the insight that the problem of ground is somehow
connected with the phenomenon of truth, that the dimension of
the problem indicated by the terms "truth" and "essence of truth"
is at the same time that dimension where the problem of ground
can be posed. We distinguished, in the making of judgments, a
multiplicity of "grounds" which refer to something different, so
that "ground" itself means different things. All these kinds of
grounds are somehow related to ground and truth. In the foregoing
we always somehow understood "ground," and yet we have not
properly clarified it. Little is gained even by suggesting that
ground is somehow connected with truth, as long as we have not
sufficiently clarified the essence of truth itself with regard to the
problem under consideration.

§9. The essence of truth and its essential relation to "ground"

a) The essence of propositional truth

Our task of exposing the essential connection between truth and ground does not deal with the demonstration of the grounds for specific truths; it deals rather with showing in what way truth as such, in its essence, has a relation to what we rightly call "ground." The essential relation truth has to anything like ground as such provides the intrinsic possibility for every truth being ideally provable. And at the same time the essential relation of truth as such and ground as such provides anchorage for the correctness of the demand, necessary in some respects, that true statements be grounded.

The essential relation truth has to something like "ground" becomes visible only when the essence of truth itself is sufficiently clear. We need therefore first a general characterization of the essence of truth, but, besides that, we need an exposition of the intrinsic possibility of the essence of truth. When we inquire and seek answers in this direction and clarify the intrinsic possibility of the essence of truth, then this means we are also describing the dimension within which the problem of ground must be posed. First, then, a general characterization of the essence of truth.

We have already emphasized that truth has its locus in the judgment, in the proposition; truth is not only to be found in the judgment, but the essence of truth is to be gathered from the essence of judgment. All this we admit on the supposition that the traditional claim is correct. It became clear from Leibniz's doctrine of judgment that truth is defined by the judgment. Judgment means *nexus, connexio, inclusio, identitas:* the cohesion of subject and predicate, of concepts, representations. Already in antiquity judgment is a σύνθεσις νοημάτων, a "combination of representations." Truth is equated with the belonging together of subject and predicate. What rightly belongs together is correct. Truth is *the validity of a combination of representations.* Among other things and by inference, truth is characterized as validity [Gültigkeit]. But does this characterization touch the essence of truth? What is valid is what rightly belongs together. How then is it decided that some things belong together? How can we assess what is appropriate for an assertion for it to be true? How do we define the correctness of what belongs together? If *veritas* is equivalent to *identitas,* then the question of truth is answered only halfway. It is typical for the mathematical mode of thought that, for his purposes, Leibniz defines truth as *identitas,* without inquiring any further into the *possibilitas* of this *identitas.*

What determines the correctness of a combination of representations, i.e., their coherence as a harmony? What decides whether a combination is correct or not? An assertion is harmonious, i.e., is correct, when the relation of representations agrees with that about which the judgment is made. The harmony (the *identitas* of the *nexus*) draws it correctness and validity from the *correspondence* of what is thought in judgmental thinking with that about which judgment is made, the object of judgment. The regulation of harmony takes place in and through correspondence. Truth qua validity, coherence, *identitas,* rests on the correspondence between representation and object, between νόημα and πρᾶγμα. From ancient times this correspondence is characteristic of truth. Truth was defined as ὁμοίωσις, *adaequatio,* as adequation to something, as measurement by something. But why and how does this character of adequation to something belong to the essence of truth? Why is it that the essence of truth is defined along the lines of the idea of adequation, of being measured by something? How does this traditional definition of the essence of truth, the idea of *adaequatio,* arise?

It is clear first off that the character of truth as identity is reduced to truth as *adaequatio.* At the same time it appears that the attempt to conceive the essence of truth by way of the judgment is not immediately successful, or in any case does not come out unequivocally. We have, in fact, up to now only exchanged one conception for another, namely for one which also relates to the assertion: the correspondence of a combination of representations. On what has our question about the essence of truth now focused? On the correspondence which representations have to their objects, with the subject and its consciousness in relation to what lies "outside consciousness." Thus truth as correspondence somehow concerns this relation of representations to their objects. How can we further define this relation? In posing this question we enter a playground for every possible theory. Can we settle the essence of truth in this dubious area? Should we base our clarification of the essence of truth on a dubious epistemological theory?

Both proponents and opponents of this traditional characterization of truth overlook the fact that the description is only a starting point for clarifying the essence of truth. It is a start which in no way guarantees, as the history of the concept of truth shows, that it will be developed correctly; it can also become a starting point for erroneous theories. The definition of truth as *adaequatio* is the starting point, not yet the answer; it is the point of departure for posing the problem, but is not yet the solution!

On the other hand, this approach for clarifying the essence of truth through the proposition, through λόγος, has been used repeatedly from early on in the philosophical tradition. It cannot be rejected simply because it leads to difficulties. What is in the end important is that this approach be undertaken in the right way and then carried out beyond the point where it is first supposed to lead, to the essence of truth as the characteristic of propositions.

Still, what does it mean "to proceed in the right way" in an interpretation of the proposition with the intention of explicating the essence of truth? What does it mean to interpret the proposition as such "in the right way?" A correct interpretation of the *proposition* as such doubtless requires us to take the proposition as it is, prior to every explanation; we must therefore avoid prematurely constructing a theory of the proposition without first adequately ascertaining the properties of the proposition as such which is to be explained, without taking it as it primarily presents itself. But a question nevertheless arises as to the meaning of "primarily presents itself." How does the proposition present itself to us, when we comport ourselves prior to all theories of judgment, prior to all philosophical questions about propositions?

Now one answer can be that the proposition is a verbalized judgment, a statement pronounced in speech, an utterance in words; words present themselves as sounds, pitches, noises, and from these we arrive at articulation, at the word; from there we arrive at meaning, thinking, representing, and this transpires in the soul and the representation in the soul is related to the object outside. Already in Aristotle we find the sequence: noise, [phonetic] sound (φθόγγος, φωνή), articulation, word, meaning, thinking, representing, soul. So, as a result, we have here a rigorous and exact approach to what is immediately given: noises from which we ascend step-by-step. Furthermore, this starting point and path lead us to the problem we have already described, the correspondence of representation to object. The more exactly we pursue and explain in detail the relationship between noise, sound, word, meaning, thinking, and representing, the more scientific will be our explanation of what is generally called the correspondence of thinking with the object.

Does beginning with the phonetic articulation then grasp what immediately presents itself to us? In no way. Suppose someone here in the classroom states the proposition "the board is black" and does so in an immediately given context of question and answer. To what do we then attend in understanding the statement? To the phonetic articulation? Or to the representation that performs the making of the statement and for which then the sounds uttered are "signs"? No, rather we direct ourselves to the blackboard itself, here on the wall! In the perception of this board, in making present and thinking about the blackboard and nothing else, we participate in the performance of the statement [vollziehen wir die Aussage mit und nach]. What the statement immediately presents is that *about which* it states something.

But do we gain much by this for furthering our inquiry? Certainly not, if we mean constructing premature theories. For the latter are undercut by this procedure. But something indeed has been gained, if the point of departure for every genuine clarification of a phenomenon lies in first grasping and holding onto what presents itself. To be sure, the difficulties of an appropriate interpretation are just beginning. It is important to maintain the primary givenness and from there to inquire into the full structure of the phenomenon in question.

What primarily presents itself to us in our natural hearing and understanding of statements? In what respect do we grasp them? With regard to that about which something is stated. We thus grasp the statement as a statement about something.

We have already mentioned this, but now we are interpreting it more sharply. What takes place in our completing the performance of a statement (about the board) is not that we first transport ourselves, as it were, into the soul of the individual who makes the statement and then put ourselves somehow in relation to the external object spoken of. We are rather always already comporting ourselves towards the beings around us. Statements do not first bring about this relation, but rather the converse is true. Statements are first possible on the basis of an always latent comportment to beings. Dasein, the "I" that makes statements, is always already "among" beings about which it makes statements. A first consequence is that making statements, as a stating about something, is not at all a primordial relation to beings but is itself only possible on the basis of our already-being-among-beings, be this a perceptual or some kind of practical comportment. We can say that making statements about X is only possible on the basis of *having to do with X*.

What does this imply for our problem? Can the essence of truth be described along the lines of the proposition? If truth means correspondence, adequation to beings, then this assertion measuring itself on beings is evidently founded on the fact that, in our intercourse with beings, we have already, as it were, come to an understanding with beings; beings not ourselves, with which we in some way have to deal, are disclosed to us. So an assertion can finally be true, be adequate in propositional content to that about which the statement is made, only because the being it speaks of is already in some way disclosed. That is, a statement about X is only true because our dealing with that X has already a certain kind of truth. The usual argument against *adaequatio* points to the superfluity, the impossibility, of correspondence; but that argument rests on the presupposition that the correspondence of a statement must have first produced the subject-object relationship.

Propositional truth is more primordially rooted, rooted in already-being-by-things. The latter occurs "already," before making statements—since when? Always already! Always, that is, insofar as and as long as Dasein exists. Already being with things belongs to the *existence* of Dasein, to its kind and mode of being.

Existence is the term for the sort of being we ourselves each are, human Dasein. A cat does not exist, but it lives; a stone neither lives nor exists but is present before us [vorhanden]. Among other things, being-already-by-things belongs to existence. This is to be taken in the sense that Dasein, as existent, exists by way of this being-by-things, and is disclosed in and for being-by-things. Being-by is not being alongside, next to something, as a bench stands next to one's house. A bench does not exist; it has no proper "being by the house," for that would mean the house would appear and manifest itself to the bench as a house.

As characteristic of existence, being-by-things is *disclosive*, it allows one to encounter things. As such, being-by is disclosive, not occasionally, but essentially. Being disclosive is the genuine sense of being-true. If we go back to the original meaning of the concept of truth, we find the elemental understanding shaped by the Greek word ἀ-ληθεύειν. The Greeks saw this character of truth, though they did not bring their insight to fruition, but covered it over with theories. It is important to make an explicit problem of the negativity residing in the concept of truth as ἀ-λήθεια.

Being-already-by-things, having to do with them, is of itself disclosive. This mode of disclosing is, as disclosure of what is objectively present, discovery in the broadest sense. Making statements about objective things [Vorhandenes] discovers them in a mode peculiar to it, namely, as a *determining* of something as something. That is the real sense of synthesis (συμπλοκή, *connec-tio*). "Something as something" is of itself irreducible but never-theless founded. It is only possible on the basis of the disclosing that is already to be found in our having to do with things [Umgang-mit]. This discovering performed in the proposition is always in reference to something; it is nurtured by the primordial discovering that is there in our intercourse with things.

We have gained several points:

1)   Being-true means being-disclosive.

2)   The being-true of statements is not primary but is founded upon the disclosure in our being-by-things, in our having to do with things. The latter mode of disclosure is a discovering.

3)   Being-true as disclosure belongs to the existence of Dasein as such.

With this the principal question is at hand. If truth belongs de-rivatively, not primarily, to the proposition, and it does so only because it is an essential feature of being-by-things as a basic characteristic of existence, then does being-true only belong to existence insofar as Dasein relates to what is objectively present [Vorhandenes], or does truth belong just as primordially to other essential structures of Dasein as well? Is being-true only a disclo-sure qua discovery, or should it be conceived still more broadly and primordially?

It further becomes clear that if the being-true of a statement is not primordial, and if ground is, however, essentially related to truth, then also the primordial problem of ground cannot be con-ceived on the basis of propositional truth.

b)   Intentionality and transcendence

Before pursuing the essence of truth more radically we must as-similate still more clearly what we found in the foregoing. We must relate it to traditional opinions which are still prevalent and which thoroughly shape logic.

One could believe there is a being-by-things and then also a being-present-on-hand [Vorhandensein], the former belonging to the subject's subjectivity. But subjectivity, it is believed, is char-acterized by the positing of a subject-object relation. The latter is understood as the being-present-on-hand together of subject and object, in the sense that neither one is without the other; there is (1) an object on hand with every subject, and (2) a subject on hand with every object.

Regarding claim (2), "There is no object without a subject," the term "object" here is ambiguous. It is something on hand by itself, and, taken in its objectivity as an object, it is supposed and grasped in its objectivity as a being such that it is of itself on hand and, in being on hand, need not be grasped. In grasping something on hand as on hand, there is, in other words, a withdrawing release of what is on hand; grasping it has the character of allowing what is grasped to abide by itself, and this grasping understands itself as an acceptance. Now if, by "object," is meant what is on hand of itself, what needs not be grasped, then the claim is false. Such a something on hand is not in need of a subject, and its being on hand does not establish a subject's being on hand. This thesis also fails to understand the essence of the subject; it takes the subject as merely something which grasps. The subject can be what it is, Dasein exists, without grasping beings merely qua objects. Objectification, or even theoretical consideration, does not necessarily belong to being-by-things. (Nevertheless, if one were to take the object with regard to its objectification, then it is correct that this objectification is dependent on a subject which grasps.)

Regarding the claim (1), "There is an object on hand with every subject." From what we have said, this claim is also dubious. It is particularly important to see that the thesis says nothing at all about the subjectivity of the subject. The subject can very well be without an object; this does not mean, however, the subject could exist without a being-by-things, for the latter belongs to being a subject as such. In other words, with the existence of Dasein, insofar and as soon as Dasein exists, something occurs, has begun to have a history, something startling, namely, that a being happens for another being and can happen for another, without the subject explicitly having this in mind.

When appeal is made to the subject-object relation, especially for characterizing subjectivity, then it must be said that, in this subject-object relation and in the appeal to it, something essential is omitted and something crucial has been missed. The characteristics of this "relation between" are omitted, the very thing to be explained. The genuine concept of subjectivity is lacking, insofar as it goes unnoticed that the "relationship to" belongs to the essence of subjectivity. To be sure, not all is clear about this claim that the relationship to possible objects belongs to subjectivity. One can maintain this claim without realizing its properly ontological sense, which is that a disclosive being-by-things belongs to existence.

Our theme is to clarify the essential connection between truth and ground. To do so we need to clarify the essence of truth, first along traditional lines which hold that truth is equivalent to propositional truth. Our interpretation of the proposition showed it to be founded in being-already-by-things. In the latter, primordial truth is to be found. Being-by as existential is of course itself a problem. It is a problem precisely because of the seeming self-evidence of the premise of a subject-object relation.

It is remarkable that the problem addressed by this claim cannot be budged. It is as old as philosophy and appears already in Parmenides. The view, developed early and easily in the prephilosophical understanding of Dasein, that the soul, thinking and representing, consciousness, establishes a relationship to objects, or put conversely, that beings occur before and lie opposite to (ἀντίκειται) thinking, seeing, and representing; this view, this understanding of Dasein also persisted for a long time in this general and vague form. The problem offers the seductive look of the obvious and simple. Thus the problem has been discussed since antiquity, in the Middle Ages and in modern philosophy, until Hegel's dialectic; especially in Kant, the relation of consciousness to the object becomes a problem. In a letter (to Marcus Herz, February 21, 1772) Kant wrote: "I asked myself, on what basis rests the relation of that in ourselves called 'representation' to the object?"

But it is typical of Kant, as well as his successors, all the more so of the contemporary epigones, to ask all too hastily about the ground of the possibility of the relation of consciousness to the object, without clarifying sufficiently beforehand what is meant by this relation whose possibility is to be clarified, what this relation is standing between, and what sort of being is applicable to it.

What "relation" really means remains vague. The vagueness falls back on the vagueness of that which stands in relation. It emerges particularly in the vagueness of the concept of the subject, and on the other hand, in the naiveté and presumptive obviousness of the being of the being. The being's "independence" is only a negative determination, and yet it can only mean non-dependence from the subject, while this non-dependence precisely in relation to the subject is what is to be explained, to be made as such into a problem.

Two things are to be kept in mind regarding the "relation" of subject and object. The problem we are touching on has a simplicity in its breadth and primordiality, and, correspondingly, it is to be conceived as a whole or not at all. Herein lies the difficulty, since the obviousness of the starting point misleads one into regarding the solution's premise and conditions as just as self-evidently given.

The theory of knowledge in the second half of the nineteenth century and in the last decades has repeatedly made the subject-object relation the basis of its inquiries. But both idealist and realist explanations had to fail because the explicandum was not sufficiently definite. The extent to which the above clarification of the problem determines all efforts to pose the problem is evident in the fact that the consequences of the first refinement of our problem, where it is really carried out and achieved, lead to the disappearance of a possible problem in the sense of the idealistic or realistic theories of knowledge.

The most recent attempts conceive the subject-object relation as a "being relation." Here, in particular, we see the misguided incomprehension of the central problematic. Nothing is gained by the phrase "being relation," as long as it is not stated what sort of being is meant, and as long as there is vagueness about the sort of being of the beings between which this relation is supposed to obtain. But leaving indifferent the being of the relation as well as the mode of being of subject and object, one believes he can pose the problem with the greatest possible neutrality. The opposite is the case. The earlier formulation is more self-critical, insofar as it does not speak of a being relation, because being, even with Nicolai Hartmann and Max Scheler, is taken to mean being-on-hand [Vorhandensein]. This relation is not nothing, but it is still not being as something on hand. Thus Hartmann too is pushed back into "critical realism," (probably the least philosophical of all approaches to the question).

One of the main preparatory tasks of *Being and Time* is to bring this "relation" radically to light in its primordial essence and to do so with full intent (cf. §§12 and 13 as the first introductory characterizations). Max Scheler came to similar insights by another path and with another purpose, and he ultimately planned, partially with reference to my investigations, a large treatise, "Idealism—Realism."[4] But the plan for this exchange came to naught.

In our last long conversation in December 1927, we agreed on four points: 1) The problem of the subject-object relation needs to be raised completely afresh, free of the previous efforts to solve it. 2) It is not a question of so-called epistemology; that is, it is not to

---

4. Parts II and III appeared in *Der philosophische Anzeiger*, volume 2, issue 3, 1927–28, pp. 253–324. [Now to be found in *Gesammelte Werke*, volume 9, *Späte Schriften*, edited by Manfred Frings, Bern and Munich, 1976, pp. 185–241.]

be raised primarily with regard to a subject that grasps an object; such a grasping may not be presupposed from the outset. 3) The problem has central import for the possibility of metaphysics and is intimately related to its basic problem. 4) the fourth and most important point of accord was that the moment is here, now when the official philosophical situation is hopeless, to risk again the step into an authentic metaphysics, that is, to develop metaphysics from the ground up. This was the atmosphere in which we parted, the glad mood of a propitious struggle; destiny wanted it otherwise. Scheler was optimistic and believed he had found the solution, while I was convinced we had not yet even raised and developed the problem radically and totally. My essential intention is to first pose the problem and work it out in such a way that the essentials of the entire Western tradition will be concentrated in the simplicity of a basic problem.

In the treatise mentioned, Scheler rejects two pathways, realism and idealism, as impossible, and seeks at the same time to provide a reason why both must fail. He shows the πρῶτον ψεῦδος [the primary error] of both to be vagueness about the relation between *essentia* and *existentia*. Here one thing is clear: the problem is connected with a central question of general ontology. Remarkably, Scheler believed this problem was decided, while in fact the whole problematic begins at this point and can only begin when the basic problem of being in general is unfolded. However unequivocally Scheler rejects the traditional attempts on the problem and also, more or less, sees the reason for their failure, he still accepts, from the tradition, theses that are even less grounded and problematized than those treated in epistemology. Because Scheler no longer saw any problem in the real sphere of the problem, he was then also led to misunderstand the central formulation of the problem in my effort.

Our meeting was, nevertheless, not a chance encounter. For one thing, because I myself have learned from Scheler, but particularly because both endeavors grew out of phenomenology, and especially out of its understanding of *intentionality*. But here again we have a term and concept taken so much for granted that no one lingers with it for long and, even in a preparatory stage, assumes it is the solution to the problem, as if it were surely the key to all doors. On the contrary, we should make what is itself meant by the term into the problem.

We will now give a condensed orientation to the problem. The "relatedness" of looking at, thinking about, of νόησις, to the νόημα [that which is thought about] emerges already in Aristotle. In the

nineteenth century, Franz Brentano made the concept of intentionality the center of his *Psychologie vom empirischen
Standpunkt* of 1874. "From an empirical standpoint," this is crucial for the manner in which he poses the problem. His methodological principle is to bring the psychical into view, prior to all
the explanations of the natural sciences. "Intentional being-in the
object" is characteristic of everything psychical. Everything psychical relates to something. Following the traditional division of
the faculties, Brentano distinguishes three kinds of relating-to,
three irreducible basic classes of the pyschical: representation,
judgment, and interest. His purpose is to classify psychical
phenomena, but the concept of the psychical remains itself untested. Intentionality remains an affair internal to psychology and
attains no fundamental significance.

Husserl brought the problem out of these straits with his concept of intentional consciousness in the fifth of the *Logical Investigations* (volume 2). He prepares a new stage, insofar as he
shows that intentionality determines the essence of consciousness
as such, the essence of reason. With his doctrine of the immanent
intentionality of the *cogitationes*, he brings out the problem's
connection with the basic questions of modern philosophy since
Descartes. But just as Brentano leaves the concept of the psyche
itself untested, so too, in his idealistic epistemology, Husserl does
not further ask the question about the being constituted as consciousness. The insight into intentionality does not go far enough
to see that grasping this structure as the essential structure of Dasein must revolutionize the whole concept of the human being.
Only then, however, does its central philosophical significance
become clear. On the basis of his first realistic position, Scheler
took up the phenomenon of intentionality, not so much as a
definition of reason as such, but as a structural moment of the act
that belongs essentially to a person. Inasmuch as he conceived
intentionality as an essential moment of the personality, Scheler
himself saw the decisive meaning of intentionality. Though he did
not make it further into a problem, through this insight he was
able to see beyond the alternatives of idealism and realism. To be
sure, he did not also make personality a further problem but
allowed it to be conceived as the center of intentional acts.

When relating-to, which is what is meant by the term "intentionality," is correctly understood, then it cannot be taken to be a
feature of representing, a representing that remains within the
psychical, as it would seem to be in Brentano. Otherwise we land
in the problematic situation where we have to posit a sphere of the

soul within which representations arise that refer intentionally to images also belonging to the psychical. In that case we, like Brentano, are faced with the problem: How does the sphere of the psychical relate to that of the physical? Yet the intentionality of perceiving is not directed to an image in the soul, which then would first be brought into relation with something on hand, but it is rather related to what is on hand itself. Only when we stick to this natural sense of intentionality do we have the necessary basis for an appropriate approach. The objection could be raised that then the problem of the subject-object relation vanishes. Certainly— but to supplant the pseudo-problem is precisely what is aimed at with the conception of intentionality.

We must nevertheless make intentionality itself into a problem. Intentionality is indeed related to the beings themselves and, in this sense, is an ontic transcending comportment, but it does not primordially constitute this relating-to but is founded in a being-by beings. This being-by is, in its intrinsic possibility, in turn grounded in existence. In this way the limitations of the earlier interpretation and function of the concept of intentionality become clear, as does its fundamental significance. This concept not only brings a modification of the traditional concept of consciousness and of mind; the radical formulation of the intended phenomenon in an ontology of Dasein leads to a fundamental, "universal" overcoming of this position. From there the previous concept of intentionality proves to be a contracted conception, inasmuch as it understands intentionality to be an active relating to something on hand. This also explains the inclination to take self-reflection for an ontic intentionality directed inwards. Furthermore, because of this contraction, intentionality is conceived primarily as "to intend" [Meinen, connoting "opinion"], where intention is understood as a neutral characteristic of knowing. Thus every act of directing oneself toward something receives the characteristic of knowing, for example, in Husserl, who describes the basic structure of all intentional relating as νόησις [thinking]; thus all intentionality is first a cognitive intending, upon which other modes of active relation to beings are later built. Scheler first made it clear, especially in the essay "Liebe und Erkenntnis,"[5] that intentional relations are quite diverse, and that even, for example, love and hatred ground knowing. Here Scheler picks up a theme of Pascal and Augustine.

---

5. [Now contained in *Gesammelte Werke*, volume 6, *Schriften zur Soziologie und Weltanschauungslehre*, edited by Maria Scheler, Bern and Munich, 2nd edition, 1963, pp. 77–98.]

Concerning the traditional concept of intentionality we maintain: 1) it is only an ontic transcendence; 2) it touches on existing relations to beings only with a certain restriction; 3) it comes to view only in the narrowing theoretical conception, as νόησις.

Underneath the entire earlier problem of the "relation" of "subject" to "object" is the undiscussed problem of *transcendence*. The term can at first be understood in the quite common sense of a being (Dasein) rising over to another being (Dasein or something on hand), crossing over in such a way that, in transcending, that to which Dasein transcends is disclosed for it in a rather broad sense. It is worthwhile to first understand this most proximate aspect of transcendence, its common conception. The common phenomenon of transcendence means the transcendence in which Dasein moves essentially in an immediate way. This is difficult to see, as was shown in the earlier discussions, and it requires openness and sharpness of vision. The preparatory work for it has been done by working out the problem of intentionality.

On the other hand, for a radical posing of the problem, it is essential to lay bare the primordial phenomenon of transcendence. This phenomenon of transcendence is not identical with the problem of the subject-object relation, but is more primordial in dimension and kind as a problem; it is directly connected with the problem of being as such, (cf. *Being and Time*, §§12 and 13; and repeatedly made more primordially visible in stages, cf. §§69 and 83.) The transcendence of Dasein is the central problem, not for the purpose of explaining "knowledge," but for clarifying Dasein and its existence as such, and the latter in turn with fundamental-ontological intent.

The problem of transcendence as such is not at all identical with the problem of intentionality. As ontic transcendence, the latter is itself only possible on the basis of original transcendence, on the basis of *being-in-the-world*. This primal transcendence makes possible every intentional relation to beings. But this relation occurs in such a way that beings are in the "there" of Da-sein in and for Dasein's comportment with beings. The relation is based on a preliminary understanding of the being of beings. This understanding-of-being, however, first secures the possibility of beings manifesting themselves as beings. The understanding-of-being bears the light in whose brightness a being can show itself. If then primordial transcendence (being-in-the-world) makes possible the intentional relation and if the latter is, however, an ontic relation, and the relation to the ontic is grounded in the understanding-of-being, then there must be an intrinsic relationship between primordial transcendence and the understanding-of-being. They must in the end be one and the same.

We saw earlier (section a) that being-true belongs to being-by something on hand and that the "discovery" of what is on hand is a basic form of the comportments in which we deal with things. The essence of truth as a whole is thus only to be clarified as the problem of transcendence as such.

§10.   The problem of transcendence and the problem of Being and Time

The understanding-of-being forms the basic problem of metaphysics as such. What does "being" mean? This is quite simply the fundamental question of philosophy. We are not here about to present the formulation of the problem and its "retrieval" in *Being and Time*. We wish instead to make an external presentation of its guiding principles and thereby pin down the "problem of transcendence."

a) First, a general description. Fundamental ontology, as the analysis of the existence of Dasein, constitutes the approach to the problem. The analysis proceeds solely with the purpose of a fundamental ontology; the point of departure, execution, limit, and mode of concretizing certain phenomena are governed by this purpose. The understanding-of-being is to be brought to light by way of Dasein's mode of being, which is primarily existence. The constitution of Dasein's being is such that the intrinsic possibility of the understanding-of-being, which belongs essentially to Dasein, becomes demonstrable. The issue is therefore neither one of anthropology nor of ethics but of this being in its being as such, and thus one of a preparatory analysis concerning it; the metaphysics of Dasein itself is not yet the central focus.

b) the guiding principles:

1. The term "man" was not used for that being which is the theme of the analysis. Instead, the neutral term *Dasein* was chosen. By this we designate the being for which its own proper mode of being in a definite sense is not indifferent.

2. The peculiar *neutrality* of the term "Dasein" is essential, because the interpretation of this being must be carried out prior to every factual concretion. This neutrality also indicates that Dasein is neither of the two sexes. But here sexlessness is not the indifference of an empty void, the weak negativity of an indifferent ontic nothing. In its neutrality Dasein is not the indifferent no-

body and everybody, but the primordial positivity and potency of the essence.

3. Neutrality is not the voidness of an abstraction, but precisely the potency of the *origin*, which bears in itself the intrinsic possibility of every concrete factual humanity.

4. Neutral Dasein is never what exists; Dasein exists in each case only in its factical concretion. But neutral Dasein is indeed the primal source of intrinsic possibility that springs up in every existence and makes it intrinsically possible. The analysis always speaks only in Dasein about the Dasein of those existing, but it does not speak to the Dasein [being-there] of those who exist; this would be nonsense, since one can only speak to those that are existing. The analysis of Dasein is thus prior to all prophesying and heralding world-views; nor is it wisdom, something available only in the structure of metaphysics. The philosophy of life, *Lebensphilosophie*, has a prejudice against this analysis as a "system of Dasein." This arises from an uneasiness with concepts, and shows a misunderstanding of concepts and of "systematicity" as an architectonic that is thoughtful while nevertheless historical [geschichtlich].

5. Nor is this neutral Dasein the egocentric individual, the ontic isolated individual. The egoity of the individual does not become the center of the entire problematic. Yet Dasein's essential content, in its existence to belong to itself, must be taken up along with the approach. The approach that begins with neutrality does imply a peculiar isolation of the human being, but not in the factical existentiell sense, as if the one philosophizing were the center of the world. Rather, it is the *metaphysical isolation* of the human being.

6. As such, Dasein harbors the instrinsic possibility for being factically dispersed into bodiliness and thus into sexuality. The metaphysical neutrality of the human being, inmost isolated as Dasein, is not an empty abstraction from the ontic, a neither-nor; it is rather the authentic concreteness of the origin, the not-yet of factical dispersion [Zerstreutheit]. As factical, Dasein is, among other things, in each case dispersed in a body and concomitantly, among other things, in each case disunited [Zwiespältig] in a particular sexuality. "Dispersion," "disunity" sound negative at first, (as does "destruction"), and negative concepts such as these, taken ontically, are associated with negative evaluations. But here we are dealing with something else, with a description of the multiplication (not "multiplicity") which is present in every factically individuated Dasein as such. We are not dealing with the notion of

a large primal being in its simplicity becoming ontically split into many individuals, but with the clarification of the intrinsic possibility of multiplication which, as we shall see more precisely, is present in every Dasein and for which embodiment presents an organizing factor. Nor is the multiplicity, however, a mere formal plurality of determinations, but multiplicity belongs to being itself. In other words, in its metaphysically neutral concept, Dasein's essence already contains a primordial *bestrewal* [Streuung], which is in a quite definite respect a *dissemination* [Zerstreuung]. And here a rough indication is in place. As existing, Dasein never relates only to a particular object; if it relates soley to one object, it does so only in the mode of turning away from other beings that are beforehand and at the same time appearing along with the object. This multiplicity does not occur because there are several objects, but conversely. This also holds good for comportment toward oneself and occurs according to the structure of historicity in the broadest sense, insofar as Dasein occurs as stretching along in time. Another essential possibility of Dasein's factical dissemination is its spatiality. The phenomenon of Dasein's dissemination in space is seen, for example, in the fact that all languages are shaped primarily by spatial meanings. This phenomenon can be first explained only when the metaphysical problem of space is posed, a problem that first becomes visible after we have gone through the problem of temporality, (radically put, this is the metontology of spatiality; cf. the Appendix).

7. The transcendental dissemination proper to the metaphysical essence of neutral Dasein, as the binding possibility of each factical existential dispersion and division, is based on a primordial feature of Dasein, that of *thrownness*.

8. This thrown dissemination into a multiplicity is to be understood metaphysically. It is the presupposition, for example, for Dasein to let itself in each case factically be governed by beings which it is not; Dasein, however, identifies with those beings on account of its dissemination. Dasein can be governed, for example, by what we call "nature" in the broadest sense. Only what is essentially thrown and entangled in something can be governed and surrounded by it. This also holds true for the emergence in nature of primitive, mythic Dasein. In being governed by nature, mythic Dasein has the peculiarity of not being conscious of itself with regard to its mode of being (which is not to say that mythic Dasein lacks self-awareness). But it also belongs essentially to factical dissemination that thrownness and captivation remain deeply hidden from it, and in this way the simplicity and "care-lessness" of an absolute sustenance from nature arise in Dasein.

9. The essentially thrown dissemination of Dasein, still understood as completely neutral, appears, among other ways, in Dasein's being-with with Dasein. This being-with with X does not emerge on account of factically existing together; it is not explained solely on the basis of the supposedly more primordial species-being of sexually differentiated bodily creatures. Instead, the species-like unification metaphysically presupposes the dissemination of Dasein as such, that is, being-with as such. But this basic metaphysical characteristic of Dasein can never be deduced from the species-like organization, from living with one another. Rather, factical bodiliness and sexuality are in each case explanatory only—and even then only within the bounds of the essential arbitrariness of all explanation—to the extent that a factical Dasein's being-with is pushed precisely into this particular factical direction, where other possibilities are faded out or remain closed.

10. Being-with as a comportment of authentic existence is only possible in such a way that every existing-with can be and is authentically itself. This freedom of with-one-another, however, presupposes the possibility of the self-determination of a being with the characteristics of Dasein as such, and it is a problem how Dasein can exist as essentially free in the freedom of the factical ties of being-with-one-another. Insofar as being-with is a basic metaphysical feature of dissemination, we can see that the latter ultimately has its ground in the freedom of Dasein as such. The basic metaphysical essence of metaphysically isolated Dasein is centered in *freedom*. But how can we conceive of freedom metaphysically? It seems too empty and too simple. Nevertheless, ontic inexplicability does not preclude an ontological-metaphysical understanding! Freedom is the term for central problems (non-dependence, obligatoriness, regulation, standards), some of which we touch on in treating the concept of world (§ 11c).

The above puts into theses what we treated in the analysis of Dasein. We still need two further guiding statements to make clear how the analysis is carried out.

11. This metaphysics of Dasein, first as an analysis, can be attained only in the free projection of the being-constitution itself. Dasein always exists as itself, and being-a-self is in every case only in its process of realization, as is also existence. For this reason, projection of the basic ontological constitution of Dasein must arise by constructing one of the most extreme possibilities of Dasein's authentic and total capability of being. The projection is directed towards Dasein, as a whole, and towards the basic determinations of its wholeness, even though Dasein in each case is only

as existent. To put it another way, attaining the metaphysical neutrality and isolation of Dasein as such is only possible on the basis
of the extreme existentiell *involvement* [Einsatz] of the one who
himself projects.

This involvment is necessary and essential for the metaphysical
project, for metaphysics as such. But it is, therefore, as an individual existentiell component, not authoritative and obligatory within
the many concrete possibilities of each factical existence. For the
metaphysical project itself reveals the essential finitude of Dasein's existence, which can only be understood existentielly in the
inessentiality of the self that only becomes concrete—as can be
proven metaphysically—through and in the service of each possible totality, a whole which becomes manifest in a rather special
way in metaphysical inquiry. Nevertheless, it is a problem in its
own right: to what extent there is an existentiell guidance, an indirect guidance, in the metaphysical project and in the existentiell
involvement of the person who philosophizes.

12. The ontological interpretation of Dasein's structures must
be concrete with regard to the metaphysical neutrality and isolation of Dasein. Neutrality is in no way identical with the vagueness of a fuzzy concept of a "consciousness as such." Real
metaphysical generalization does not exclude *concreteness*, but is
in one respect the most concrete, as Hegel had seen, though he
exaggerated it. However, concreteness in the analysis of the Dasein phenomena, which give direction and content to Dasein's
metaphysical projection, easily misleads one, first, into taking the
concrete phenomena of Dasein by themselves and, second, into
taking them as existentiell absolutes in their extreme, fundamental-ontological conceptualization. The more radical the existentiell involvement, the more concrete the ontological-
metaphysical project. But the more concrete this interpretation of
Dasein is, the easier it becomes to misunderstand in principle by
taking the existentiell involvement for the single most important
thing, whereas this involvement, itself becomes manifest in the
project, with all its indifference to the particularity of the person.

The existentiell involvement of fundamental ontology brings
with it the semblance of an extremely individualistic, radical
atheism—this is at least the interpretation groped for when fundamental ontology is taken to be a world-view. Yet that interpretation must be tested for its legitimacy, and if it is correct, it must be
examined for its metaphysical, fundamental-ontological sense.
One may not, nevertheless, lose sight of the fact that with such a
fundamental-ontological clarification nothing has yet been de-

cided, and what furthermore ought to be shown is that nothing is decidable in this manner. Yet there is also always the factical necessity of the "presupposition" of a factical situation.

These guiding principles should indicate briefly the sort of intent behind the analysis of Dasein and the requirements for carrying out the analysis. The basic intent of the analysis is to show the intrinsic possibility of the understanding-of-being, which means at the same time the possibility of transcendence.

But why is the preparatory analysis of Dasein with regard to revealing the possibility of the understanding-of-being an exposition of the *temporality* of Dasein? Why does the metaphysical projection of Dasein move in the direction of time and the radical interpretation of time? Possibly because relativity theory treats time or the principle of an objective measurement of time? Or maybe because Bergson and, following him, Spengler deal with time? Or because Husserl worked at the phenomenology of internal time consciousness? Or because Kierkegaard speaks, in the Christian sense, of temporality in contradistinction to eternity? Or maybe because Dilthey considers the historicity of Dasein to be central, and historicity is connected with time? Was the analysis of Dasein then projected on the backdrop of time because it was believed the result would be good if the above-mentioned were fused together? In short, because one can get the idea of mixing together these various treatments of the problem of time and, as the phrase has it, "think them out to the end"? This is all too much the simpleton's notion of philosophy, the one who believes that out of five authors you can make a sixth. (I was already confronting the works of Kierkegaard when there was as yet no dialectical literature, and treating Dilthey when it was still not respectable to mention him in a philosophical seminar.) Furthermore, the so-called thinking out to the end has its own special difficulty. In order to think something out to the end, especially taking in Kierkegaard, Husserl, Bergson, and Dilthey, one must first be in possession of that end toward which one is supposed to think them out; and still the question always remains: Why just these particular thinkers mentioned?

Furthermore, the analysis of Dasein as temporality, developed with respect to revealing the intrinsic possibility of the understanding-of-being, is not determined by anything other than the content of this basic problem of metaphysics. More precisely, it is determined by the basic insight that the understanding-of-being stands in a primordial relation to time, a relation at first, however, completely obscure and mysterious.

Once the analysis of temporality has first received its direction from the basic metaphysical problem, the previous interpretation of time, from Aristotle through Augustine to Bergson, can be highlighted in its decisive contents and appropriated. And it would be remarkably naive to reject the aid to be found in Aristotle, be it only indirect, for Aristotle defined the problematic of time for every subsequent thinker, and not least of all for Bergson.

But why is time connected with the understanding of being? This is not obvious. Yet there are suggestive references to and indications of this connection—since nothing accessible is hidden, pure and simple, otherwise it would not be accessible at all for finite Dasein. Before following up on these indications, we present here a recollection which will serve to give us a sharper formulation of the problem of the understanding-of-being.

Parmenides had already recognized and focused on the correlation between εἶναι and νοεῖν: τὸ γὰρ αὐτὸ νοεῖν ἐστίν τε καὶ εἶναι (Frag. 3). Here it is important to first eliminate misunderstandings. There were attempts in the nineteenth century to claim this statement for various conceptions in the theory of knowledge. In it was seen "the first glimmerings of idealism," as if Parmenides had held that the subject is what first posits beings as beings, or as if Parmenides had thought, as one takes Kant to hold, that objects order themselves according to our knowledge. All this contains a certain kernel of truth, inasmuch as it was first stated by Parmenides that being is related to the subject. But here it is important to realize that the εἶναι correlated with the νοεῖν is not yet clearly differentiated from the ὄν; but this certainly does not mean the ὄν would only be a being insofar as it were caused and produced by a νοεῖν. There is no causal ontic dependency or "positing" intended. It would be just as premature to seek in Parmenides the so-called predeliction for critique, i.e., epistemological intent in the sense of the Copernican revolution, which, moreover, rests on a misunderstanding of Kant.

Opposing interpretations of this sort, one can point out that there is no such idealism in all of ancient philosophy. To this it must be added, however, that interpretations of Parmenides' thought as "realism" are equally untenable. For we are not dealing with a position taken regarding the relation of beings as such to a subject that has being, but rather we have here the first dawning of the real metaphysical problem of being as such. The point is not whether the subject posits beings or whether it, as knowing subject, directs itself toward beings, but the point is rather the way in which the human being as such understands anything like being at all. Whoever does not think idealistically in his epistemology believes himself, especially nowadays, superior to the so-called critical theories and believes he is the guardian of the medieval and ancient tradition, whereas he only represents the reverse side of idealism; he also thinks in epistemological terms and cannot, even less than others, grasp the problem.

If one then has any grasp at all of the basic problems of ancient philosophy and seizes them at their roots with sufficient radicality, then it cannot be the case that the issue is a position or viewpoint, in the sense of a realism or idealism. And this is so not only because both are equally untenable as epistemological formulations of the problem, but because the basic problem (being) is not at all a problem of epistemology; the problem of being is prior to every problem of epistemology. To see this, one has to have truly grasped the basic problems of ancient metaphysics and to understand them concretely.

An easily accessible reflection in the *Theaetetus* (185a ff.) shows how Plato develops the claim of Parmenides regarding νοεῖν and εἶναι as the problem of the relation of being to the soul, the ψυχή. There Socrates explains to Theaetetus that "you cannot grasp being, otherness, sameness, and equality by hearing or sight. And yet you do say 'they are,' though you neither see nor hear them. If you say 'salty,' you know which capacity, namely taste, you must depend on. For being, on the contrary, no bodily organs are to be found, but it seems to me that the soul of itself takes everything into view that we say about everything insofar as it is." This passage shows that we do not attain the primary kind of being-determinations through the bodily organs, but the soul itself, purely of itself, according to its intrinsic freedom, relates to being. Of itself the soul extends itself out of itself toward being, i.e., it is the soul, purely by itself, that, in the manner of ἐπόρεξις [stretching out towards], understands anything like being.

To understand Parmenides' approach and his development in Greek philosophy we have to keep two things in mind: 1) The ὄν [being] is not ontically derived from νοεῖν or λέγειν (These latter are, moreover, a δηλοῦν, a making manifest); 2) We are not dealing with an epistemological claim concerning an inversion of the standard by which knowledge is measured. Both misinterpretations rest metaphysically on the subject-object relation and take the problem too lightly. As the passage in the *Theaetetus* showed, the problem instead concerns being, though only incipiently, and this problem is oriented to the "subject" as ψυχή. In this, what we call subjectivity is still tenuous. We must accordingly distinguish what is expressly, consciously recognized as subjectivity, in terms such as νοεῖν, νοῦς, λόγος, ψυχή, νόησις, and ὄρεξις; but how subjectivity nevertheless functions quite differently in τέχνη and πρᾶξις, this, too, is also recognized, though not in its ontological function. The positive result for the problem of being is that some special connection obtains between being and subjectivity (Dasein).

With this recalled, we can follow up the suggestions concerning the connection of time and the understanding-of-being. There is first a more external indication (a) and (b) the one which points to the center of the problem.

a) In respect to time, being is divided into the following regions of being: 1) What is in time (nature and history); 2) what is outside time; 3) what is above time, these latter two being the non-temporal.

One can object here that this suggestion proves even more that beings outside and above time are without time, thus that not all beings are "in time." Of course! But the question is whether this exhausts the relation beings have to time. For the important thing is to see that this question is completely different; it is not whether beings are in time or not. It is rather whether the being of beings gets understood by reference to time. And we have, as a result, that what is outside and above time is intended ontically as not in time, but this "non-temporal" quality is precisely a definite mode of relation to time, just as immobile rest is a mode of movement, though a still more radical relation obtains in the former. We need here an explanation of why and how this relation is possible, and with what intrinsic necessity the commonplace understanding of the being of beings can be traced back to time. Further, the time relation in question in not exhausted, not even touched at all, by time in the sense of being in time. This understanding-of-being is itself in need of clarification. Even beings that are not "in time," and especially these, can be understood, in their being, on the basis of time; but here time must be conceived more radically. Being gets understood by way of the time relation, but the problem of this relation of being and time is the "and."

b) Our question is, to what extent has a connection been seen between being and time? After the first rough indication, we shall now follow a second which is twofold (α and β).[6]

α) The term for the being of beings, just as often used for beings

---

6. Cf. also "Kants Lehre vom Schematismus und die Frage nach dem Sinn des Seins," the Cologne lecture held on January 26, 1927.

themselves, is οὐσία, being-ness. It is what constitutes a being as being, the ὄν ἦ ὄν, being. And, not accidentally, οὐσία itself has a twofold meaning, and this first comes out clearly in Aristotle, but it can be discerned already everywhere in Plato.

Οὐσία is being in the sense of *modus existendi* [the mode of existence], of being on hand. For example, in the *Theaetetus* (155e 4ff.) εἰσὶν δὲ οὗτοι οἱ οὐδὲν ἄλλο οἰόμενοι εἶναι ἢ οὗ ἂν δύνωνται ἀπρὶξ τοῖν χεροῖν λαβέσθαι, πράξεις δὲ καὶ γενέσεις καὶ πᾶν τὸ ἀόρατον οὐκ ἀποδεχόμενοι ὡς ἐν οὐσίας μέρει; "There are those who believe nothing exists [vorhanden] unless they can grasp it with their hands; everything else does not belong in the realm of οὐσία, of being objectively present [Vorhandensein]."

Οὐσία is being in the sense of *modus essendi*, the what-being, the what-contents, essence, that which makes something be what it is whether it "exists" or not. The Latin translation *essentia* (since Boethius) does not therefore describe the Greek οὐσία; the latter is richer and also means *existentia*. Aristotle intends both meanings, inasmuch as he distinguishes the πρώτη οὐσία [first οὐσία], this being as it exists, the that-being, and the δευτέρα οὐσία [second οὐσία], what-being, essence.

Both of these basic meanings take their orientation from time. *Existentia* is that which really "exists"; being qua *existentia* occurs in that which always is, the ἀεὶ ὄν, which never in any now does not exist, which is there "at any time." *Essentia* means the what, the ἰδέα, that which determines every being in advance as a being, and hence as ὄντως ὄν ["beingly being"], which is properly ἀεὶ ὄν [always being]. The time relation becomes apparent not only in this characteristic of *constant duration*, of the ἀεί, but even more primordially, though less obviously, in another characteristic.

Οὐσία, the term for a being and its being (at once the what and the that) is also an ontic term, one used [by the Greeks] for that which is always available in the everyday Dasein of humans: useful items, the homestead, property assets, possessions, that which is at hand anytime for everyday use, that which is immediately and for the most part always present [Anwesende]. The temporal significance of οὐσία comes out even more clearly in this prephilosophical meaning. What is present [Gegenwärtige] in this sense is not only and not so much ἀεί, but it is *present* in every now, present however as a temporal feature in the sense of *presentness* [Anwesenheit]. Frequently οὐσία is only a shortened form of παρουσία, presentness. παρά as the term for being-present-to, for the constant present of something in closest proximity, occurs in all of Plato's main ontological problems.

Being is what is always present, in constant presentness. *Duration* and *presentness* possess a temporal feature, in a sense that is at first problematic. (Here we refer to the previously mentioned expressions in Thomas Aquinas: *intuitus praesens, omme praesentialiter subjectum, esse Dei* as *actus purus,* where in principle the same conception of being occurs.)

β) But the connection of being and time came to the fore also in another respect, though it did not then become a problem but was merely taken for granted. In ancient ontology (Aristotle), being (as ἰδέα and γένος), or that which defines a being as a being, is said to be πρότερον [earlier] than beings, and something prior in a unique way. As πρότερον φύσει [prior by nature], it is to be distinguished from the πρότερον γνώσει [what is prior by knowledge], the πρότερον πρὸς ἡμᾶς [prior with regard to us]. Being is earlier than beings; this "earlier than," attributed to being, is a distinguishing "feature," and it does not apply to γνῶσις [knowledge], as the ordering of our conceptualization of beings. Being is earlier than, is that which is essentially "earlier"; it belongs to what is prior, in the language of later ontology: a priori. All ontological questioning is inquiry into and definition of the "a priori."

"Prior to" is obviously still a temporal determination, there being no "earlier" without time. But prior to every possible "prior to" is time! Thus if being is the πρότερον, the a priori, then it stands in a primordial connection with time. Of course, what we mean here by "earlier," by time, is obscure and remains completely enigmatic if we try to go ahead with the common conception of time. We see immediately it will not work; it would have been repudiated already by the Greeks through the distinction we have mentioned.

Being is πρότερον not as πρότερον πρὸς ἡμᾶς [earlier with regard to us], not in the sense of our knowing it as such prior to beings. We always grasp being immediately, and this mostly remains the case, without our conceiving being as such. In the order of conceptualization, then, being is not the earlier but the last of all. And yet it is the earlier φύσει [by nature] (this is why there are beings as object), it is earlier of itself. What this means is assuredly obscure and ambiguous; all of it is ontologically, metontologically, unclarified and so gets understood ontically. Though it does receive the rank of ὄντως ὄν [beingly being], being is not a being. Nor does its priority mean being is something existing on hand earlier, as a being in a certain sense before other beings. What is prior thus belongs neither to the order of conceptualization nor to the order of being on hand; it is neither logically nor ontically earlier, neither of the two. And yet!

We have already said frequently before that being is already understood in advance in grasping beings; the precursive
understanding-of-being provides light, as it were, for every grasp
of beings. "In advance," "precursive"—are these not the prior?
Certainly! But we said too that the prior does not pertain to the
order of conceptualization, and now we are speaking of a precursive understanding-of-being, an understanding in advance. The
πρότερον of οὐσία, of the ἰδέα, is nevertheless not a πρότερον
γνώσει [prior by knowledge]. We should note that γνῶσις here
always means knowing beings, and the rejection of this kind of
πρότερον has only a negative meaning, when understood correctly.
It means being is not a being and its conceptualization is not of
the order of conceiving beings. Thus being is, in the end, indeed
prior with regard to its being grasped in the broadest sense of the
term, prior to grasping beings. And, in the end, being is [gibt sich
das Sein] in a way that differs totally from our grasping of beings.
Being is *"in itself"* [gibt sich *'an sich'*] in an original sense: it is a
πρότερον φύσει and πρὸς ἡμᾶς—only if understood correctly, and
not as one ontic thing among others. Being is the solely and
genuinely "in itself"; and hence the originary nature of the
understanding-of-being and (as we shall see) of freedom.

Being is prior neither ontically nor logically, but prior in a
primordial sense that precedes both. It is prior to each of them in a
different way; neither ontically nor logically prior but ontologically. But this is the problem. It is precisely the problem of how
being is "earlier," how it, qua being, originally relates to time.
Being and time, this is the basic problem! And as long as this
problem is not posed or only relatively solved, even the use of the
term "a priori" remains unjustified and unwarranted, as does the
talk of "a posteriori" and the distinction in general.

In an obscure sense, being is prior. It grows clearer, in a certain
way, if we refer to something else that Plato, in particular, saw in
his doctrine of ἀνάμνησις. Being is what we recall, what we accept
as something we immediately understand as such, what is always
already given to us; being is never alien but always familiar,
"ours." Being is, accordingly, what we always already understand,
and we only need to recall it once again to grasp it as such. In
grasping being we do not conceive anything new, but something
basically familiar; we always already exist in an understanding-
of-being, insofar as we relate to what we now call "beings." This
recollection pertains to being and thus reveals an original connection of being with time: always already there and yet always
grasped only in coming back to it. This is not the common recollection of something ontic that happened, a being; it is rather

metaphysical recollection, in which that original connection of being with time emerges. In this metaphysical recollection the human being understands himself in his authentic essence, as the being that understands being and relates to beings on the basis of this understanding.

According to Plato (in the *Phaedrus,* 249b5-c6), a living thing that has never seen the truth can never take on the shape of a human. For, corresponding to its mode of being, the human must understand and know in such a way that he thereby addresses what he knows with regard to its being (κατ᾽ εἶδος λέγειν). The human can have truth about something only in understanding beings in their being. Understanding-of-being is a recollection of that which our soul saw previously; that is, previously when the soul still wandered together with God and looked beyond what we now call beings. In the phenomenon of recollection, Plato sees a relation of the understanding-of-being to time, even though it could only be made clear through the use of a myth.

These are references for connecting the problem of being with time.

The problem of being, however, is the basic problem of philosophy as such, and closely connected to it is the guiding problem of transcendence, to which our inquiry into the essence of grounds and the essential connection of ground and truth has led us, according to our theme: logic as the metaphysics of truth guided by the problem of ground. If, then, the being problem as such is absolutely central, especially for our inquiry, and if this relation of being to time obtains, but has hitherto remained obscure and taken for granted, then it is important really to pose this central question of being and its relation to time. This means the central problem, in its fundamental significance for philosophy as such, must be posed and worked out 1) radically, and 2) universally.

1) *Radicalizing* the problem of being. A reference was made to the relation between εἶναι and ψυχή and between εἶναι and χρόνος, as well as between the ψυχή and χρόνος in ἀνάμνησις. The relation between being and the soul must be conceived more primordially, as must that between being and time. But this means the relation between the soul and time must be clarified.

To clarify the relation of being to the soul means to show how there is an understanding-of-being in the soul, in that being whose being is characterized primarily by the soul; this requires a primordial and appropriate interpretation of Dasein. This interpretation, because it is undertaken on account of the question of being, is therefore also metaphysical, ontological; that is, the interpretation aims at bringing to light the specific mode of being peculiar to Dasein in order to make clear how this special mode includes something like the understanding-of-being. In attempting an ontologically primordial and appropriate interpretation of Dasein, however, it emerges that the philosophical tradition interpreted this being, metaphysically, in a way that is not primordial and appropriate and not at all in the context of the basic problem. And this the tradition did, not out of negligence and incompetence, but for grounds that rest in the nature of the genesis of the understanding-of-being itself.

An ontologically primordial interpretation of Dasein means a primordial interpretation of time as well. The latter, too, gets interpreted as something present-at-hand, taken according to the traditional concept of time, as something explained out of the perspective of the now.

Our task is then to undertake a primordial interpretation of time as well as of Dasein, which means a primordial clarification of how both are connected. It is an ancient insight (cf. Aristotle and Augustine) that time is ἐν τῇ ψυχῇ, *in anima*. But time is regarded as something present-at-hand, which is on hand somehow in the soul. This is still completely unclarified in Kant (as the problem of the connection of time and the "I think") and in his successors. Recently Bergson tried to conceive the concept of time more originally. He made it more clear than any previous philosopher that time is interwoven with consciousness. But the essential thing remained unresolved in Bergson, without even becoming a problem. He developed his interpretation of time on the basis of the traditional concept of consciousness, of Descartes' *res cogitans*. The basic metaphysical problem of the primordial connection between Dasein and temporality he does not pose, and even less does he pose the problem of being, for which the other problem is only a preparation.

But if being has a primordial relation to time, and if the understanding-of-being belongs primordially to the essence of Dasein, to its intrinsic possibility, then time must co-determine this intrinsic possibility of Dasein. That is, directed toward and by the problem of being, temporality must be shown to be the basic constitution of Dasein. The concept of time itself, though, becomes transformed by this. An original position towards the history of metaphysics, as such, then emerges. We talked about being as a priori. If a-prioricity is a basic characteristic of being, and if a-prioricity is a time designation, and if being is connected with time in such a way that the understanding-of-being is rooted in the temporality of Dasein, then there is an intrinsic connection between the a priori and temporality, the being-constitution of Dasein, the subjectivity of the subject. In the end, then, it is no arbitrary idealistic prejudice, as people nowadays like to pronounce, that the problem of the a priori in Plato and Aristotle, as well as in Descartes, Leibniz, Kant and German idealism has closest ties with the problem of the subject, however obscure the connection may have remained heretofore.

2) *Universalizing* the problem of being. Here too the problem has become alien to our age and is made even more alien by a movement that seemingly wishes to renew ontology and metaphysics. It is a widespread misunderstanding, one derived from Kantianism, to hold that, if an ontological problem is to be posed, then one has opted for an epistemological realism, since the latter still allows for beings-in-themselves.

Contemporary interest in ontology was revived mainly by phenomenology. But even Husserl and Scheler, and certainly the others, did not see the full scope of ontology. By ontology they understand—as one does everywhere today, as in Rickert—an inquiry that problematizes the being-in-itself of things in their so-called independence of the subject. The inquiry into subjectivity is not then a question for ontology, but belongs in the theory of knowledge. Ontology is taken to mean an emphasis on the object, after the subject alone has been emphasized heretofore. In this sense, ontology is linked with the epistemological position of realism—in opposition to idealism. Ontology must then disregard the subject as far as possible, while, conversely, the basic necessity in fact lies in making subjectivity problematic. But in the current understanding, on the contrary, ontology is taken, first, not as the science of being but of beings, and, second, as a science of objects, of nature in the widest sense of the term.

The revival of ontology is considered to be a return to medieval realistic Scholasticism and to Aristotle, to Aristotle disguised as one of the Fathers of the Church. One can look for the thread of ontology, in this sense of the term, in Kant as well. There is a notion in Scheler, Nicolai Hartmann, and Heimsoeth that, besides his epistemological-idealistic lines of thinking, Kant has tendencies toward a so-called ontological realism, tendencies that still concede the existence of an objective world. This notion of ontology is nonsense and is neither Aristotelian nor Kantian.

What the supposedly ontological interpretation of Kant takes to be a theory of knowledge is precisely genuine ontology. Metaphysics is not to be opposed to the theory of knowledge.

Moreover, it is necessary to show that the analytic of the *Critique of Pure Reason* is the first attempt since Plato and Aristotle to really make ontology a philosophical problem. But such an attempt is presumed impossible, because Kant is of course a critical thinker, i.e., the Kantian opinion holds that knowledge is not ordered to the object, but the object is ordered according to knowledge.

In the first place, the ontological problem has nothing at all to do with the acclaimed pseudo-problem of the reality of the external world and the independence of beings-in-themselves from the knowing subject. The ontological problem consists, rather, in seeing that this so-called epistemological problem cannot be posed at all if the being-in-itself of existing things is not clarified in its meaning. But this cannot even be posed as a problem, much less solved, if it is not yet clear how the question about the meaning of being as such must be posed.

But our reference to a widespread error, one which makes all the so-called interest in metaphysics a fundamentally fruitless endeavor, remains merely negative. To universalize the problem of being in a positive way means to show which basic interdependent questions are contained in the question of being. What basic problems are indicated with the simple term "being" when we ask about being and time?

The ontological problem is not only not identical with the question about the "reality" of the external world, but the latter question presupposes a genuine ontological problem. It presupposes the clarification of the existence mode of things and their regional constitution. Furthermore, the existence of the material things of nature is not the only existence; there are also history and artworks. Nature has diverse modes: space and number, life, human existence itself. There is a multiplicity of modi existendi, and each of these is a mode belonging to a being with a specific content, a definite quiddity. The term "being" is meant to include the span of all possible regions. But the problem of the regional multiplicity of being, if posed universally, includes an investigation into the unity of this general term "being," into the way in which the general term "being" varies with different regional meanings. This is the problem of the *unity of the idea of being and its regional variants*. Does the unity of being mean generality in some other form and intention? In any case, the problem is the unity and generality of being as such. It was this problem that Aristotle posed, though he did not solve it. The important thing is, in every case, how the universality of the concept of being is conceived.

But regional multiplicity is only one aspect in which the problem of being must be universalized beforehand. In clarifying the meaning of οὐσία, we already noted that being also refers to that-being in general and to what-being. This articulation of being has been accepted since antiquity. One takes it for granted as obvious, without asking for its source, for the intrinsic possibility of articulating the idea of being as such. Why is every something that is, whatever its specific subject-matter, determined by its what-character and by a possible that-it-is? For even something formal, something we say exhibits no definite material content, is distinguished precisely by the fact that it lacks a definite inherent content. (We cannot explore the problem of the formal at this point.)

Being means not only the multiplicity of regions and their respective *modi existendi* and *essendi,* but the idea intends being in its essential articulation into *existentia* and *essentia.* This articulation is a basic problem of ontology, the problem of *the basic articulation of being.*

Up to now we have adduced two basic problems pertaining to being itself, without attending to the fact that being is, as such, always the being of beings, just as it is in each case articulated into *essentia* and *existentia* and regionalized. Being is, as such and in its every meaning, the being of beings. Being is different than beings, and only this difference in general, this possibility of distinction, insures an understanding-of-being. Put another way, in the understanding-of-being this distinction of being from beings is carried out. It is this distinction that makes anything like an ontology possible in the first place. We thus term this distinction that first enables something like an understanding-of-being the *ontological difference.*

We purposely use the neutral expression "distinction," since the real problem is the manner in which what is distinguished here, being and beings, are different or even separate. Clearly, with the problem of the ontological difference, the primordial problem of being and the center of the investigation of being comes to the fore. Needless to note, this ontological difference must, furthermore, be taken in the entire scope of the aforementioned problems of basic articulation and regionalization.

Closely linked with this problem of the ontological difference, and the others mentioned, is the problem toward which we have been constantly moving, though from the opposite direction, as it were: the intrinsic connection of being and truth, the truth-character of being. The investigation into the primordial connection of truth and being, the problem of *the veridical character of being* belongs to logic as metaphysics.

The general term "being" includes these four basic problems: 1) the ontological difference, 2) the basic articulation of being, 3) the veridical character of being, 4) the regionality of being and the unity of the idea of being.

The being problem has been thus clarified as central, universal, and radical. We gained some insight into what it means, in general, to investigate the intrinsic possibility of there being something like an understanding-of-being, an understanding which is the essential prerogative of human existence. But, in characterizing the commonly understood, ontic transcendence as it occurs in intentionality, we saw that the relationship to beings, the ontic relationship, presupposes an understanding-of-being; we saw that ontic transcendence is itself based on primal transcendence, which is thereby related to the understanding-of-being. The structure of this problem has now been shown, and this indicates in retrospect that the problems of transcendence, of truth, of reason [grounds], can only be investigated in the dimension adumbrated by the problem of being in general. In other words, the problem of transcendence must be posed as universally and radically as the problem of being as such. It is, therefore, not a problem that could be restricted to the relation the subject has to things independent of it, and it is not only a question about a certain region of beings. Nor may one stop or start with a subject-object relation, as if it somehow fell from heaven; but for transcendence, as for the problem of being, it is the subjectivity of the subject which is itself the central question.

Three claims may be added here:

1) Beings are in themselves the kinds of beings they are, and in the way they are, even if, for example, Dasein does not exist. 2) Being "is" not, but being is there [es gibt], insofar as Dasein exists. In the essence of existence there is transcendence, i.e., a giving of world prior to and for all being-toward-and-among intra-worldly beings. 3) Only insofar as existing Dasein gives itself anything like being can beings emerge in their in-themselves, i.e., can the first claim likewise be understood at all and be taken into account.

N.B. Because being "is" not, and thus is never along with other beings, there is no proper sense at all or legitimacy in asking what being is with respect to beings in themselves. One could ask, however, what, in beings, corresponds to the being (that is not, but) which is "only" there. Being is there [gibt sich] primordially and in itself, when it gives access to its beings. Nor with regard to these beings can one investigate their being in itself. We always know only beings, but never being as a being. This becomes clear from the nature of transcendence and the ontological difference.

And so we have attained what we wanted in the first section of the second main part, the exposition of the dimensions of the problem of ground—which is none other than the dimensions of an area of inquiry in the central direction of metaphysical inquiry as such. Before proceeding to the second section to develop the problem of ground itself within the dimension we attained, we should first briefly, in a sort of appendix, describe this dimension more closely and indicate the way it may be worked out. We designate this problem dimension, and its explanation a fundamental ontology.

APPENDIX:
DESCRIBING THE IDEA AND FUNCTION
OF A FUNDAMENTAL ONTOLOGY

By a fundamental ontology we mean the basic grounding of ontology in general. This includes: 1) a grounding that exhibits the intrinsic possibility of the being question as the basic problem of metaphysics—the interpretation of Dasein as temporality; 2) an explication of the basic problems contained in the question of being—the temporal exposition of the problem of being; 3) the development of the self-understanding of this problematic, its task and limits—the overturning.

For what follows, and in the context of this lecture course, a rather general sketch must suffice. It is important not to conceive fundamental ontology too narrowly or from a single standpoint. The guiding questions here are: Why is fundamental ontology from the outset an existential analysis? What is meant here by "existence"? And to what extent does existential analysis as metaphysical history and "humanitas" get its sense from the full concept of metaphysics?

Only with and through this fundamental ontology do we grasp, from a definite viewpoint, the inner and hidden life of the basic movement of Western philosophy. We saw in several ways how the basic features of this problematic become manifest from the beginning. And it is important to bring these features to light as far as possible and not allow them to remain concealed by indifference. And this we should do, not because these problems have been repeatedly touched upon in previous ages, nor because of their venerable antiquity, which gives them a certain respectability, but the reverse, because fundamental ontology comprises problems which, in their problematic character, themselves belong to the existence of human beings, to the metaphysical essence of Dasein, as it becomes visible to us; and it is only and precisely for this reason that these problems came to light in a specific, concrete shape at the beginning of Western philosophy.

Fundamental ontology is always only a repetition of this ancient, early [manifestation]. But what is ancient gets transmitted to us by repetition, only if we grant it the possibility of transformation. For by their nature these problems demand as much. All this has its basis as we will show in detail, in the historicity of the understanding-of-being. And characteristically, the tradition, i.e., the externalized transmission, deprives the problem of this very transformation in a repetition. Tradition passes down definite propositions and opinions, fixed ways of questioning and discussing things. This external tradition of opinions and anonymous viewpoints is currently called "the history of problems" [Problemgeschichte]. The external tradition, and its employment in the history of philosophy, denies problems their life, and that means it seeks to stifle their transformation, and so we must fight against the tradition.

Not that antiquity should be overcome—if in this regard there is any sense to "criticism" (something which is not primary but which is nonetheless demanded in every situation). But it is the inept guardians of tradition who should be fought against. This can happen only if we ourselves strive to create an occasion for the transformation of the basic problems, for the *metaphysica naturalis* in Dasein itself. This is what I mean by the destruction of tradition. It is not a matter of doing away with two millenia and setting up oneself in their place.

But, as decidedly as we must find our way back to the elemental force of central problems conceived in their universality and radicality, so would it be fatefully misguided were we to absolutize these very problems and so negate them in their essential function. We humans have a tendency, not just today and just on occasion, by which we either mistake what is philosophically central for that which is interesting or easily accessible, or we absolutize a central point immediately, blindly, and once we grasp it, we fixate on a single potential stage of the originating problematic and make it an eternal task, instead of summoning and preparing the possibility of new originations. To do the latter, one need not foresee these originations. One just needs to work continually at factical possibilities, because of Dasein's finitude. Since philosophizing is essentially an affair of finitude, every concretion of factical philosophy must in its turn fall victim to this facticity.

The shortwindedness proper to questioning and thinking cannot be surmounted, but we must take pains not to yield to it unawares. Only rarely are we capable of running the whole gamut of a problem and preserving it in its vitality and potential for transformation. Or, if we can do so, we may then no longer have the strength to draw breath again for other equally important possibilities. Or, if we can do that, then the elaboration required is more difficult, because it is at bottom intrinsically impossible to dissociate the problem from previous ones. And so there is in every case a breaking open of horizons; what is important or essential is always handed over to the future as the real heritage. But what is essential is not what can be refuted and discussed by the times. (If Kant had been merely he whom his contemporaries took him to be, one whom they refuted right and left, he would indeed be in a sorry state.)

The finitude of philosophy consists not in the fact that it comes up against limits and cannot proceed further. It rather consists in this: in the singleness and simplicity of its central problematic, philosophy conceals a richness that again and again demands a renewed awakening.

What must be kept in mind, particularly with regard to fundamental ontology, is that it is precisely the radicality and universality of this central problematic, and it alone, which brings us to realize that these problems are indeed central; but for that very reason they are in their import and essentiality never the sole problems. In other words, fundamental ontology does not exhaust the notion of metaphysics.

Since being is there only insofar as beings are already there [im Da], fundamental ontology has in it the latent tendency toward a primordial, metaphysical transformation which becomes possible only when being is understood in its whole problematic. The intrinsic necessity for ontology to turn back to its point of origin can be clarified by reference to the primal phenomenon of human existence: the being "man" understands being; understanding-of-being effects a distinction between being and beings; being is there only when Dasein understands being. In other words, the possibility that being is there in the understanding presupposes the factical existence of Dasein, and this in turn presupposes the factual extantness of nature. Right within the horizon of the problem of being, when posed radically, it appears that all this is visible and can become understood as being, only if a possible totality of beings is already there.

As a result, we need a special problematic which has for its proper theme beings as a whole [das Seiende im Ganzen]. This new investigation resides in the essence of ontology itself and is the result of its overturning [Umschlag], its μεταβολή. I designate this set of questions *metontology*. And here also, in the domain of metontological-existentiell questioning, is the domain of the metaphysics of existence (here the question of an ethics may properly be raised for the first time).

Positive sciences also have beings for their subject matter, but metontology is not a summary ontic in the sense of a general science that empirically assembles the results of the individual sciences into a so-called "world picture," so as to deduce from it a world-view and guide for life. Something of the sort is, in a certain way, current in prescientific Dasein, although the latter has a different structure; the possibility and structure of the natural world-view is a problem in its own right. The fact that attempts are repeatedly made to summarize ontic information and call it "inductive metaphysics" points to a problem that of necessity arises repeatedly throughout history.

Metontology is possible only on the basis and in the perspective of the radical ontological problematic and is possible conjointly with it. Precisely the radicalization of fundamental ontology brings about the above-mentioned overturning of ontology out of its very self. What we seemingly separate here, by means of "disciplines," and provide with labels is actually one—just as the ontological difference is one of, or *the*, phenomenon of human existence! To think being as the being of beings and to conceive the being problem radically and universally means, at the same time, to make beings thematic in their totality in the light of ontology.

It would be superficial and pedantic to believe that once fundamental ontology is founded as a discipline, a further ontology with a new title would be adjoined to it. Fundamental ontology, moreover, is not a fixed discipline which, once the baby is named, should now for good occupy the previously empty place reserved for it in some putative system of philosophy—a discipline which is now to be developed and completed so as to bring philosophy to a happy ending in a few decades (as the layman or positivist imagines). In fact, that "place" is, in every philosophy, an occupied place, and it is in each case transformed.

The pedantry of a schematic system should not be confused

with the rigor of questioning. One must keep clearly in mind that in the analytic we grasp only that which every analytical approach implies as its originary unity and wholeness, as a synthesis we have not previously carried out explicitly but which, nevertheless, insofar as we exist, is always already carried out simultaneously with and by us.

Not only do we need analysis in general, but we must produce the illusion, as it were, that the given task at hand is the one and only necessary task. Only the person who understands this art of existing, only the person who, in the course of action, can treat what is in each case seized upon as wholly singular, who at the same time nonetheless realizes the finitude of this activity, only such a one understands finite existence and can hope to accomplish something in it. This art of existing is not the self-reflection that hunts around uninvolved, rummaging about for motives and complexes by which to obtain reassurance and a dispensation from action. It is rather only the clarity of action itself, a hunting for real possibilities.

Our results are that the basic problem of metaphysics demands, in its radicalization and universalization, an interpretation of Dasein on the basis of temporality; and, from this interpretation, the intrinsic possibility of the understanding of being and thereby of ontology should become evident—but not merely in order to make this intrinsic possibility known. The latter is rather understood only in carrying out, in working out, the basic problematic itself (in the four main problems presented). Fundamental ontology is this whole of founding and developing ontology; the former is 1) the analysis of Dasein, and 2) the analysis of the temporality of being. But the temporal analysis is at the same time the turning-around [Kehre], where ontology itself expressly runs back into the metaphysical ontic in which it implicitly always remains. Through the movement of radicalizing and universalizing, the aim is to bring ontology to its latent overturning [Umschlag]. Here the turn-around [Kehre] is carried out, and it is turned over into the metontology.

In their unity, fundamental ontology and metontology constitute the concept of metaphysics. But herein is expressed the transformation of the one basic problem of philosophy itself, the one touched upon above and in the introduction under the dual conception of philosophy as πρώτη φιλοσοφία and θεολογία. And this is only the particular concretion of the ontological difference, i.e., the concretion of carrying out the understanding-of-being. In other words, philosophy is the central and total concretization of the metaphysical essence of existence.

This necessarily general and brief indication of the idea and function of fundamental ontology was needed so that we might see the breadth of the problem's horizon, and also not lose sight of the narrow path upon which we must necessarily move in the concrete treatment of the following problem.

SECOND SECTION:
THE PROBLEM OF GROUND

§11. *The transcendence of Dasein*

a) On the concept of transcendence

We are asking about the essence of ground [or reason], i.e., the intrinsic possibility of anything like ground as such. The development of this question led us to the insight that asking and answering the question can only take place within the dimension of the question of being as such. The steps by which we went back into this dimension are indicated by the following terms: grounds, principle of reason, law of thought, judgment, proposition, truth, intentional relation, ontic transcendence, ontological transcendence, ontology, the problem of being as such, metaphysics.

The approach to the concrete treatment of the problem of ground lies in the problem of being as such. The latter is prepared, however, by the analysis of Dasein, and the analysis reveals transcendence to be a basic phenomenon. So as not to traverse now the whole way again from its beginning, we will start with the problem of transcendence, treating it not, however, solely and primarily in view of the analysis of Dasein, fundamental ontology. Instead, we will treat it in relation to the problem of ground. From what was said previously, we can expect that an adequate interpretation of transcendence will of itself, as it were, run up against the phenomenon and essence of ground.

Now we must preserve the perspective on the problem, as given above, while at the same time allowing it to fade out, so that we can concentrate our focus on the phenomenon of transcendence. What is the general meaning of this word, what is its verbal definition, and what does it mean as a philosophical term?

We will proceed from the verbal definition and then try to set down the meanings found in usages of the expression "transcendence." The verbal meaning comes from *transcendere* [Latin]: to surpass, step over, to cross over to. Thus *transcendence* means the surpassing, the going beyond. And the transcendent means that toward which the surpassing takes place, that which requires surpassing in order to be accessible and attainable, the beyond, that which is over against. Finally, that which does the transcending is what carries out the stepping-over. The verbal meaning then includes the following: 1) an activity in the broadest sense of the term, a doing, 2) in the formal sense, a relation: the crossing over to X, from Y, 3) something which is to be surpassed, a limit, a restriction, a gap, something "lying between." These are only part of a general clarification of the range of our notions when we understand the meaning of "transcendence."

We must now describe its word usage as a term in philosophy. We need not go into all its variants; it will suffice to examine two main meanings from which all the others are derived, and we will treat the concept of the transcendent and characterize its philosophical meaning with regard to its important conceptual contraries. The term means: 1) the transcendent in contradistinction to the *immanent*, 2) the transcendent in contradistinction to the *contingent*.

Regarding 1), the transcendent in contradistinction to the immanent, the latter is what remains within, by which is meant that which is in the subject, within the soul, remaining in consciousness. The transcendent is therefore that which does not remain within but is without, what lies *outside* the soul and consciousness. What is outside the borders and encompassing wall of consciousness has then, spoken from the innermost yard of this consciousness, surpassed the enclosing wall and stands outside. Now insofar as this consciousness has cognition, it relates to what is outside, and so the transcendent as something on hand outside is, at the same time, that which *stands over against*.

Here the subject is thought of as a sort of box with an interior, with the walls of a box, and with an exterior. Of course the crude view is not put forth that consciousness is in fact a box, but what is essential to the analogy and what belongs to the very conception of the transcendent is that a barrier between inner and outer must be crossed. This means that the inner is, first of all, really restricted by the barrier and must first break through it, must first *remove the restrictions*.

Transcendence, then, is taken to be the relationship that somehow or other maintains a passageway between the interior and exterior of the box by leaping over or pressing through the wall of the box. So the problem arises of how to explain the possibility of such a passage. One tries to explain it either causally, psychologically, or physiologically; or one somehow summons the aid of intentionality; or one holds the enterprise to be hopeless and one stays in the box, trying to explain, from inside it, how to understand what enters into our ideas from what is supposed to be outside.

In the latter case, still another standpoint of immanence is taken up, and the conception of consciousness also varies accordingly. But however and wherever the problem of transcendence is posed, whether in express or implicit orientation on the contrary concept of immanence, there is, in principle, the notion of the subject, of Dasein, as box-like at its basis. Without it, the problem of crossing a barrier or border would be nonsense! And it will become clear that the problem of transcendence depends on how one defines the subjectivity of the subject, the basic constitution of Dasein. Does this box-notion have any a priori validity at all or not? If not, however, why does it arise with such persistence?

To put it another way, it is clear by now that transcendence is not an additional attribute I ascribe to a subject, but the question becomes whether the essence of subjectivity can be grasped, first and foremost, through a rightly understood transcendence.

On the basis of the concept of transcendence we described, the one having immanence for its contrary, it becomes possible to have what is known as a theory of knowledge [epistemology]. So we call this conception *epistemological* transcendence. If this conception were to prove unjustified, because it rests on a hasty assumption, then the same thing is proved of epistemology as such. This is not to say that cognition would not be a philosophical problem. From this epistemological conception of transcendence, we distinguish the broadly *theological* conception of transcendence.

2) Transcendence can be considered the opposite of contingency. The contingent is what touches us, what pertains to us, that with which we are on the same footing, that which belongs to our kind and sort. The transcendent, on the contrary, is what is beyond all this as that which conditions it, as the unconditioned, but at the same time as the really unattainable, what exceeds us [das Überschwängliche]. Transcendence is stepping-over in the sense of lying beyond conditioned beings.

In this case, transcendence is also a relational concept, but not between subject and object. The relation is between conditioned beings in general, to which belong subjects and all possible objects, and the unconditioned. In this case, contrariwise, the concept of transcendence is defined essentially by the formulation and notion of that to which transcendence transcends, by what lies beyond the contingent. Being-beyond, in this case, expresses at the same time a difference in the degree of being, or better, the infinite difference of the created from the creator, were we to substitute God, as understood by Christians, for the transcendent, which we need not do. Insofar as the transcendent, in this second concept, always means the unconditioned, the Absolute in some form or other, and the latter means predominantly the divine, we can speak here of a theological conception of transcendence.

Now both conceptions of transcendence, the epistemological and the theological, can be conjoined—something that has always happened and always recurs. For once the epistemological conception of transcendence is granted, whether expressly or implicitly, then a being is posited outside the subject, and it stands over against the latter. Among the beings posited opposite, however, is something which towers above everything, the cause of all. It is thus both something over against [the subject] and something which transcends all conditioned beings over against [the subject]. The transcendent, in this double sense, is the Eminent, the being that surpasses and exceeds all experience. So, inquiry into the possible constitution of the transcendent in the epistemological sense is bound up with inquiry into the possibility of knowing the transcendent object in the theological sense. The latter inquiry, in fact, is, in a certain sense, the impulse for the former. Therefore, the problem of the existence of the external world and whether it can be known is implicated in the problem of the knowledge of God and the possibility of proving God's existence.

All theological metaphysics, but also all systematic theology, operates through the entanglement of both problems of transcendence. Were we additionally to assign the distinction between the rational and the irrational to that between the transcendent and the contingent, then the confusion would be complete. This tangle of partially and falsely posed problems is continually confused in ontological philosophy and systematic theology; the tangle gets passed along from hand to hand and the state of entanglements gets further confused by receiving a new name.

It is not worth the effort for philosophy to pursue the thread of this confusion or even to disentangle it. I am referring to it for another reason and with a view to our central problem. Seen roughly, this intertwining of both problems of transcendence is an urgent impulse even and especially in the framework of Kant's investigations, and this is true of every period of his philosophizing. It is nevertheless a fundamental distortion to place these commonplace connections at the basis of Kant interpretation. It is more important to see just how Kant tried to free himself from these shackles on the problem of transcendence, an effort which succeeded only in part and did not make the transcendence problem central for him.

We will give a brief reference to the transcendence problem in Kant, beginning with a passage where he asserts the double meaning for the expression "outside us" in connection with the distinction between appearance and the thing-in-itself:[7]

> The expression "outside us" is thus unavoidably ambiguous in meaning, sometimes signifying what as thing in itself exists apart from us, and sometimes what belongs solely to outer appearance. In order, therefore, to make this concept, in the latter sense—the sense in which the psychological question as to the reality of our outer intuition has to be understood—quite unambiguous, we shall distinguish empirically external objects from those which may be said to be external in the transcendental sense, by explicitly entitling the former "things which are to be found in space." (Critique of Pure Reason, A 373; not found in B) [N. K. Smith translation]

"Outside us" means, therefore, 1) the independent being itself, 2) the being itself conceived of, however, as possible object of an absolute knowledge not possible for us, conceived of as outside our possibility of experience. "Outside us" means, in one sense, that which we ourselves are not, extant things which can, however, only become manifest as such within the ecstatic transcendence of Dasein thrown as a being-in-the-world. But "outside us" can also mean that which we ourselves not only are not, but also that which lies outside the access of a finite, ecstatic transcendence—namely, appearances [Erscheinungen], insofar as they are considered in-themselves. "Outside us" in this case means outside "us," in the sense of the whole of finite Dasein and its possibilities. Appearance itself has "two sides" (A 38, B 55): the thing itself as a being that exists by itself and which is manifest to me, a finite subject. This means, first, the object is considered in

---

7. Cf. the lecture in *Phänomenologische Interpretation von Kants Kritik der reinen Vernunft, Winter-Semester 1927–28* [published as volume 25 of the *Gesamtausgabe*, ed. I. Gorland, Frankfurt a.M., 1977].

itself, regardless of the way in which it is intuited through the affection [of the sensibility]; it is intuited in the infinite understanding, in the *intuitus originarius*. Second, the consideration is of the form in which the being becomes accessible for a finite subject; then the being-in-itself is an appearance. (Cf. also A 251 f.)

One of the crudest misunderstandings by the otherwise most accurate and profound of Kant interpretations, that of the Marburg School, consists in its having understood the thing-in-itself as something separate and in then having sought to interpret it away. In the *Opus Postumum* Kant says: The thing-in-itself is no other being than the appearance, but both only express "another regard (*respectus*) the representation has to the same object." The same being can be the correlate of an *intuitus originarius* or an *intuitus derivatus;* the difference resides "merely in the difference of the relationship, how . . . the subject . . . is affected."[8]

Transcendence, in the Kantian sense, is, above all, oriented to the two possible ways of grasping the being-in-itself, on two essentially different sorts of intuition. This formulation of transcendence is important because it is not developed in relation to a psychological theory, but bases itself instead on the immediate relation a subject has to the being itself. The concept of the thing-in-itself cannot be set aside by solving it epistemologically, but this concept (as correlate of an absolute understanding) can only be removed if one can show that the presupposition of an absolute understanding is not philosophically necessary.

We must therefore distinguish the thing itself qua appearance and qua thing-in-itself. 1) Proceeding from the correctly understood concept of the thing-in-itself, one can validly deduce the concept of appearance qua "finite" object. 2) Proceeding from appearance, one can show the "X" immanent in it qua thing itself, which is not, however, the "thing-in-itself" in the strict sense.

N.B. Two questions arise here: 1) To what extent is "infinity" to be presupposed as a guiding notion? 2) To what extent do we find in Kant a still more basic problematic function which the ontic has for the ontological? Ontology is grounded in the ontic, and yet the transcendental problem is developed out of what is thus grounded, and the transcendental also first clarifies the function of the ontic.

The whole of Kant's *Critique of Pure Reason* is a circling around

---

8. *Kants Opus postumum,* arranged and edited by E. Adickes, Berlin, 1920, p. 653 (C 551) and p. 695–96, note 5 (C 565). [*Akademie* edition, volume 22, contains the hand-written manuscripts in the *Nachlass*, volume 9, pp. 26 and 43.]

the problem of transcendence—which in its most primordial sense is not an epistemological problem, but the problem of freedom—without Kant's having secured this transcendence phenomenon radically from the ground up. He must be read, however, for what he wanted to say. The import of these distinctions is, on the balance, missing in Hume, Leibniz, Wolff and others.

Against both conceptions of transcendence, the epistemological and the theological, we must in principle say that transcendence is not a relation between interior and exterior realms such that a barrier belonging to the subject would be crossed over, a barrier that would separate the subject from the outer realm. But neither is transcendence primarily the cognitive relationship a subject has to an object, one belonging to the subject in addition to its subjectivity. Nor is transcendence simply the term for what exceeds and is inaccessible to finite knowledge.[9]

1) Transcendence is rather the primordial constitution of the *subjectivity* of a subject. The subject transcends qua subject; it would not be a subject if it did not transcend. To be a subject means to transcend. This means that Dasein does not sort of exist and then occasionally achieve a crossing over outside itself, but existence originally means to cross over. Dasein is itself the passage across. And this implies that transcendence is not just one possible comportment (among others) of Dasein toward other beings, but it is the basic constitution of its being, on the basis of which Dasein can at all relate to beings in the first place. Dasein can learn to relate to beings in diverse ways and to confront beings

---

9. The problem of transcendence must be drawn back into the inquiry about temporality and freedom, and only from there can it be shown to what extent the understanding of being qua superior power [Übermachtig], qua holiness, belongs to transcendence itself as essentially ontologically different. The point is not to prove the divine ontically, in its "existence", but to clarify the origin of this understanding-of-being by means of the transcendence of Dasein, i.e., to clarify how this idea of being belongs to the understanding-of-being as such. (Compare now also Scheler's idea of such a genesis.) The idea of being as a superior power can only be understood out of the essence of "being" and transcendence, only in and from the full dispersal belonging to the essence of transcendence (see §10, heading 6), and not by an interpretation referring to an absolute Other [*Du*], nor to the *bonum* [the good] as value or as the Eternal. (Still remaining for consideration is being and δαιμόνιον, the understanding of being and δαιμόνιον. Being qua ground! Being and nothingness—*Angst*.)

The above is purposely not dealt with in the lectures, because precisely here and now, with the enormously phony religiosity, the dialectical illusion is especially great. It is preferable to put up with the cheap accusation of atheism, which, if it is intended ontically, is in fact completely correct. But might not the presumably ontic faith in God be at bottom godlessness? And might the genuine metaphysician be more religious than the usual faithful, than the members of a "church" or even than the "theologians" of every confession?

only because Dasein, as existing, is in a world; but it does not thereby first arrive at beings.

2) Transcendence does not mean crossing a barrier that has fenced off the subject in an inner space. But what gets crossed over is the being itself that can become manifest to the subject on the very basis of the subject's transcendence. Because the passage across exists with Dasein, and because with it beings which are not Dasein get surpassed, such beings become manifest as such, i.e., in themselves. Nothing else but transcendence, which has in advance surpassed beings, first makes it possible for these, previously surpassed *as beings,* to be ontically *opposite* [Dasein] and as opposite to be apprehended in themselves.

Therefore, what Dasein surpasses in its transcendence is not a gap or barrier "between" itself and objects. But beings, among which Dasein also factically is, get surpassed by Dasein. Objects are surpassed in advance; more exactly, beings are surpassed and can subsequently become objects. Dasein is thrown, factical, thoroughly amidst nature through its bodiliness, and transcendence lies in the fact that these beings, among which Dasein is and to which Dasein belongs, are surpassed by Dasein. In other words, as transcending, Dasein is beyond nature, although, as factical, it remains environed by nature. As transcending, i.e., as free, Dasein is something alien to nature.

3) That "toward which" the subject, as subject, transcends is not an object, not at all this or that being—whether a certain thing or a creature of Dasein's sort or some other living being. The object or being that can be encountered is that which is surpassed, not the towards-which. That towards which the subject transcends is what we call *world.*

4) Because transcendence is the basic constitution of Dasein, it belongs foremost to its being and is not a comportment that is derived later. And because this primordial being of Dasein, as surpassing, crosses over to a world, we characterize the basic phenomenon of Dasein's transcendence with the expression *being-in-the-world.*

Insofar as Dasein exists, i.e., insofar as a being-in-the-world is existent, beings (nature) have also already been overleapt, and beings thus possess the possibility of manifesting themselves in themselves. Insofar as Dasein exists, objects have already also become accessible to Dasein, though the mode of possible objectivity by which the objects are grasped is completely left open and variable; there are different stages of possibility by which things themselves [Dinge selbst] are discoverable in the way they are in themselves [entdeckbar in ihrem An-sich-sein].

Scheler had not actually seen this intrinsic connection, but he was the first to gain some insight into what he calls the "Dasein-relativity of things" (where here "Dasein" means merely extant-ness). According to Scheler it is misleading to posit things and then investigate their objectivity. Beings have stages of dis-coverability, diverse possibilities in which they manifest them-selves in themselves. There are diverse stages—and one cannot say that, for example, physics has the genuine knowledge of the solar sphere, in contrast to our natural grasp of the sun.

Inasmuch as Dasein exists qua being-in-the-world, it is already out there with beings; and even this manner of speaking is still imprecise since "already out there" presupposes Dasein is at some point on the inside. Even if I say, Dasein's intentional activ-ity is always already open towards beings and for beings, there is still at bottom the supposition that it was once closed. What we mean by transcendence cannot be made compatible with the pre-vious formulations of it and is very difficult to see, in light of the usual deadlocked version of the problem. Neither Bergson—and he least of all, along with Dilthey—nor Husserl sees the problem and the phenomenon; two years ago Husserl vehemently opposed the problem from the start.

But if transcendence in the sense of being-in-the-world is the basic metaphysical constitution of Dasein, then a metaphysics of Dasein, one with a fundamental-ontological intent, must neces-sarily refer to this basic constitution. And we are required to try to clarify this basic constitution, first of all, by proceeding from the traditional concept of the epistemological subject-object relation. Thus the investigation in *Being and Time,* after the exposition and first chapter, begins with: "Being-in-the-world in general as basic constitution of Dasein" and §§12 and 13 present an outline and a first acquaintance with the phenomenon. Had one the least sen-sitivity to method, one could conclude that this basic constitution is obviously central for a metaphysics of Dasein, that it returns continually and does so even more primordially in the course of the interpretation; this means the phenomenon comes more and more to light as central. Therefore the attempt is then made, after a first description of the basic constitution, to articulate its struc-tural moments and to elaborate them as a whole in further detail through the connections that provide the greatest access. But, in-sofar as the entire investigation tries to highlight temporality as the metaphysical essence of Dasein, transcendence becomes itself conceived by way of temporality; but, as basic constitution, tran-scendence must always come into central focus along the whole path of the investigation. The analysis of *Angst* (§40), the problems of Dasein, worldhood, and reality, as well as the interpretation of conscience and the concept of death—all serve the progressive elaboration of transcendence, until the latter is finally taken up anew and expressly (§69) as a problem, "The Temporality of Being-in-the-World and the Problem of Transcendence of World." Here again is transcendence, for the first time a problem. By making this reference I want to say that the problem must not be underestimated and that one must have long wind, so as not to be exhausted just when the problem is first beginning. And right at this point it is stated (p. 363, note) that intentionality is based upon transcendence and is focused on as an ontological problem.

Transcendence, being-in-the-world, is never to be equated and identified with intentionality; if one does so, as often happens, one proves only that he is far from understanding this phenomenon and that the latter cannot be grasped immediately. It is not the basic constitution itself, in its contents and structure, that increases the difficulty of a correct understanding, but the fact that we are weighed down with prejudices and want to finish matters too hastily, or that one does not take with sufficient seriousness what cannot be grasped immediately. So the expenditure of effort on concrete interpretations cannot be large enough, nor can the way be laid out rigorously enough for clarifying this basic phenomenon of transcendence (cf. *Being and Time*, p. 351 ff.). I am far from believing I have worked out this basic constitution in such a way that one need only look at it, as if at a blackboard, in order to "confirm" it. There are no findings in this sense here at all! But a result of the second part is that an interpretation is possible that is still more radical than my previous interpretations; that this is even necessary, however, can be seen from the fact that even Scheler did not see what was meant by transcendence.[10]

We want now to try to interpret more closely this basic constitution of Dasein, and this implies the rejection of likely misunderstandings. At first one might wonder why so much has been made of transcendence, even as a problem, if transcendence means being-in-the-world. The claim asserts what seems the most evident thing there could be. The being-in-the-world of Dasein—sure: a factually existing Dasein, an actually existing human is, as actual being, naturally there amidst other beings; humans stand on the earth, walk under trees, and move among other humans. Dasein is in a world, i.e., factually existing humans happen to be

---

10. Cf. *Idealismus–Realismus*, op.cit., p. 293 above [*Gesammelte Werke*, volume 9, p. 215 below].

among other beings, within the totality of other beings. This is all so clear that one cannot see at all what the problem is supposed to be; one could at best say that the statement, "Dasein is constitutionally, according to its essence, in a world," is evidently false, since it is just as evident that it is not essentially necessary that this or that human being exist; it is not contained in the idea of human being that a human actually exist, i.e., be in a world; but to say the essence of Dasein resides in its being-in-the-world is ostensible nonsense.

Now this is correct, it is not intrinsic to the essence of Dasein as such that it factually exist; it is, however, precisely its essence that in each case this being can also not be extant. The cosmos can be without humans inhabiting the earth, and the cosmos was long before humans ever existed.

But then how can we maintain that being-in-the-world belongs to the essence of Dasein? If this statement is nevertheless supposed to be true, then being-in-the-world must mean something else. And what it does mean is in principle asserted when we emphasize: being-in-the-world is the *basic constitution* of Dasein. For the crucial aspect lies in the negative: If I say of Dasein that its basic constitution is being-in-the-world, I am then first of all asserting something that belongs to its essence, and I thereby disregard whether the being of such a nature factually exists or not. In other words, the statement, "Dasein is, in its basic constitution, being-in-the-world," is not an affirmation of its factual existence; I do not, by this statement, claim that my Dasein is in fact extant, nor am I saying of it that, in accord with its essence, it must in fact exist. Rather, I am saying: If Dasein in fact exists, then its existence has the structure of being-in-the-world, i.e., Dasein is, in its essence, being-in-the-world, whether or not it in fact exists.

Dasein is therefore not a being-in-the-world because it in fact exists, but conversely. It can only exist in fact as Dasein because its essence is being-in-the-world. It is accordingly important to distinguish sharply and in principle between: 1) the existential statement of fact, that this particular Dasein exists now. What is crucial here is whether a Dasein in fact exists or not, and with regard to its existing; 2) the metaphysical statement of essence, that being-in-the-world belongs to the essence of Dasein as its constitution, whether it in fact exists or not. Crucial here is not whether or not it in fact exists, but what is presented is that which belongs to the intrinsic possibility of Dasein, if it should be able to exist. Being-in-the-world characterizes the basic mode of being, the existence of Dasein, and does not say whether or not it exists.

An analogue is the statement, "body is extended," which is a statement of essence and not a statement of fact; the statement does not say that one particular body or other is extant. The statement about transcendence is an existential (ontological) assertion, and not an existentiell (ontic) assertion.

To be sure, all this only serves to define, in principle, the meaning of the statement and to remove distortive interpretations. But what it means as to content is not yet clear, and here we need patience, step-by-step preparatory work, and especially the will to look toward that to which our indications point. The statement, "it belongs to the essence of Dasein that it is in the world," means that it is in fact extant among other things. Contrariwise, the statement that being-in-the-world belongs to the essence of Dasein characterizes its essential constitution. In both cases "world" means something fundamentally different. What is therefore decisive is, first: What does world mean (as a wherein)? Second: What is meant here by being-in?

The statement, "Dasein has, as the basic constitution of its being, a being-in-the-world," is thus supposed to be a statement of essence. It implies that Dasein "has," in its essence, something like world, and it does not obtain a world by the fact that it exists, that other beings of its kind and of other kinds are also factually with Dasein (or that it is among them). Rather, conversely, Dasein can, in each case, exist as this particular Dasein, insofar as it has, as Dasein as such, something on the order of world.

We find, by this, that the difficulty of seeing and understanding this basic constitution of transcendence obviously lies in the peculiarity of the concept of world. We wish therefore to try now to clarify the structure of transcendence as being-in-the-world by defining and explaining the concept "world."

b) The phenomenon of world

Our aim is to look more closely at what is signified by "world" as a feature of transcendence as such. Transcendence is being-in-the-world. Because it pertains to transcendence as such, world is a transcendental concept in the strictest sense of the term. In Kant "transcendental" has a meaning equivalent to ontological but pertaining to the ontology of "nature" in the broadest sense. For us the term has a meaning equivalent to "fundamental-ontological."

The expression "world" has many meanings, but this multiplicity of meaning is not accidental. We must first trace the traditional concept along the lines of its many meanings, i.e., investigate all it means and how it is in each case taken. From these we will be able to gather some indications of what we mean by the concept "world," as it really pertains to transcendence. The multiplicity characteristic of the concept of "world" becomes especially understandable if we take a look at the history of the concept. For us, of course, this can only mean the treatment of some few typical references.

If we look to ancient philosophy, especially in its decisive beginnings (Parmenides and Heraclitus), we immediately notice something remarkable. The Greek expression for "world" is κόσμος. And what does the term mean? Precisely not what is usually believed; it does not mean extant beings as such, heavenly bodies, the stars, the earth, even a particular being. Nor does κόσμος mean something like all beings together; it does not at all mean beings themselves and is not a name for them. Κόσμος refers rather to "condition" [Zustand]; κόσμος is the term for the mode of being [Weise zu sein] not for beings themselves. Κόσμος οὗτος means this particular condition of beings, this world of beings in contradistinction to another. Beings themselves remain the same, while their total condition, their world, can differ; or, one can hold the view that the world of beings always remains the same. To express this mode of being we use (already in my Freiburg lectures) the verb "to world," [welten]. This basic meaning of κόσμος—in principle first suggested by Karl Reinhardt (*Parmenides und die Geschichte der griechischen Philosophie*, 1916, p. 174 f. and p. 216, note)—appears in several fragments of the pre-Socratic philosophers.

In Fragment 7 of *Melissos*: ἀλλ᾿ οὐδὲ μετακοσμηθῆναι ἀννστόν [τὸ ὄν] · ὁ γὰρ κόσμος ὁ πρόσθεν ἐὼν οὐκ ἀπόλλυται οὔτε ὁ μὴ ἐὼν γίνεται; it is even impossible that beings have their world changed, for the previously worlding world does not perish, nor does the world arise that is not yet worlding. In Fragment 4 Parmenides speaks of κατὰ κόσμον with regard to τὸ ἐόν: Use understanding (instead of your eyes) and see what is ever so far as something present (in its real being); for the understanding will not scatter the coherence of beings, whilst it neither in any away scatters them with reference to their collective constitution, κατὰ κόσμον, nor does it arrange them in some other manner. Anaxoagoras, Fragment 8: It is not completely separated or sliced apart with a hatchet, i.e., scattered, τὰ ἐν τῶι ἑνὶ κόσμωι: the beings that are in a world; this means here what worlds as a whole in a definite manner, what has a definite basic condition and context. Κόσμος, as the "how" of the totality, is at the basis of every partitioning.

Partitioning does not eliminate world, but it is itself possible only on the basis of world. (Every "part" of the world is finite.) *Heraclitus*, Fragment 89: ὁ Ἡρακλειτός φησι τοῖς ἐγρηγορόσιν ἕνα καὶ κοινὸν κόσμον εἶναι, τῶν δὲ κοιμωμένων ἕκαστονεἰς ἴδιον ἀποστρέφεσθαι; a single and common world belongs to the awake, but each of the sleeping turns to his own world. Here world is related to being awake and sleeping, as basic modes proper to factical Dasein. Awakeness is a condition of Dasein in which beings manifest themselves for everyone as one and the same within the same world-character; beings manifest themselves in a thorough-going harmony accessible to everyone and binding for everyone. In sleep, on the contrary, self-manifesting beings have their own peculiar world-character for the individual, in each case a completely different way in which they world.

From these examples we can extract several points: 1) world is a term for the mode of the being of beings (even though the concept of world is not yet expressly an ontological problem); 2) world means the totality, the unification and possible dispersal of beings; 3) each mode of being is either changeable or not; world has a connection with movement, change, and time; 4) world is somehow relative to Dasein and to the mode in which it currently exists and with regard to 5) whether the world is a common world, one and the same, i.e., whether beings are allowed to manifest themselves in the same harmonious mode for all or only for every individual in his own manner—the world of everyman or of the lone self.

Further references will not only confirm these meanings but will refine them even more. As a whole, they will clarify the single main point of this preliminary set of reflections, that the concept "world" has a peculiarly universal character (qua totality relative to dispersion) and yet a character essentially related to human Dasein. This is only preliminary for the genuinely transcendental meaning we will give to this term later, in interpreting transcendence.

At this point it is good to notice, with regard to the foregoing as well as to what follows, that concepts like "world" which express a condition of beings, the how of beings (beings can world in such-and-such a way), easily and often—indeed usually for the most part—are used to describe beings themselves. "Stream," for example, means what flows, this particular stream that flows here, the creek; but "stream" means also the "how" of the being of beings, for example, to flow instead of to roll with waves. The Greek φύσις also means nature in a material and formal sense as the ἀρχή κινήσεως; even linguistically the ending –ις indicates a how or manner. Correspondingly, "world" primarily and properly means the mode of beings—and means, at the same time, these beings themselves. Both meanings can be used together compatibly, "world" meaning beings in a certain mode.

For example, when Paul in the *First Letter to the Corinthians* and in the *Letter to the Galatians speaks of* κόσμος οὗτος, this world, it means this total condition of beings, and not only and in the first instance nature, the "cosmic," in our sense. "This world" means this condition and this situation of human beings, this sort and way of their Dasein, indeed the way they act towards virtues and works, towards nature and everything, their way of evaluating goods. Indeed, κόσμος is the direct term for the way in which human Dasein is, for its attitude, its way of thinking, ἡ σοφία τοῦ κόσμου. This κόσμος, this how, is defined by its relation to the κόσμος, already dawning, to the αἰὼν ὁ μέλλων [age to come]. The condition of all beings is regarded in relation to the ἔσχατον, the final situation. Again it is clear that κόσμος means a how and is essentially related to Dasein and to time. Κόσμος is the world, in the sense of humanity, the community and society of humans in their attitude of forsaking God, i.e., in their basic stance toward themselves and all beings. "Worldly" then becomes the expression for a basic sort of human existence. Cf. especially *First Corinthians* 1, 28: καὶ τὰ ἀγενῆ τοῦ κόσμου . . . ἐξελέξατο ὁ θεὸς τὰ μὴ ὄντα, ἵνα τά ὄντα καταργήσῃ; and so God has chosen the low-born of the world, the lowly, the things that are not, so that he may annul the things that are, the predominant.

Inasmuch as we are concerned only with principles, we find in the development of the Christian concept the direct way that "world" means 1) a mode of being and this mode 2) with primary reference to human beings, pertaining to their comportment to beings.

For *Augustine, mundus* [world] means the whole of creation. But just as often *mundus* stands for the *mundi habitatores*, the inhabitants of the world, those who settle themselves in the world. But this does not only mean that they too are there, along with mountains and rivers. Settling themselves in is characterized primarily by certain basic comportments, evaluations, ways of behaving and approaching things, by the "attitude," *corde esse cum mundo* [to be with the world in one's heart]. The *habitatores mundi* are the *dilectores mundi* [enjoyers of the world], the *amatores vel impii vel carnales* [the lovers or impious or carnal]. *Mundus non dicuntur justi, quia licet carne in eo habitent, corde cum deo sunt (Opera,* ed. Migne, tom. IV; 1842) [The just are not spoken of as the world, because while they may in the flesh live in the world, they are in their hearts with God]. Here "world" is clearly the term for the God-forsaking way of behaving towards beings among which humans exist. Thus "world" is 1) a collective designation for the human community living in a certain way and means, 2) primarily the mode of this definite sort of existence wherein and for which all beings manifest themselves in a definite evaluation and context. In general, world is the how, not the what.

So too for *Thomas Aquinas,* world is equivalent in meaning to the *universum,* the *universitas creaturarum* [the universe of creatures]. But it is also equivalent to *saeculum, secundum quod mundi nomine amatores mundi significantur* ("children of the world"), [the age insofar as the term "world" designates those who love the world]. *Mundanus* [worldly] is equivalent to *saecularis* [secular], worldly in attitude, in contradistinction to *spiritualis* [spiritual]. Thus comes the term *astutia mundana,* worldly cleverness, the slyness of those who have a worldly attitude.

The following will show what meaning accrues to the concept *mundus* in modern metaphysics. Metaphysics became divided into *metaphysica generalis* and *metaphysica specialis,* and the latter into *cosmologia, psychologia,* and *theologia.* The definition of *cosmologia* according to *Baumgarten (Metaphysia* §351), is: *Cosmologia generalis est scientia praedicatorum mundi generalium* [General cosmology is the science of the general attributes of the world]. *Mundus* he defines as (*Ibid,* §354): *Mundus (universum, παν) est series (multitudo, totum) actualium finitorum, quae non est pars alterius.* "The world (totality of beings) is the series (multiplicity, totality) of finite existing things, the series which is itself not in turn a part of another." In this contrived definition, all definite features are confused and lumped together in the superficial sense of a summation. World is simply the sum of the actually extant. Thus the discriminations that were possessed by antiquity are here completely lost. Kant first mentions the essential distinctions,

By world, Kant understands quite clearly a how, a totality, in the ontological-metaphysical sense. This is found in 1) his remarks on Baumgarten, 2) his distinction between world and nature, 3) the way he divides philosophy into the academic and worldly conceptions.

1) From Kant's marginalia to Baumgarten's *Metaphysics,* we find in note #4085 (Akademie edition, volume XVII—manuscript remains, volume IV): "The idea of world is not accidental ⟨but

indeed a necessary concept⟩. For just as I must conceive in a finite way of a part that is not further a whole ⟨in which totality is conceived⟩, so must I conceive of a whole that is no part." We must necessarily have a conception of world insofar as we think a whole; but here Kant gives no further justification of why it is we must think a whole. In #4329 we read: "The world is finite because it is a totum of beings [Wesen] which restrict one another," and in #4521: "The current concept of world serves more to organize the idea of a substantial and isolated whole ⟨thus an ontological conception of world⟩ than it does to prove thereby the existence of any certain cause." #4522:

"The world that cannot be part of another ⟨more primordial⟩ whole is the world in the transcendental understanding. The world that is not part of an actual whole is world in the physical understanding. Because the possible is distinguished from the actual only inasmuch as, in the former, the *conditiones* [conditions] are not considered in their full determination, therefore a whole world that has no other conditions besides itself in its absolutely necessary essence must also have no other limits to actuality than the intrinsic conditions of possibility. From a world, in this understanding of it, one would be able to infer a single cause and its complete sufficiency, and further infer the unity of this world. But from a world that is not the absolute cosmos [Weltall], one could no longer draw such inferences than one could, in general, from a *composito substantiali* [substantial composite]. Finite from a mere *multitudo rerum finitarum* [multiplicity of finite things] no more than from a single *finito* [finite].

The Kantian conception of world becomes especially clear in the last remark above, which is directed against dogmatic theoretical metaphysics. World means not only wholeness, such as the wholeness of a particular aggregate of ontically extant things, so that world reaches only as far as the single whole of actual beings reaches. But world is the wholeness, the universality of which is determined by the whole of intrinsic possibilities. Thus Kant goes unequivocally beyond the ontic concept of world as a *series actualium finitorum* [series of finite actualities] to a transcendental conception. This is also the positive work and metaphysical content of the Kantian transcendental dialectic. Only from a conception of this sort can we infer an absolute cause, if this inference is supposed to make any sense at all. This transcendental conception of world, however, is an idea, and the inference is therefore essentially impossible. An actuality cannot be inferred from something possible, even from the totality of possibilities, but only the idea of an absolute ground can be inferred: the transcendental ideal.

In another remark (*op. cit.*, #3799) Kant summarizes the meaning of the conception of world in the following manner: "If the concept of world meant the whole of all possible things, namely, those which are possible in connection with an all-sufficient ground, then it would be a fruitful concept." He is saying here that the pre-philosophical, superficially ontic concept of world as a series means nothing at all. This concept is even essentially inferior to the ancient concept of κόσμος. Nor is the latter, on the other hand, identical with Kant's transcendental conception of world. In the transcendental dialectic Kant gives this concept still another meaning which we can only suggest here.

2. Kant says in the *Critique of Pure Reason* (A 418/19, B 446/47):

> We have two expressions, *world* and *nature*, which sometimes coincide. The former signifies the mathematical sum-total of all appearances and the totality of their synthesis, alike in the great and in the small, that is, in the advance alike through composition and through division. This same world is entitled "nature," when it is viewed as a dynamical whole. We are not then concerned with the aggregation in space and time, with a view to determining it as a magnitude, but with the unity in the *existence* of appearances. [N.K. Smith translation]

Immediately striking here is that the concept world is further narrowed down to the *totum* of beings, but it is nevertheless not understood ontically but ontologically, in distinction to nature. To put the differentiation into a formula, world is the mathematical whole (the mathematical totality) and nature is the dynamic totality of appearances. Accessible beings come under both these transcendental, ontological determinations. To understand them correctly, we need a clarification of the terms "mathematical" and "dynamic."

Kant employs this distinction not only here, but throughout the *Critique of Pure Reason*. In fact he uses it to divide the whole of the categories into two classes; the mathematical categories of quantity and quality, and the dynamic categories of relation and modality. And insofar as the ontological principles are articulated along the lines of the categories, Kant speaks of mathematical and dynamic principles; the former are the axioms of intuition and the anticipations of perception, and the latter are the axioms of the analogies of experience and the postulates of empirical thinking in general. The (mathematical) principles of intuition have an intuitive certainty, and the (dynamic) principles of thinking are capable of a discursive certainty; in each case the certainty is a "full" certainty (A 162, B 201).

What Kant means by the terms "mathematical " and "dynamic" has, as far as content goes, nothing directly to do with either the mathematics or the dynamics of physics. Both terms are nevertheless chosen to decribe something (categories, principles, ideas) which in its possible application, i.e., insofar as it deals with the ontological, is describable with regard to its use, its completion, in determining the ontical. "In the application of pure concepts of understanding to possible experience, the employment of their synthesis ⟨the principles⟩ is either *mathematical*, or *dynamical*; for it is concerned partly with the mere *intuition* of an appearance in general, partly with its *existence* (A 160, B 199).

> I shall therefore entitle the former principles *mathematical*, and the latter *dynamical*. But it should be noted that we are as little concerned in the one case with the principles of mathematics as in the other with the principles of general physical dynamics. We treat only of the principles of pure understanding in their relation to inner sense (all differences among the given representations being ignored). It is through these principles of pure understanding that the special principles of mathematics and of dynamics become possible. I have named them, therefore, on account rather of their application than of their content. [Smith translation] (A 162, B 201/2, compare the division of *conjunctio* into *compositio* or *nexus* in the note to B 202.)

For Kant's general ontology, the exemplary being is, of course, nature, i.e., beings-in-themselves as discovered by the mathematical science of nature. Thus the ontological determinations in general have possible application to these beings and can themselves be designated by the names for the beings to which they are applicable. "Mathematical" and "dynamical" are not primarily ontological terms, but they designate something ontological from the perspective of the beings that are ontologically based. By his choice of these determinations, it is clear that, with his general ontology, Kant had at the same time a positive interest in creating the ontological foundation for "physics," as the science of beings in general, but this does not mean a theory of the science of physics.

Now insofar as the what-content of a natural thing is defined by its extensive and intensive magnitude (in Descartes only by *extensio*), and magnitude is what is determined mathematically, and the a priori foundations of these determinations are space and time as pure intuitions, the mathematical categories coincide with the categories of the essence of nature, its *essentia*. Those categories which Kant calls dynamic, on the other hand, deal with the nature of beings not in their what-being but in their that-being, their *modus existendi*. Dynamic categories are categories of "existence." The mathematical principles are ontological-essential principles, and the dynamic principles are ontological-existential principles.

Just as world and nature relate to the same, so too do mathematical wholeness and dynamical wholeness. World is the wholeness that presents the totality of those a priori determinations which state what belongs to a possible being in its what-contents. Nature is the corresponding wholeness which delimits the *modus existendi*. Here nature is understood (cf. note to A418, B446) in the primordial sense of φύσις, as the how of the extantness (*natura formaliter spectata*) of that which we also call nature materially. World designates the region, nature, with regard to the essential contents of its pertinent thinghood, therefore not even the essential and existential totality of beings; not even the totality of possibilities (*omnitudo realitatis*), as mentioned in the marginalia to Baumgarten. World is the sum-total of the a priori essential contents of that which belongs to nature—regardless of whether it exists or not!

There is indeed a difficulty here. An ontology of the *modus existendi* is plainly a priori as well, and this *modus* also pertains to nature; only what remains undecided is whether or not the *modus* is actualized. This is, in general, a difficulty prevalent in traditional metaphysics and ontology and in the consideration of essences, particularly in Husserl. By suspending what is actual (in the phenomenological reduction) the what-character is set forth—but, in suspending the actual, the actuality, i.e., the *modus existendi*, and its intrinsic connection [Wesenszusammenhang] with the essential contents in the narrower sense, is not suspended. Essence has here a double meaning: it means the a priori of *essentia* and of *existentia*.

This conception of world as mathematical sum-total, as transcendental ideal without a concomitant conceptualization of *existentia*, indicates that the concept of world in Kant is, as a whole, unrefined and still too narrow, however its particular meanings might be defined.

3. There is, however, yet another use Kant makes of the concept of world. Kant distinguishes in the essence of philosophy a double concept which we found already several times in this lecture course: *metaphysica generalis* and *metaphysica specialis*; metaphysics as preparatory and metaphysics as final purpose—πρώτη φιλοσοφία and θεολογία. Philosophy as *metaphysica specialis*, as genuine metaphysics, is philosophy "according to the concepts of the world." It treats the questions: What can I know?

What should I do? What may I hope? But why is this real metaphysics called philosophy according to the concept of world (*in sensu cosmico*)? It deals precisely not with nature, but with human beings and with the existence and essence of humans; cf. the fourth question: What is the human being? in the Introduction to the *Logikvorlesung* (Section III, Akademie edition, Volume IX, p. 25). And yet this is philosophy according to the concept of world! Once again here we see this other remarkable relation the concept "world" has to the existence of human Dasein and to the essence of humans in the whole, but we also see the meaning of the aforementioned Kantian concept of the world as totality. Thus Kant says (*C.P.R.*, A839, B867 note):

> By 'cosmical concept' [Weltbegriff] ⟨of philosophy with a view to the "world citizen"⟩ is here meant the concept which relates to that in which everyone necessarily has an interest; and accordingly if a science is to be regarded merely as one of the disciplines designed in view of certain optionally chosen ends, I must determine it in conformity with *scholastic concepts*.

For this reason Kant considers "logic" and even, in a certain sense, "ontology" to be propaedeutic (cf. the *Lectures on Logic*, Intro. III).

The expression "world-view," found already in Kant but not yet in our contemporary meaning, points in the direction of this use of the concept "world." By "world-view" we do not mean contemplating the world in the sense of nature, but view here means, as *repraesentatio singularis*, representing, thinking, knowing some whole in which every human existence as such has an interest. The term "world-view" must also be taken in this sense in the work by Karl Jaspers, *Psychologie der Weltanschauungen* (3rd edition 1925); the latter psychology is the endeavor to show "what the human being is."

In the contemporary meaning of the term, we include in world-view the taking up of a certain position, or the means provided for taking up a position, and a position which is, in each case, a distinct existentiell stance. Philosophy itself never gives a world-view nor does it have the task of providing one. On the contrary, philosophy is one possible form of existence that, ideally, in itself requires no world-view, because it moves in the possibilities of world-views. (To what extent, though, it requires "involvement," cf. above § 10, heading 11.) "World-view philosophy" is in general a nonsensical phrase; it can only have meaning as a discussion of the essence of world-views, their intrinsic necessity and possible forms. But equally nonsensical at bottom is the expression "scientific philosophy," because philosophy is prior to all science, and can be so only because it is already, in an eminent sense, what "science" can be only in a derived sense. The alternatives, either a scientific or a world-view philosophy, are just as superficial as is a combination of both.

What Kant, on the contrary, means by dividing philosophy into the academic conception and the world conception coincides in a certain way with the difference already mentioned. "In a certain way," because the idea of metaphysics is not correspondingly grounded and developed in a positive manner, as the foundation itself is.

We now summarize this orientation in the history of the concept of world. "World" as a concept of the being of beings designates the wholeness of beings in the totality of their possibilities, a wholeness which is itself, however, essentially related to human existence, and human existence taken in its final goal. For preparing the following phenomenological clarification of the transcendental concept of world, and at the same time as a systematic summary of what was said, we can distinguish four concepts of world (cf. *Being and Time*, p. 64 f.):

1. An ontical concept: "world" is simply the term for what is extant itself together as a whole, for "nature." This pre-philosophical, naive concept of world can thus also be called the ontic-natural concept.

2. An ontological (in a certain way) concept which is subordinate to the aforementioned concept. It is "world" as the region of nature, as the totality of what belongs to a nature as such.

3. There is a further ontical concept: "world" here means not nature (inorganic and organic) but means existing humans as existing; it is in this sense we speak of "the wide world," of a woman or man "of the world." This pre-philosophical concept of world is the ontic-existentiell (or human) concept, in contradistinction to the ontic-natural concept.

Anticipating, we can name the fourth the ontological concept of world that indicates, not human society in an ontical way, but indicates ontologically the metaphysical essence of Dasein as such with respect to its basic metaphysical constitution, i.e., transcendence.

The transcendental concept of world is evidently related, in its own way, to the other conceptions. On the other hand, none of the concepts mentioned, from 1 to 3, nor even their sum, exhausts the concept "world" as a constituent of transcendence.

Something important remains to be noticed about both pre-philosophical ontical concepts of world. Take the existentiell concept of world which was mentioned as number 3. For example, in the expression, "the fashionable world," we understand not only, say, a gathering or even a society of well-dressed human beings. Constitutive for the expression "world" is that we mean the people designated precisely in their comportment; all that among which they move, hotels and race-tracks, etc., also belongs to them as world. It would be a complete misconstrual of the pre-philosophical concept of world were one to think that the concept designates (according to 1) only extant things and, in particular, useful things and that this concept of world had to be then supplemented or replaced, inasmuch as one says world is a human concept and designates the surrounding or remote human environment. Instead, "world" just as little designates things in isolation as it does humans in isolation. The importance of the pre-philosophical concept is the relationship that human Dasein has to things or that things have to humans.

In other words, the prephilosophical-ontic concept has, for its primary significance, not a particular being but the how of Dasein's existing—namely, taken in its totality, the active comportment toward beings and toward itself. The mode of human existing consists in defining itself in and by the whole. Dasein's being-in-the-world means to be in the whole, specifically with respect to the how. Even if Dasein were to conform itself to a single part and expect everything from it, this very expectation would nonetheless witness to existence and its wholeness.

We cannot accordingly understand world as the ontical context of useful items, the things of historical culture, in contradistinction to nature and the things of nature. Yet the analysis of useful items and their context nevertheless provides an approach and the means for first making visible the phenomenon of world. World is therefore not beings qua tools, as that with which humans have to deal, as if being-in-the-world meant to move among cultural items. Nor is world a multiplicity of human beings. Rather, all these beings belong to what we call intra-worldly beings, yet they are not the world itself. But what and how is world?

As was mentioned several times, we cannot unravel the problem in its entire scope here, nor do we have enough time to develop concretely the context of the problem in a balanced way. In the following I will try to make headway with the aid of a necessarily only vague historical orientation to *Plato's doctrine of ideas*. Conversely, by working out the original phenomenon of transcendence, we obtain the perspective for a renewed penetration into the Platonic doctrine of ideas and for clarifying μέθεξις [participation] and the μεταξύ [the between].

In our last considerations, we realized that the character of wholeness belongs in some way to the concept of world, and we know that world should be constitutive for the transcendence of Dasein. Dasein transcends beings, and its surpassing is surpassing to world. The beings surpassed in transcendence are not, however, only those which are not Dasein. In transcendence Dasein surpasses itself as a being; more exactly, this surpassing makes it possible that Dasein can be something like itself. In first surpassing itself, the abyss [Abgrund] is opened which Dasein, in each case, is for itself. This abyss can be covered over and obscured, only because the abyss of being-a-self is opened up by and in transcendence.

But the question becomes unavoidable: What then is the world to which Dasein transcends? How is this wholeness related to Dasein itself? Is world a realm of ideas, in some ὑπερουράνιος τόπος [super-heavenly place], that is looked at and contemplated by a reason built into Dasein? Or is the world the totality of the ideas innate in the subject? It is already evident from these questions how the problem of the concept of world, as a transcendental concept, is fully intertwined with the problem of the subjectivity of the subject and, at the same time, with the basic ontological inquiry into being as such.

If the phenomenon which we designate as a transcendental concept is central, then it must have already come to light in some form, even if quite veiled and not formulated as such, in all genuine philosophy. There can be no doubt that the conception of the doctrine of ideas was prompted by a transcendence which was as such still latent. But it is just as evident that the conception of the doctrine of ideas could not attain the concept of world, because the ideas themselves and the relationship to them consisted solely in an intensification of one particular grasp of beings—and this grasp is *intuition* [Anschauung]. The look to which everything here reverts has for its correlate a definite, quite one-sided conception of being. In ἰδέα, θεωρία, *intuitus*, essential intuition, recourse is had to a consciousness that looks, a recourse so incapable of solving the problem of transcendence, that it is not even capable of seeing the phenomenon of transcendence.

The connection between ideas and looking, θεωρία, intuitus (referred to already in the word ἰδέα), is essential, since the source of the doctrine of ideas is expressed in it. Insofar as being is attrib-

uted to the ideas themselves, they are only a reduplication of beings, as Aristotle saw. Besides this, what is seen in contemplation,
the ideas, as eternal, are elevated above change. Hence the doctrine of ideas implies a replication of the basic way of relating to
beings, theoretical contemplation, and the doctrine is one with
that replication. If the doctrine of ideas is related to the phenomenon of transcendence, and if the idea is the correlate of intuition,
then there is, in the doctrine, a tendency to conceptualize the
problem of transcendence along the lines of looking. This is prepared already in antiquity and later leads to orienting the problem
of transcendence to the epistemological relationship of subject to
object.

Further, because looking was, as αἴσθησις is, connected with
grasping the beautiful, one is inclined to conceive or explain transcendence not only by measuring it in reference to θεωρεῖν, but
also by patterning it on aesthetic activity. This inclination finds
support in the opinion that things are seen most primordially in
aesthetic intuition, seen as they are—an opinion which is based
on the erroneous view that in aesthetic intuition the subject is
supposed to be disinterested in the being looked at.

One cannot pack transcendence into intuition, in either the
theoretical or the aesthetic sense, because it is not even an ontic
activity. Even less can it be packed into a practical comportment,
be it in an instrumental-utilitarian sense or in any other. The central task in the ontology of Dasein is to go back behind those divisions into comportments to find their common root, a task that
need not, of course, be easy. Transcendence precedes every possible mode of activity in general, prior to νόησις, but also prior to
ὄρεξις.

The phenomenon of world gets approached ontically and gets
diverted into an extant realm of ideas accessible to a mere looking.
This is because, among other reasons, transcendence was from
early on taken primarily in the sense of θεωρεῖν, which means that
transcendence was not sought in its primordial rootedness in the
real being of Dasein. Nevertheless, Dasein was known to antiquity also as genuine action, as πρᾶξις. If we now pose the problem of transcendence in connection with the problem of freedom,
we must not take freedom in a narrow sense, so that it pertains to
πρᾶξις in contradistinction to θεωρία. The problem of freedom
remains ambiguous up through Kant's doctrine of the primacy of
practical reason, and especially in Neo-Kantianism. One must
understand Kant's effort to take theoretical comportment back into
πρᾶξις—Kant's giving primacy to practical over theoretical

comportment—against the background of the division of the faculties into imagination, intuition, thinking, and against the background of his positing an either-or of receptivity and spontaneity. Kant was, however, moving towards grounding both more primordially, even though he had never posed the problem radically in a completely conscious way. But the problem is the common root of both intuition, θεωρεῖν, as well as action, πρᾶξις.

We noted that ἰδέα is correlated to an ἰδεῖν [seeing]. In the initial approach of Western philosophy in general, intuition, mere looking, is the basic act wherein transcendence is to a certain extent localized. Even later, when theoretical comportment is apparently supplanted by the practical (primacy of practical reason), even then the ancient approach remained directive. The genuine phenomenon of transcendence cannot be localized in a particular activity, be it theoretical, practical, or aesthetic. All these, as relationships to beings, are only possible on the basis of transcendence itself.

Though in Plato transcendence was not investigated down to its genuine roots, the inescapable pressure of the phenomenon nevertheless brought to light the connection between the transcendent intended by the idea and the root of transcendence, πρᾶξις. The idea is the correlate of intuition, but there is a passage in Plato according to which *the idea of the good*, the ἰδέα τοῦ ἀγαθοῦ, still lies beyond beings and οὐσία, *beyond the ideas*, ἐπέκεινα τῆς οὐσίας. Here a transcendence emerges that one must consider the most primordial, insofar as the ideas are themselves already transcendent with regard to the beings that change.

What the idea of the good means is not simple to ascertain on the basis of what we have from Plato. It is certain that this ἰδέα τοῦ ἀγαθοῦ still has, in the end, a mythic quality such that the philosophical point is not yet exposed by this suggestion. Nor, however, should we take the path that is particularly tempting today, simply to read our concept of value into the idea of the good. For the concept of value, having a necessary function within set limits, derives from the same traditional metaphysics, whose real ontological foundations are unclear and ungrounded.

What we must, moreover, learn to see in the ἰδέα τοῦ ἀγαθου is the characteristic described by Plato and particularly Aristotle as the οὖ ἕνεκα, the *for-the-sake-of-which*, that on account of which something is or is not, is in this way or that. The ἰδέα τοῦ ἀγαθοῦ, which is even beyond beings and the realm of ideas, is the for-the-sake-of-which. This means it is the genuine determination that transcends the entirety of the ideas and at the same time thus organizes them in their totality. As ἐπέκεινα, the for-the-sake-of-which excells the ideas, but, in excelling them, it determines and gives them the form of wholeness, κοινωνία, communality. If we thus keep in mind the οὗ ἕνεκα characteristic of the highest idea, the connection between the doctrine of ideas and the concept of world begins to emerge: the basic characteristic of world whereby wholeness attains its specifically transcendental form of organization is the for-the-sake-of-which. World, as that to which Dasein transcends, is primarily defined by the for-the-sake-of-which.

But a for-the-sake-of-which, a purposiveness [Umwillen], is only possible where there is a willing [Willen]. Now insofar as transcendence, being-in-the-world, constitutes the basic structure of Dasein, being-in-the-world must also be primordially bound up with or derived from the basic feature of Dasein's existence, namely, *freedom*. Only where there is freedom is there a purposive for-the-sake-of, and only here is there world. To put it briefly, Dasein's transcendence and freedom are identical! Freedom provides itself with intrinsic possibility; a being is, as free, necessarily in itself transcending.

c) Freedom and world

But now the puzzles begin anew! What is the intrinsic connection between Dasein's freedom, being-in-the-world, and the primary character of world, the purposive for-the-sake-of?

Let us start with the last of these. In our previous account it seemed to be only a formal determination. Dasein, we can say, exists for the sake of something, and now we must still ascertain that for-the-sake-of-which Dasein exists, in terms of its content. What is the final purpose for which humans exist? Here we would seem to have the decisive question. But just seemingly. For the question is ambiguous. By itself, it seems to go directly to the whole, yet the question is premature. It assumes that it can be somehow decided objectively, while, in the final analysis, the sense of the question itself is such that it is, in each case, only the questioner alone who can pose the question in its real sense and answer it. But if this is the case, then we must show why it is so. In other words, it must become clear from the metaphysics of Dasein why, in conforming to the essence of its being, Dasein must itself take over the question and answer concerning the final purpose, why searching for an objective answer is in itself a or *the* misunderstanding of human existence in general.

In contrast to truth about extant things, truth about what exists is truth for that which exists. The latter truth consists only in being-true qua existing. And questioning too must be understood accordingly, not as an inquiry-about but as a questioning-for, where the questioner's situation is included in the question.

Before then one sets out prematurely to give an answer to the question about the final human purpose—an answer which would be at bottom none at all—before we try to fill in the content of the formal for-the-sake-of, we must first examine more closely this for-the-sake-of itself, so as to avoid an inadequate construal of for-the-sake-of as the constituent of worldhood.

The existence of Dasein is determined by the for-the-sake-of. It is Dasein's defining characteristic [Auszeichnende] that it is concerned with this being, in its being, in a specific way. Dasein exists for the sake of Dasein's being and its capacity-for-being. But, one might immediately object, here we have just provided a determination of the contents of the for-the-sake-of, and we have pinned down the final purpose that is one-sided in the greatest degree; it is an extreme egoism, the clearest delusion to assert that all beings, including nature and culture and whatever else there might be, only exist in each case for the individual human being and his egotistic goals. In fact, if this were the sense of the claim of the ontology of Dasein, then it would indeed be madness. But then neither would it be explicable why one would need an analysis of Dasein in order to assert such outrageous nonsense. On the other hand, finally, Kant has said that man exists as an end in himself.

But things are not finally so simple if the statement of essence, "It belongs to Dasein's essence to be concerned about its own being," occurs within a metaphysics of Dasein. In that case it would be completely superfluous were one to correct the statement by pointing to the many humans who sacrifice themselves for others and who perish in friendship and community with others. To correct the statement in this way is superfluous, because such a correction would correct something it cannot correct. For the aforementioned statement is not at all an ontic assertion claiming that all existing humans in fact use or even should use all that surrounds them solely for their own particular egotistic aims. The ontological statement, "It belongs to the essence of Dasein that its own being resides in its for-the-sake-of," does not exclude humans from being in fact concerned about the being of others; this ontological statement, moreover, supplies the metaphysical ground of the possibility for anything like Dasein to be able to be with others, for them and through them. In other words, if the state-

ment, "It belongs to Dasein's essence that in its being it is concerned with this being itself," is located at the beginning of an
ontological analysis of Dasein and in direct connection with the
statement of transcendence, then it is a simple imperative of even
the most primitive methodology to at least ask whether or not this
ontological statement of essence does or could present an ontic
claim from a world-view that preaches a so-called individualistic
egoism.

This statement, and all those connected with it, does not deal
with an existentiell, ethical egoism, but it deals rather with the
ontological-metaphysical description of the egoicity [Egoität] of
Dasein as such. Only because Dasein is primarily determined by
egoicity can it factically exist as a thou for and with another Dasein. The thou is not an ontic replicate of a factical ego; but
neither can a thou exist as such and be itself as thou for another
ego if it is not at all Dasein, i.e., if it is not grounded in egoicity.
The egoicity belonging to the transcendence of Dasein is the
metaphysical condition of the possibility for a thou to be able to
exist and for an I-thou relationship to be able to exist. The thou is
also most immediately thou if it is not simply another ego, but
rather a "you yourself are." This selfhood, however, is its freedom,
and this freedom is identical with egoicity, on the basis of which
Dasein can, in the first place, ever be either egoistic or altruistic.

Indeed, the very fact that we can make the I-thou relation into a
problem at all indicates that we are transcending each factual ego
and factual thou and that we grasp the relation as a relation of
Dasein as such, i.e., we grasp the relation in its metaphysical neutrality and egoicity. Of course we usually do so without suspecting
anything of these presuppositions we take for granted. However
rich and interesting the analysis of possible I-thou relationships
may be, it cannot solve the metaphysical problem of Dasein, because it cannot even pose the problem. With its first approach,
such an analysis already presupposes, in some form, the entire
analysis of Dasein and constantly employs it. Today, for quite a
variety of reasons, the problem of the I-thou relation is of great
interest to world-views. There are sociological, theological, political, biological, and ethical problems which ascribe a prominence
to the I-thou relation; yet the philosophical problems are thereby
concealed.

Here we see then a new difficulty characteristic of the problem
of subjectivity and of every ontology of Dasein. The first difficulty
was with regard to illegitimately roping the closed subject off from
all objects, the misguided view that the most presuppositionless

approach is the one beginning with a worldless subject. The difficulty we are considering now, however, is with regard to the view that an approach beginning with a subject, though in the end a transcending subject, is an even more individualistic, more egotistic subjectivism; that the more radically one makes an ontology of Dasein into a problem and task, the more extremely must one embrace individualism—let us correct this—the more such individualism *seems* to obtrude, along with the difficulty of holding and maintaining the ontological intent.

If we say "Dasein is in each case essentially mine," and if our task is to define this characteristic of Dasein ontologically, this does not mean we should investigate the essence of my self, as this factical individual, or of some other given individual. The object of inquiry is not the individual essence of my self, but it is the essence of mineness and selfhood as such. Likewise, if "I" is the object of the ontological interpretation, then this is not the individual I-ness, of my self, but I-ness in its metaphysical neutrality; we call this neutral I-ness "egoicity." But here too there is danger of a misunderstanding. One could say, Must not thou-ness, too, become likewise a topic and must not thou-ness be taken together with I-ness as equiprimordial? This is certainly a possible problem. But I-ness, as the phenomenon correlative to thou-ness, is still not metaphysical egoicity. Here it becomes clear that the term "I" always pushes in the direction of the isolation of my self in the sense of a corresponding severance from the thou. Contrariwise, I-ness does not mean the factical ego distinguished from the thou; egoicity means, rather, the I-ness also at the basis of the thou, which prevents an understanding of the thou factically as an alter ego. But why is thou not simply a second ego? Because being an ego, in contradistinction to being a thou, does not at all pertain to the essence of Dasein, i.e., because a thou is what it is, only qua its self, and likewise for the "I". Therefore I usually use the expression *"selfhood"* [Selbstheit] for metaphysical I-ness, for egoicity. For the "self' can be said equally of the I and the thou: "I-myself," "you-yourself," but not "thou-I."

Pure selfhood, understood as the metaphysical neutrality of Dasein, expresses, at the same time, the metaphysical isolation of Dasein in ontology, an isolation which should never be confused with an egoistic-solipsistic exaggeration of one's own individuality. We suggested earlier, however, (§ 10, heading 11) how individuality necessarily has a function in involvement. Because selfhood is the basic character of existence, but to exist means, in each case, a capability-to-be, one of the possibilities of existence must serve for the concrete exposition of ontological selfhood, and for this reason the approach using an extreme model was chosen (cf. *Being and Time* §64). Nor did I for a moment believe that this problematic and its inherent task would be quickly comprehended today or that it would even have to be comprehended by the multitude. What Hegel says in the preface to his *Phenomenologie* is even more accurate today than it was in his time: "It is not a pleasant experience to see ignorance, and a crudity without form or taste, which cannot focus its thought on a single abstract proposition, still less on a connected chain of them, claiming at one moment to be freedom of thought and toleration, and at the next to be even genius."[11]

To be for its own sake is an essential determination of the being of that being we call Dasein. This constitution, which we will now, for brevity, call the for-the-sake-of, provides the intrinsic possibility for this being to be itself, i.e., for *selfhood* to belong to its being. To be in the mode of a self means to be fundamentally towards oneself. Being towards oneself constitutes the being of Dasein and is not something like an additional capacity to observe oneself over and above just existing. Existing is precisely this being towards oneself, only the latter must be understood in its full metaphysical scope and must not be restricted to some activity or capability or to any mode of apprehension such as knowledge or apperception. Moreover, being toward oneself as being a self is the presupposition for the various possibilities of ontic relations to oneself.

Furthermore, only because this being is, in its essence, defined by selfhood can it, in each case, as factical, expressly choose itself as a self. The "can" here includes also its flight from choice. What then is implied by this possibility grounded in selfhood, this possibility of choosing oneself expressly or of fleeing the choice? What essentially is concomitantly chosen in the express choice of oneself?

Here, however , is the orgin of "possibility" as such. Only through freedom, only a free being can, as trancending, understand being—and it must do so in order to exist as such, i.e., to be "among" and "with" beings.

Several times we mentioned how all these metaphysical, ontological statements are exposed to continual misunderstanding,

---

11. *Werke* (*Vollst. Ausg. durch e. Verein v. Freunden des Verewigten*), volume 2, edited by J. Schulze (Berlin, 1832), p. 54. [*Philosophische Bibliotek*, volume 114, 6th edition, Hamburg, 1952, edited by J. Hoffmeister, p. 55.]

are understood ontically and existentielly. One main reason for this misunderstanding lies in not preserving the proper metaphysical horizon of the problem. And there is a particular danger of this at the present stage of our exposition. We said that Dasein chooses itself. One inadvertently then fills in the term Dasein with the usual concept of the isolated, egoistic subject and then interprets Dasein's choosing itself as a solipsistic-egoistic contraction into oneself. In the genuine metaphysical sense precisely the reverse is the case. Dasein, and only Dasein qua Dasein, should choose itself (Dasein). Many times, even ad nauseam, we pointed out that this being qua Dasein is always already with others and always already with beings not of Dasein's nature. In transcending, Dasein transcends every being, itself as well as every being of its own sort (Dasein-with) and every being not of Dasein's sort. In choosing itself Dasein really chooses precisely its being-with others and precisely its being among beings of a different character.

In the express self-choice there is essentially the complete self-commitment, not to where it might not yet be, but to where and how it already always is, qua Dasein, insofar as it already exists. To what extent this may, in fact, transpire in each case is not a question of metaphysics but a question and affair of the individual person. Only because Dasein can expressly choose itself on the basis of its selfhood can it be committed to others. And only because, in being toward itself as such, Dasein can understand anything like a "self" can it furthermore attend at all to a thou-self. Only because Dasein, constituted by the for-the-sake-of, exists in selfhood, only for this reason is anything like human community possible. These are primary existential-ontological statements of essence, and not ethical claims about the relative hierarchy of egoism and altruism. Conceived in an existential-ontological way, the phenomenon of authentic self-choice highlights, in the most radical way, the metaphysical selfhood of Dasein, and this means transcendence as transcending ones's own being, transcending being as being-with others, and transcending beings in the sense of nature and items of use. Again, we are here suggesting, methodologically, an extreme existential-ontological model.

N.B. In Kierkegaard there is much talk of choosing oneself and of the individual, and if it were my task to say once again what Kierkegaard has said, then it would not only be a superfluous endeavor, but would be one which necessarily in essence lagged behind Kierkegaard with regard to his purpose. His purpose is not ours, but differs in principle, something which does not prevent us from learning from him, but obliges us to learn what he has to offer. But Kierkegaard never pushed onward into the dimension of this problematic, because it was not at all important for him, and his work as an author had a completely different basic purpose, that also required different ways and means.

The statement, "For-its-own-sake belongs to the essence of Dasein," is an ontological statement. It asserts something about the essential constitution of Dasein in its metaphysical neutrality. Dasein is for its own sake and herein, in the for-the-sake-of, lies the ground of the possibility for an existentiell, egoistic or non-egoistic, for-my-own-sake. But herein lies, just as primordially, the ground for a for-him-or-her-sake and for every kind of ontic reason-for. As constituting the selfhood of Dasein, the for-the-sake-of has this universal scope. In other words, it is *that towards which* Dasein as transcending transcends.

In the context of the inquiry about transcendence, we began with the problem of world and came, by way of the realm of ideas and the ἐπέκεινα τῆς οὐσίας, up against for-the-sake-of, as the basic character of world. This for-the-sake-of is to be understood as the metaphysical structure of Dasein, not, however, with regard to a factual existent's setting up particular egoistic goals. We must pursue more sharply this for-the-sake-of, as metaphysical constitution and basic structure of world, so that we have an understanding of being-in-the-world as transcendence.

The for-the-sake-of is what it is in and for a willing. But the latter does not mean the existentiell-ontic act of will, but means rather the intrinsic possibility of willing: *freedom*. In freedom, such a for-the-sake-of has always already emerged. This self-presentation of the for-the-sake-of resides in the essence of freedom. There is not something like for-the-sake-of somewhere extant, to which then freedom is only related. Rather, freedom is itself the origin of the for-the-sake-of. But, again, not in such a way that there was first freedom and then also the for-the-sake-of. Freedom is, rather, one with the for-the-sake-of. It is unimportant here to what extent something defined as free is, in fact, free or to what extent it is aware of its freedom. Nothing is said here regarding the extent to which it is free or only latently free, bound or enthralled by others or by beings not of Dasein's kind. Only a free being can be unfree.

Here we also have to remove freedom from the traditional perspective where emphasis is placed on self-initiating spontaneity, *sua sponte*, in contrast to a compulsive mechanical sequence. But this initiative "from itself" remains indefinite without selfhood.

And this means that one must take transcendence back into free-dom; one must seek the basic essence of transcendence in freedom.

In other words, the world described primarily by the for-the-sake-of is the primordial totality of that which Dasein, as free, gives itself to understand. Freedom gives itself to understand; freedom is the primal understanding, i.e., the primal projection of that which freedom itself makes possible. In the projection of the for-the-sake-of as such, Dasein gives itself the primordial *commitment* [Bindung]. Freedom makes Dasein in the ground of its essence, responsible [verbindlich] to itself, or more exactly, gives itself the possibility of commitment. The totality of the commit-ment residing in the for-the-sake-of is the world. As a result of this commitment, Dasein commits itself to a capability of being toward-itself as able-to-be-with others in the ability-to-be-among extant things. Selfhood is free responsibility for and toward itself.

As free, Dasein is world-projection. But this projecting is only projected in such a way that Dasein holds itself in it and does this so that the free hold binds Dasein, i.e., so that the hold puts Da-sein, in all its dimensions of transcendence, into a possible clear-ance space for choice. Freedom itself holds this binding opposite to itself. The world is maintained in freedom counter to freedom itself. The world is the free counter-hold of Dasein's for-the-sake-of. Being-in-the-world is accordingly nothing other than free-dom, freedom no longer understood as spontaneity but as defined by the formulation of Dasein's metaphysical essence, which we have described (which is, to be sure, not as yet fully defined).

The free counter-hold of the for-the-sake-of has, however, as transcendence, the character of leaping over each factical and fac-tual being, as was pointed out earlier. World, as the totality of the essential intrinsic possibilities of Dasein as transcending, *surpass-es* all actual beings. Whenever and however they are encountered, actual beings always reveal themselves—precisely when they are disclosed as they are in themselves—only as a restriction, as one possible realization of the possible, as the insufficient out of an excess of possibilities, within which Dasein always maintains it-self as free projection.

Dasein is in itself *excessive*, i.e., defined by a primary insatia-bility for beings—both metaphysically as such and also existen-tially, in factic individuation. This primary insatiability can be seen in a definite, ontic, existentiell comportment. Only on the basis of insatiability can there be any settling-down-with, any exis-tentiell peace-of-mind or dissatisfaction. The latter dissatisfaction should not be confused with insatiability, in a metaphysical sense. The essence of freedom, which surpasses every particular factic and factual being, its surpassive character, can also be seen particularly in despair, where one's own lack of freedom engulfs a Dasein absorbed in itself. This completely factical lack of freedom is itself an elemental testimony to transcendence, for despair lies in the despairing person's vision of the impossibility of something possible. Such a person still witnesses to the possible, inasmuch as he despairs of it.

The surpassing of factic beings that is peculiar to the world as such, and thereby to transcendence and freedom corresponds to the *epekeina* [beyond]. In other words, the world itself is surpassive; beings of Dasein's character are distinguished by upswing or *élan* [Uberschwung]; world is the free surpassive counter-hold of the for-the-sake-of.

Only insofar as Dasein in its metaphysical essence, freely presenting its own for-the-sake-of, overshoots itself, does Dasein become, as upswing toward the possible, the occasion (from a metaphysical viewpoint) for beings to emerge as beings. Beings of Dasein's nature must have opened themselves as freedom, i.e., world must be held out in the upswing, a being must be constituted as being-in-the-world, as transcending, if that being itself and beings in general are to become apparent as such. Thus Dasein, seen metaphysically as this being-in-the-world, is therefore, as factically existent, nothing other than the existent possibility for beings to gain *entry to world*. When, in the universe of beings, a being attains more being [seiender] in the existence of Dasein, i.e., when temporality temporalizes [Zeitlichkeit sich zeitigt], only then do beings have the opportunity to enter the world. Entry into world, furthermore, provides the possibility for beings to be able to be revealed.

Before proceeding to clarify transcendence in its intrinsic possibility, so as to see then the rootedness of the essence of ground in transcendence, we must first make transcendence more intelligible by briefly characterizing the entry into world.

So far as we have succeeded in clarifying transcendence, one thing must be clear. The world does not mean beings, neither individual objects nor the totality of objects standing opposite a subject. Whenever one wishes to express transcendence as a subject-object relation, especially as in the movement of philosophical realism, the claim is frequently made that the subject always already presupposes the "world" and, by this, one means objects that are. We maintain that this claim is far from even seeing the real phenomenon of transcendence and even further from saying anything about it.

What is it supposed to mean that the subject "presupposes" objects that are, "presupposes" that these objects are? There is no sensible meaning to connect with this statement, aside from the fact that we never run across any such pre-supposing. Is it supposed to mean that "we" make in advance the assumption that objects are? On account of some stipulation? By what right do we make that assumption? How did we come to it in the first place? But only on the supposition of the isolated subject. And do those particular beings show themselves as such to us that we only out of kindness, as it were, permit to exist. There is nowhere the trace of any such presupposition. And only one thing is apt in all the talk about presupposing the "world," presupposing objects, and that is that factically existing Dasein always already comes across extant things, has always already in advance come across beings. But beings and their already being in advance do not rest upon a presupposition; nor, as it were, upon a metaphysical fraternizing: let's presuppose beings are and then we want to try to exist amidst them. Our very encounter with extant things sharply contravenes our having presupposed they exist. It implies on the contrary that, as existents, we have no prior need to presuppose objects beforehand.

At any rate, beings (extant things) could never get encountered had they not the opportunity to enter a world. We are speaking therefore of the possible and occasional entrance of beings into world. When and how is this possibility realized? Entry into world is not a process of extant things, in the sense that beings undergo a change thereby and through this change break into the world. The extant's entry into world is "something" that happens to it. World-entry has the characteristic of happening, of history [Geschichte]. World-entry happens when transcendence happens, i.e., when historical Dasein exists. Only then is the being-in-the-world of Dasein existent. And only when the latter is existent, have extant things too already entered world, i.e., become intraworldly. And only Dasein, qua existing, provides the opportunity for world-entry.

Intraworldliness is accordingly not an extant property of extant things in themselves. Extant things are beings as the kind of things they are, even if they do not become intraworldly, even if world-entry does not happen to them and there is no occasion for it at all. Intraworldliness does not belong to the essence of extant things as such, but it is only the transcendental condition, in the primordial sense, for the possibility of extant things being able to emerge as they are. And that means it is the condition for existing Dasein's experience and comprehension of things as they are.

World-entry and its occurrence is the presupposition *not* for extant things to become first extant and enter into that which manifests itself to us as its extantness and which we understand as such. Rather, world-entry and its occurrence is solely the presupposition for extant things announcing themselves in their not requiring world-entry regarding their own being.

As being-in-the-world, transcending Dasein, in each case, factically provides beings with the opportunity for world-entry, and this provision on the part of Dasein consists in nothing other than in transcending.

If, however, intraworldliness is not a property of intraworldly extant things as extant, where does it belong then and how is it itself? It obviously belongs to world and only is along with it; it only happens insofar as being-in-the-world happens. There is world only insofar as Dasein exists. But then is world not something "subjective"? In fact it is! Only one may not at this point reintroduce a common, subjectivistic concept of "subject." Instead, the task is to see that being-in-the-world, which as existent supplies extant things with entry to world, fundamentally transforms the concept of subjectivity and of the subjective.

When Dasein exists, world-entry has simultaneously also already happened together with it, and it has happened in such a way that extant things entering there in principle undergo *nothing*. They remain so completely untouched that it is on account of world-entry that Dasein can, on its part, approach, encounter, and touch them. But if what enters world undergoes nothing in the occurrence of world-entry, is then the world itself nothing? In fact the world is nothing—if "nothing" means: not a being in the sense of something extant; also "nothing" in the sense of no-thing, not one of the beings Dasein itself as such transcends; but Dasein transcends itself as well. The world: a nothing, no being— and yet something; nothing of beings—but being. Thus the world is not nothing in the sense of *"nihil negativum."* What kind of *"nihil"* is the world and then ultimately being-in-the-world itself?

Here we come upon the question about the intrinsic possibility of transcendence itself, of being-in-the-world as the upswing to a surpassive counter-hold, wherein Dasein makes itself known to itself in its metaphysical essence, so as to bind itself primordially as freedom in this self-understanding. I maintain that the intrinsic possibility of transcendence is time, as primordial temporality!

§ 12   Transcendence and temporality
(nihil originarium)

As free, Dasein projects itself on the for-the-sake-of-itself, as the whole of the essential possibilities in its capacity-to-be. Suspending before itself this for-the-sake-of-itself and existing in this suspension, this being applies itself, in its mode, for itself. This self-application for itself can not, as we noted above, mean a solipsistic selfishness. Moreover, only because Dasein as such, as free, applies itself for itself, is Dasein essentially such that in each case it factically stands before the choice of how it should, in a particular case, in the ontic-existentiell sense, apply itself for others and for itself. Or—what is also only possible for freedom as its lack—Dasein comports itself indecisively and lets things matter in each case according to circumstances. The fact that we are only seldom free existentielly, factically, does not contradict the metaphysical essence of Dasein, but supports it. It is misguided to think one understands freedom most purely in its essence if one isolates it as a free-floating arbitrariness. Moreover, the task is precisely the reverse, to conceive freedom in its finitude and to see that, by proving boundedness, one has neither impaired freedom nor curtailed its essence.

What was designated as freedom, being-in-the-world, transcendence, must now, however, be also understood in the way we have shown. All this is not some hidden apparatus inside an isolated subject and its inwardness, but freedom itself transcends, and the surpassing of beings transpires and has always already transpired in freedom; and we always come across these beings as being-in-themselves in a way that we return thereafter into freedom, from out of the origin and within it. All ontic comportment to beings, whether of Dasein's kind or not, transcends, not just insofar as it opens up, insofar as it puts itself in an intentional relation to objects, but the intentional relation is only the given factical mode of appropriating what is already, on account of transcendence, overleapt and thus disclosed.

Untroubled by deeply ingrained ways of looking and questioning, we must learn to see how Dasein, on the basis of its metaphysical constitution, on the basis of being-in-the-world, is always in its very possibility already beyond all beings. And in this being-beyond it does not come up against absolute nothingness. Rather, on the contrary, in this very being-beyond Dasein holds before itself the binding commitment as world and in this counter-hold first can and even must hold itself to beings. Now we have the task of understanding temporality with regard to this basic phenomenon of transcendence.

What is temporality itself and how do we begin to analyze it? One can speculate about time in many different ways; one can start somewhere and try to analyze and interpret it. But our problem does not deal with the usual isolated philosophical speculation about time that always aims in some way toward other philosophical problems. Time, as we have shown, has some relation, however obscure it may still be, to the understanding-of-being as such. Time therefore claims a central systematic function in metaphysics as such; the interpretation of time must then be guided primarily by that central function in metaphysics. The pathway to the interpretation of time is not simple. The one I myself have taken is not the only one, but every pathway is long and runs into obstacles. I am choosing another procedure for our purposes. We will try to suggest the essence of time more directly and dogmatically, which means we will put aside the common way of posing the question about time.

I will try to enumerate briefly the main lines of the common conception of time:

1. Time is itself something extant somewhere and somehow, and it is in motion, and it flows away; as we say, "it passes."

2. As transient (to a certain extent the paradigm of transience in general), time is something "in the soul," in the subject, inside consciousness; thus to have time requires an internal consciousness. Consequently, the possibilities of conceiving and interpreting time are essentially dependent on the particular conception of soul, subject, consciousness, Dasein.

3. Time is something passing, which transpires in the soul but does not yet really belong in the center of the soul. For time has long been seen in connection with space. In space, the spatial is what we experience with our senses. This is likewise true of time. Time belongs to our sensibility (still the case also in the phenomenological conception in Husserl and Scheler). However one may understand sensibility, it remains distinct from mind and reason, which is not itself temporal but outside of time. (One could say without exaggeration that, in Kant, spontaneity as freedom stands immediately alongside of time.)

4. Since Plato, time is frequently distinguished by contrasting it with eternity, and the latter is itself conceived more or less theologically. The temporal then becomes the earthly vis-à-vis the heavenly. From this viewpoint time possesses a certain world-

view quality. This has contributed to one's never having really arrived at insight into the metaphysical significance of the phenomenon of time.

All these descriptions of time, known both to the common as well as the philosophical understanding, can not have been simply arbitrary fabrications and inventions. The essence of time must itself make these kinds of conceptions possible and even plausible. Yet none of them touches exactly the metaphysical essence of time.

If one therefore simplifies matters and from these common perspectives merely assimilates what the fundamental-ontological analysis of time discovers, instead of first appropriating this discovery independently and in terms of its own purpose, then everything falls into confusion. We want to set forth, in a positive way, the main features of the metaphysical essence of time in five points, which do not, however, directly correspond to the four mentioned above.

1. The essence of time has an ecstatic character.

2. Together with this ecstatic structure there is a horizonal character which belongs to time.

3. Time neither passes nor remains but it temporalizes itself. Temporalization is the primal phenomenon of "motion."

4. Time is not relative to sensibility but is more primordial than sensibility and than mind and reason as well. Here we suppose, of course, the only conception of reason with which we are acquainted, that of finite reason.

5. Methodologically we should note that, because it constitutes the metaphysical continuity of Dasein, time is not intelligible if Dasein is construed in some sort of theoretical scheme, whether it be as a psychical whole, as cognitive-volitional subject, as self-awareness, or as the unity of body, soul, and mind. Moreover, the analysis of Dasein must select for its guiding horizon the horizon which, in factic existence, continually guides Dasein's being-toward-itself in its being-with with others and in its relation to beings unlike Dasein prior to, outside of, and despite all theory.

The classical texts on the problem of time are the following: Aristotle's *Physics*, Δ 10–14; Plotinus' *Enneades* III,7; Augustine's *Confessiones*, Book XI; Kant's *Critique of Pure Reason*, the Transcendental Aesthetic, Transcendental Deduction, and the chapter on Schematism, the Analytic of Principles, the Doctrine of Antinomies; Hegel's *Encyclopedie der philosophischen Wissenschaften* (a prior stage in the "Jena Logic") and *Phenomenologie des Geistes*; Bergson, all his writings; Husserl, in *Ideen zu einer rein-*

en Phänomenologie und phänomenologischen Philosophie, Book
One, only brief comments; compare Oskar Becker, "Beiträge zur
phänomenologischen Begründung der Geometrie und ihrer
physikalischen Anwendungen: (in *Jahrbuch für Philosophie und
phänomenologische Forschung*, volume VI, 1923, p. 385 ff.; and
now Husserl's own *Vorlesungen zur Phänomenologie des inneren
Zeitbewusstseins*, which are appearing in Volume IX of the same
Jahrbuch (see further on this below). (The investigations into time
by Aristotle and Augustine are the important ones, and they are
decisive for subsequent periods. More unawares than with clear
intent, Kant later pushed the problem furthest into the dimension
of the truly philosophical problematic.)

We shall restrict ourselves to a discussion of the most important
aspects of the first two points.

Regarding 1, Time has an ecstatic character. We want insight
into this essential characteristic of time. For this we need to recall
briefly the common conception of time, or more precisely, our
usual relationship to time. The fact that we speak about a relationship to time already indicates that time presents itself as some
thing among many others, something to which we also relate
everyday (as we do to space, for instance). That and how we relate
to time is documented by the fact that we customarily wear a
watch on our person, a gauge of time. We do not measure time
simply out of a mere curiosity to ascertain what time it is now. We
rather measure time in such a way as to reckon by the time. "To
reckon by time" does not mean here primarily to count the time
numerically. It means instead *to take it into account*, which
means, to make the most of our time, to use it in the right way, to
lose no time. Everybody is acquainted with time and knows what
he means when he refers to time, and yet he seldom has a conception of time. We have not, however, assimilated this precon-
ceptual acquaintance with time by picking it up somewhere from
others and putting it into ourselves. We do not somehow become
acquainted with time! What we do learn is merely the manner in
which time is measured, the factical concrete ways by which we
best deal with time in a practical way. But every Dasein reveals
time itself—and yet time long remains something strange. Only
seldom do we take possession of time, which possesses our very
selves in a metaphysical sense; only seldom do we become master
of this power which we ourselves are; only seldom do we exist
freely.

However much we may occupy ourselves everyday with time,
more or less consciously, or even pedantically, as often as we talk

of time, naming and discussing it, it remains nevertheless just as indifferent and remote to us. And this is partially the reason why we are blind to its truest essence, even why, moreover, when we wish to conceptualize time, we just conceive it as we do everything directly accessible to us, as we do things.

It is important to free one's vision for the total essence peculiar to that which reveals itself as time. Here we can only place one of the phenomena before our eyes, the one that induces us most directly to conceive the ecstatic character of time, and we want to interpret at least this phenomenon in a relatively concrete way. (Cf. *Die Grundprobleme der Phänomenologie* from the summer semester of 1927, part two,[12] and *Being and Time,* part one.)

We measure time with the aid of numbers and distances, of quantities: from now to back then, from now till then, from this time to that time. We *name* time itself with "now," "then," "at that time." And it is essential to see the way in which these expressions speak of time. If I immediately, completely without reflection, say "now," then it always means: "now—the door slams," "now—I proceed to analyze the structure of time." By "now" we do not mean now, itself, truly thematically; we do not dwell on it in such a way as if we meant "this now has such-and-such a quality; it follows the preceding moment, and a forthwith follows after this now." Rather, we mean "now—the door slams"; we mean the door, and that it is slamming now. We do not mean that the now and the slamming door coincide. We rather mean this peculiar relation between both. But this relation between both, the now and the slamming door, does not first arise by both being at the same time. Instead, the relation belongs to the now as such; only what precisely takes place at this now, however, is arbitrary, i.e., it is not preordained in the now. When we say "now," we are not focused thematically on the now as an isolated now-thing, but the now itself guides and pushes us forward to that which is just transpiring there in the now. This forward-indexical function belongs essentially to the now. This means the now is, in its essence, a "now when this and that . . . ," a "now wherein. . . ." Likewise the other expressions for time: the then is always, usually without our expressing it, a "then when . . . ," the formerly is always a "formerly when. . . ."

These time designations, we said, have the character of

---

12. [*Gesamtausgabe*, volume 24, *Die Grundprobleme der Phänomenologie*, edited by F.W. von Herrmann (Frankfurt a.M., 1975)]. [*The Basic Problems of Phenomenology*, translation, introduction and lexicon by Albert Hofstadter (Bloomington: Indiana University Press, 1982).]

forward-indices, pointing onward to that which now, then, formerly is. Yet, if considered precisely, the phenomenal content of the situation is the converse: we are not focused on the now so as to be then guided onward toward things and processes that are "in" time. We are, rather, occupied with things, related to them, and we then apply to them these time designations in more or less fixed numerical measurements. "The door slams—now: now the door slams." But does the now still remain, unthematically, prior to everything? At any rate, in saying "now" I do not make the now into a thematic object; I do not address myself to it as such, as I do to the door or the blackboard.

This shows that we do not come across the now, then, and formerly as we do extant things, but that we nonetheless do say "now" with a peculiar immediacy. We do not have spread before us a so-called sequence of nows from which we then pick one, grab it, and name it. We are not even purposely focused on time, and yet we have it immediately "at hand" even when we do not even assert "now" and "formerly" on purpose. Again, the most elementary example of this is our use of the clock, and we need not even reflect on a conscious use. It belongs to the essence of using clocks that, when I read off the time, I do not ask, "How much time is it?" but rather, for example, "How much time do I still have?" I do not state the now, but I, moreover, immediately read off the time and only latently say "now." Where do we then really get that which we mean and understand, though unthematically, in our uttering "now," "then," and "formerly"?

Let us follow, for example, the interpretation of the "then." We never use "then" in isolation but, for example, in arranging and organizing: "Then this should happen," "Then that might result." Or in a reflection on our plans: "Then perhaps this will come about, and this is therefore what is to be done." Or, however, when we are involved in such deliberative considerations we ask, "What then?" In planning, we do intend something to which we are related, only what we intend remains indefinite and indeterminable. Here we utter the "then" from within a relatedness to something to which we relate as planning, deliberating, being pre-occupied [vor-sorgend]. Stated quite generally, we utter "then" from out of a *mode of existence* in which we are *expectant* of a thing to come, of something to be accomplished. Only in such expectation can I utter a "then." Expectant, we naturally say "then and then" without purposely adverting to these thens. We are always adverting to that which will be then or should be. In themselves these thens are not such that our expectation would be merely a kind of grasping of the thens, in the way that perception has access to a material thing (the blackboard). Rather, expecting *provides of itself*, as expecting, the then. The then is that in which expectation utters itself, is thus something in expectation itself. In expecting, and only in it, slumbers, as it were, the then.

But, just as we do not come across the then in an object which will be "then" or should be, neither do we find the then somewhere in the soul as a psychical process or as a property of a psychical process. Neither in objects nor in subjects (in the traditional conception), neither here nor there but, as it were, on the way from the subject to the object! But we are already acquainted with this "on-the-way," as the stepping-over, as *transcendence*. This on-the-way is only a reference to the "location" where, in the end, that "is" which we utter as time character.

The then arises from and in an expecting, and it permits of various unambiguous definitions, within certain limits, of course. These are possibilities that are not important for us now, since we are seeking something else. But what we laid out regarding the "then" is true of the "formerly" and the "now" in a corresponding way. The "formerly" always pronounces a *retention* of something previous. It is irrelevant here to what extent and how precisely we recall what is previous; we could even have forgotten it. In other words, the "formerly" is equally the utterance of a *forgetting*. The "now" accordingly pronounces being toward what presences [Anwesendes], and we term this being toward presencing things a holding in attendance or, more generally, *making present*.

Let us turn again to the phenomenon of the then. It emerges from expecting as such and is neither a property of objects nor of subjects. Yet we have not thereby finally exhausted its essential character but have, for the moment, overlooked something quite essential. The then, which is utterable and arises in making-present, is always understood as "now not yet" (but rather: then). Whichever then I may choose, the then as such always refers in each case back to a now, or more precisely, the then is understood on the basis of a now, however inexplicit. Conversely, every formerly is a "now no longer" and is as such, in its structure, the bridge to a now. But this now is, in each case, the now of a particular making-present or retention in which a "then" and a "formerly" is, in each case, uttered. With this we see a peculiar connection, still obscure in its essence, between the formerly, then, and now. In the common understanding we call time the mere sequence of nows (now, not yet now—forthwith, now no longer—just now). And in a certain way we also know that time is not an accumulation of nows but a continuum; again, not a rigid continuum, but one which flows (the "stream of time"). But, however time, thus understood, may be defined, and, whether or not a definition might be successful from this viewpoint, it has in any case become clear that then, formerly, and now emerge, and do so in their *unity*, from expectance, retention, and making-present—which obviously must first be unitary among and in themselves.

If, however, time means something we come upon here as emergent, then the origin of what emerges and what lets it emerge must evidently be that which, all the more, and in the primordial sense, deserves to be called *time*. Time is therefore originally this expectance, retention, and making-present.

N.B. Bergson first worked out the connection between a derived and an original time. But he did so in a way that went too far and said that time, once emerged, is space. Bergson thereby blocked the way to the real understanding of derived time, since he, in principle, mistakes the essence of emergent time, insofar as he does not view as emergent the time that has emerged. But, conversely, insofar as he stays merely with the time that has emerged, he does not really succeed either in clarifying primordial and genuine time in its essence. Bergson's analyses nonetheless belong to the most intense analyses of time that we possess. It has become a commonplace that Bergson (as well as Dilthey) is fuzzy and must be therefore re-examined and improved. But Bergson's "images" are the very expression of his exertions to really grasp the phenomenon within the realm he takes for his theme. The lack does not lie in an alleged fuzziness—Bergson is perfectly clear in what he sees. But it lies in the overly narrowed realm of his set of problems. Nor would this be removed by a revision for "greater exactness." As everyone knows, there are also exact trivialities in philosophy!

To repeat: expectancy, retention, and making-present are not merely the way we grasp the then, the formerly, and the now, not merely modes of being conscious of them; they are rather the very origin of the then, the formerly, and the now. Expectancy is not a mode of being conscious of time but, in a primordial and genuine sense is time itself.

In his *Vorlesungen zur Phänomenologie des inneren Zeitbewusstseins* in volume IX of the *Jahrbuch*[13] (from his Göttingen

---

13. [Published in the *Jahrbuch für Philosophie und phänomenologische Forschung*, volume 9, and, separately, Halle, 1928, edited by Martin Heidegger. Now in *Husserliana*, volume X: *Zur Phänomenologie des inneren Zeitbewusstseins* (1893–1917), edited by R. Boehm, the Hague, 1966.] [An English translation by James Churchill was published as *The Phenomenology of Internal Time-Consciousness* (Bloomington: Indiana University Press, 1964).]

lectures of 1904/05), Husserl investigated the problem of time in a rather definite context, and this context is characteristic for his line of vision. Husserl speaks of the "internal time-consciousness," and he analyzes especially, as forms of this consciousness of time, remembrance, presentification, representification, expectation [Erinnerung, Vergegenwärtigung, Wiedervergegenwärtigung, Erwartung]. These phenomena are, however, suggested to him for investigation on account of a quite different problematic, namely, that of intentionality as such, i.e., an analysis of consciousness as consciousness-of. (But even Aristotle already discussed μνήμη and ἐλπίς.) The problem of time develops, also, along with the interpretation of phenomena such as perception, phantasy, consciousness, and memory. Here memory gets conceived as a particular knowledge about what is past. So here too time still remains an efflux of the nows, just thens, and right aways, to which a quite definite sort of knowledge of them corresponds. With regard to all previous interpretations, it was Husserl's service to have seen these phenomena for the first time, with the aid of the intentional structure. A glance at contemporary psychology or epistemology suffices for assessing the importance of the step made here. Concerning the problem of time, nevertheless, everything remains, in principle, as it was, so much so that time gets understood as something immanent; it remains something internal, "in the subject." Hence the title, "internal time-consciousness." Husserl's whole investigation originated from his observations of the primary and primordial consciousness of time in the knowledge about a merely experential datum; the whole investigation thus circles continually around the phenomenon of the temporal occurrence of a sound. These lectures are important (aside from the concrete analyses of memory, perception, etc.) for the sharper development of intentionality beyond the *Logical Investigations*. That which Husserl still calls time-consciousness, i.e., consciousness of time, is precisely time, itself, in the primordial sense.

We purposely call primordial time *temporality* in order to express the fact that time is not additionally on-hand, but that its essence is temporal. This means that time "is" not, but rather temporalizes itself. Thus every attempt to fit time into any sort of being-concept must necessarily falter. If one tries to master it with the aid of dialectic, that is an escape, as is all dialectic.

Temporality in its temporalizing is the primordially self-unifying unity of expectancy, retention, and making-present. We came across this unity in our recourse to the most accessible time of the

utterance ("then," "formerly," "now"). We did so by having re-
flected on the essentials, namely, that the "then" is a "then, when
... ," which means it is in each case determinable, in essence, by
way of some being. We call this character of time its datability. In
the "then, when ... ," an onward-reference occurs in the manner
of an *indicator over to* beings, which themselves have a "when"
and can thus date the "then." This indicator must bring uttered
time along with it from out of primordial temporality, if it belongs
to its essential structure. To what extent can this indicator be made
evident in primordial temporality?

We will again proceed from the "then" as expectance. Comportment toward the sort of thing of which we say "it will be
'then'" are, for example, hoping or fearing or awaiting. We call
these modes intentional comportments toward the futural. Hoping
is not fearing and conversely; awaiting is not necessarily hoping or
fearing and can itself manifest several variations: eager impa-
tience, and indifferent letting-come-what-may. But all these comportments would not be possible, i.e., this directing oneself
toward something that will somehow be "then" would have no
open direction if the Dasein that hopes, fears, etc., did not, as Dasein as such, stretch itself into a then-quality, completely aside
from what it might encounter from the then. What we called expecting [Gewärtigen] is nothing other than that getting-carried-
away [Entrückung] into the then-quality which lies at the basis of
those comportments, which has previously already overleapt all
possible beings about which we can and must say, they will be
"then." And because the then and each particular then is essentially only the utterance and expression of this expectance that is
potentially in advance always carried away beyond all beings, for
this reason the then is, corresponding to this getting-carried-away,
in its own structure an indicator, datable.

Conversely, expecting is, as we say, ecstatic. The ecstasy mentioned here, stepping out itself (ἔκστασις) is to some extent a *raptus* [rapture]. This means Dasein does not become gradually expectant by traversing serially the beings that factually approach it
as things in the future, but this traversing rather goes gradually
through the open path made way by the raptus of temporality itself. Now this is true, in a corresponding manner, of retention and
making-present. And we therefore call these three basic
phenomena the *ecstases* of temporality. Temporality is itself the
self-unifying ecstatic unity in ecstatic temporalization.

Expectance implies a being-ahead-of-oneself. It is the basic
form of the toward-oneself, or more exactly, it enables the like as

such. Expectance means to understand oneself from out of one's own capacity-for-being; one's own capacity-for-being is in turn understood in the essential metaphysical breadth to which belong being-with and being-by. Expecting one's own capability-for-being as mine, I have also come toward myself already and precisely through expecting. This approaching oneself in advance, from one's own possibility, is the primary ecstatic concept of the *future*. We can illustrate this structure, insofar as this is possible at all, in this way (the question mark indicates the horizon that remains open):

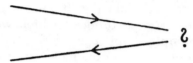

But this coming-to-oneself does not, as such, stretch over a momentary present of my own; it stretches over the whole of my having-been. More precisely—and here is our claim—this having-been-ness temporalizes itself only from out of and in the future. The having-been is not a remnant of myself that has stayed behind and has been left behind by itself. Neither is it what Bergson likes to illustrate with various images: the future unrolls, as it were, while the past is rolled up on another roll, which can be roughly illustrated in the picture below.

Presenting it this way would be correct insofar as the immanent connection of future and having-been-ness are suggested by the picture; but it would be misleading because the has-been is not something remaining by itself, nor is it an accumulating dead weight I haul behind me and to which I could occasionally relate in one way or another. Rather, my having-been only "is," in each case, according to the mode of the temporalization of the future, and only in the temporalization. What-has-been is, of course, no longer something present, and to that extent one might arrive at the common inference that nothing can be altered; it is finished. This is not the way it is. The having-been-ness, rather, of what-has-been becomes the having-been, first of all and constantly, in the respective future. The very fact that we say "we are not capable of getting rid of the past" indicates a certain mode of our having-been. What we find here expressed regarding the essence of temporality is that the future ecstasis, as a coming-towards, stretches out immediately, constantly, and primarily into the having-been.

There are indeed definite reasons why forgetting is the predominant mode of having-been. That is, it seems as if that what has been "is" no longer there, and that, in understanding itself, Dasein could indeed come back toward itself from out of its capacity-to-be, but does so toward the momentary present that has just closed the door behind itself to having-been-ness. But this closing of the door is already a way of temporalizing the having-been, a temporalizing which, in its way, brings into being the having-been. And the *making-present* first temporalizes itself in the ecstatic unity of future and having-been-ness. This basic sort of temporalization is the result of interpreting temporality in itself.

Were we to choose uttered time for our starting point, as does the common and traditional interpretation of time, then the most proximate is, as always, the present, which means "here is the now," and the no-longer-now and the not-yet-now are then the two arms which extend time, as the now, into the respective directions of non-being. This image, and the time analysis derived from it, become unavoidable as soon as one overlooks the ecstatic character of temporality and does not inquire into the unity of temporality as that which temporalizes itself ecstatically.

We say this to fend off a likely misunderstanding, namely, the belief that temporality is indeed a threefold being-carried-away, but one which operates in such a way that these three ecstases flow together somehow in one substance, just as a living animal can stretch out feelers in different directions and then retract them again. The whole of these three ways of being-carried-away does not center in a kind of thing which would of itself lack any being-carried-away, something present on hand unecstatically and which would be the common center for initiating and unfolding the ecstases. Moreover, the unity of the ecstases is itself ecstatic. It needs no support and pillars, as does the arch of a bridge. But if we may speak at all about the "being" of the ecstases, we must say that its being lies directly in the free ecstatic momentum. Bergson speaks of this phenomenon with his term "élan," and he saw something essential here too, only he applied it too hastily, in general metaphysics, to all different forms of beings, without focusing on the ecstatic structure of time and its horizonal character. As a result, élan has only an ontic character and is, so to speak, directed forwards.

Temporalization is the free oscillation of the whole of primordial temporality; time reaches and contracts itself. (And only because of momentum is there throw, facticity, *thrownness;* and only because of oscillation is there *projection.* Cf. the problem of time and being referred to in *Being and Time.*)

It is therefore essential, in first defining the unity of temporality, to eliminate the notion of anything thing-like, present on hand, which is between, as it were, having-been-ness and the future. Nor should one smuggle in any sort of personal center, an I-nucleus, but the essence of time lies in the ecstatic unitary oscillation. The unity of horizon belongs to this peculiar unity of time.

Regarding 2. What do we mean by the *horizonal character* of the ecstases? We understand "horizon" to be the circumference of the field of vision. But horizon, from ὁρίζειν, is not at all primarily related to looking and intuiting, but by itself means simply that which delimits, encloses, the *enclosure.* And the ecstases are, of course, not an awareness of, not a consciousness, and even less a looking.

Now we say each ecstasis encloses itself and does so precisely as ἔκστασις. One could believe the converse to be the case, that being-carried-away is the very leap over every barrier. Certainly there is, on its own, nothing determinate in expectance itself; it is not able to decide for itself, and certainly never unambiguously, what, on its basis, can be expected and how it can be expected. But the being-carried-away as such nonetheless provides something, just something futural as such, futurity as such, i.e., possibility pure and simple. Of itself the ecstasis does not produce a definite possible, but it does produce the horizon of possibility in general, within which a definite possible can be expected. We must keep in mind, however, that the ecstasis surpasses every being and the horizon is not located, say, in the sphere of the subject. Hence this horizon is also nowhere, since it presents no determinate being: it is neither spatially nor temporally located, in the usual sense. It "is" not as such, but it temporalizes itself. The horizon manifests itself in and with the ecstasis; it is its *ecstema* (formed analogically as, say, σύστημα is to σύστασις or σύνθημα to σύνθεσις). And, corresponding to the unity of ecstases in their temporalization, the unity of horizons is a primordial unity.

This ecstematic unity of the horizon of temporality is nothing other than the temporal condition for the possibility of *world* and of world's essential belonging to *transcendence.* For transcendence has its possibility in the unity of ecstatic momentum. This oscillation of the self-temporalizing ecstases is, as such, the upswing, regarded as [swinging] toward all possible beings that can factically enter there into a world. The ecstematic temporalizes itself, oscillating as a worlding [Welten]. *World entry* happens only insofar as something like ecstatic oscillation temporalizes itself as a particular temporality.

World-entry is based on the temporalization of temporality. The primal fact, in the metaphysical sense, is that there is anything like temporality at all. The entrance into world by beings is primal history [Urgeschichte] pure and simple. From this primal history a region of problems must be developed which we are today beginning to approach with greater clarity, the region of the mythic. The metaphysics of myth must come to be understood out of this primal history, and it can be done with the aid of a metaphysical construct of primal time, i.e., the time with which primal history itself begins.

By pointing to the ecstatic and horizonal essence-constitution of time as temporality, our aim was to suggest the intrinsic possibility of transcendence. Only through an exposition of the phenomenon of care could we, at this point, give a more concrete definition of transcendence. We would have to show how facticity and individuation are grounded in temporality, which, as temporalization, unifies itself in itself and individuates in the metaphysical sense, as *principium individuationis*. But this individuation is the presupposition for the primordial commerce between Dasein and Dasein.

Now you see a distinct correspondence between this and Leibniz's monadology, but also that wherein they differ. Our exposition of the monadology was already guided by the interpretation of Dasein as temporality, especially by an insight into the essence of transcendence. We can say, at this point, that the interpretation of the monadology as I have given it was exaggerated on purpose, and was so in two respects: 1) insofar as we conceived the basic determinations of the monad, *repraesentatio* and *appetitus*, primarily as intentional structures; 2) insofar as we clarified the latter as transcendental structures, i.e., in their relatedness to the universe, "world"; for this reason the monad can be defined as a *mundus concentratus*. The essential difference between Leibniz's interpretation of the monad and my interpretation of Dasein as temporality lies in the followng: in Leibniz the realization of the truly metaphysical sense of his conception is hindered by the fact that he, in principle, places the Cartesian *ego cogito* at the basis of his conception of the monad, of the I; that he also takes the monad as a substance enclosed in its sphere, even though he incorporates the whole world in this immanence and its [the monad's] contents. Leibniz can therefore say, Monads need no windows, because they already have everything on the interior. We would say, conversely, they have no windows, not because they have everything within, but because there is neither inside nor outside—because temporalization (drive) in itself implies the ecstatic happening of world-entry, insofar as transcendence is already in itself the possible leap over possible beings that can enter into a world. Thus time is not a *mundus concentratus* but the converse. Time is essentially a self-opening and expanding into a world. I will not go into the comparison any further, particularly the question of the extent to which one might conceive the interpretation of Dasein as temporality in a universal-ontological way—just as the monadology is presented as an exposition of the whole universe of beings. This is a question which I myself am not able to decide, one which is still completely unclear to me.

It must also have become clearer to what extent we can say about the world that it is a *nothing*. What sort of *nihil* is it? Insofar as we treat world at all, make it a problem and try to prove it is essential, for transcendence, it must be something. If it is a *nihil*, then it must not be a *nihil negativum*, i.e., not the simple pure empty negation of something. The world is nothing in the sense that it is nothing that is. It is nothing that is yet something that "is there." The "there is" ["es" of "es gibt"] which is this not-a-being is itself not being, but is the self-temporalizing temporality. And what the latter, as ecstatic unity, temporalizes is the unity of its horizon, the world. World is the nothing which temporalizes itself primordially, that which simply arises in and with temporalization. We therefore call it the *nihil originarium*.

Yet the *origo* of transcendence is temporality itself, and it is origin in such a way that transcendence too, and that means world-entry, happens with temporalization. There is time, in the common sense, only with the temporalization of temporality, with the happening of world-entry. And there are also intratemporal beings, such that transpire "in time," only insofar as world-entry happens and intraworldly beings become manifest for Dasein.

We see then the peculiar productivity intrinsic to temporality, in the sense that the product is precisely a peculiar nothing, the world. Kant, for the first time, came upon this primordial productivity of the "subject" in his doctrine of the transcendental productive imagination. He did not succeed, of course, in evaluating this knowledge in its radical consequences, by which he would have had to, as it were, raze his own building with the help of the new insight. On the contrary, this great intuition was, in principle, lost. Nevertheless, this first advance into the transcendental imagination, which was for Kant only obscurely connected with time, was the first moment in the history of philosophy in which metaphysics endeavored to liberate itself from logic, and from a logic which had not found and never did find its own essence in metaphysics, but remained a training grown superficial and formalistic. Perhaps the true happening in the history of philosophy is always but a temporalization [Zeitigung] of such "moments" in distant intervals and strokes, moments which never become manifest as what they really are. But this productivity of the subject (taken in the transcendental sense) has, as is always the case for something philosophically central, already emerged somewhere in all real philosophy. For example I refer to Heraclitus (Fragment 115): φυχῆς ἐστι λόγος ἑαυτὸν αὔξων; Dasein is the being that enriches itself out of itself in the manner of understanding. In Dasein itself is essentially the primordial intrinsic possibility of enrichment; Dasein always has the character of being-richer-than, of outstripping.

§ 13. *Transcendence temporalizing itself in temporality and the essence of ground*

Temporality temporalizes itself primarily out of the future. This means that the ecstatic whole of temporality, and hence the unity of horizon, is determined primarily out of the future. That is the metaphysical way of saying that the world, which is grounded in nothing else than the ecstatic totality of the time horizon, temporalizes itself primarily out of the *for-the-sake-of*. This for-the-sake-of is, in each case, the for-the-sake-of of willing, of freedom, i.e., of the transcending being-toward-oneself. But this for-the-sake-of has the intrinsic possibility of such a coming-toward-oneself in the mode of binding only in the ecstatic temporalization of the primordial making-present, i.e., in the future in which, or better, as which the backward movement of Dasein constitutes itself. But in its essence, the future is not an isolated or even self-isolating ecstasis. Rather, the more primordially futural, the more retrocursive temporality is, and in this way occurs the whole of temporality and the temporalization of its ecstematic horizon.

Being-in-the-world, transcending toward world, temporalizes itself as temporality and is only possible in this way. This implies that world-entry only happens if temporality temporalizes itself.

And only if this happens can beings manifest themselves as beings. But insofar as this is possible only on the basis of the understanding-of-being, the possibility of the understanding-of-being must reside in the temporalization of temporality. Beings enter "into time" in and with the temporalization of temporality and the world-entry of beings; beings become understood and determined as intra-temporal. Because the event of the world-entry of beings is the primal event and is, in essence, temporalization, there is a tendency, even in the pre-philosophical comportment to beings and in the common pre-ontological determining of being, to effect the determination of being by reference to time. In the enigmatic and not at all arbitrary tendency to understand beings as intratemporal, extra- and supra-temporal, we have a testimony to the metaphysical primal history of Dasein as temporality. Dasein as temporality thereby sets itself the task of understanding itself in its temporalization.

In other words, metaphysics belongs to the nature of human beings. And for this reason human Dasein has, in its essence, a predeliction [Vor-liebe] for metaphysics. We can also say, all existing is already a philosophizing. Philosophy, it has always been known, should not be derived from somewhere else, but it must ground itself. This "itself" arises because philosophy belongs essentially to the self-hood of Dasein. This is not to say that, in fact, a training in philosophy is simply necessary, just as, conversely, the business of philosophical erudition or the emergence of a literature calling itself philosophical does not yet, in distinction to philosophizing, vouch for the existence of philosophy. But, in order to exist, everything genuine needs semblance. There is neither a philosophy, in all its purity, nor a sophistry with a complete monopoly. Both belong together in a particular historical "culture" which is possible in many diverse ways.

The way we suggest for the self-grounding of philosophy cannot be pursued here further. Our purpose is different, though no less important. We have finally brought to light the essential connection between transcendence and temporality, of which we sought the main features. The stepping-beyond beings in transcendence, which is carried out toward all dimensions, is grounded in the ecstatic constitution of temporality. Stepping-over to world means nothing other than that the ecstatic unity of temporality has, as the unity of being-carried-away, a horizon temporalized primarily out of the future, the for-the-sake-of: the world. To transcend is to be-in-the-world. But we strove for a metaphysical clarification of transcendence for the purpose of revealing the essence of *ground*. The essence of ground, however, was a problem for us, because giving reasons and reasonableness [Begründung und Begründbarkeit] belong to *truth*. But, properly understood and taken universally, truth is the theme of logic. Clarifying the essence of ground, or the way thereto, should not only provide us with insight into this essence, but should simultaneously bring us to see that logic is nothing other than the metaphysics of truth.

What then is the essence of ground? Just as important, even more decisive than a straight, apparently reassuring and merely learnable answer to this question, is familiarity with the way it is worked out. This is because the answer can only be given in traversing and repeating the pathway of the question. Now, however, an answer should be attempted to the question about the essence of ground, with all the reservations that any such answer contains when taken as, so to speak, a definition and isolated claim.

When we inquire into the essence of ground, we are not seeking particular grounds for something, but we are rather looking for insight into that which ground as such means, for the way ground as such is intrinsically possible, and that means how it is metaphysically necessary. The inquiry into the essence of grounds can be put into a formula which formulates the problem as: Why do we ask, not just factically but essentially, qua Dasein, about the *why?* Why is there anything such as a why and a because? Because Dasein exists, i.e., because transcendence temporalizes! To transcend, however, is the ecstatic being-toward-itself in the mode of for-the-sake-of-itself. The *for-the-sake-of,* as primary character of world, i.e., of transcendence, is the primal *phenomenon of ground as such.* Because we are in the manner of an existing that transcends, in the manner of being-in-the-world, and the latter is temporalization, we therefore ask about the why.

But this statement is still misleading. It does not mean that, because we are in fact actual, we are also interested in our whence and whither. The question is, moreover: Whence arises this interest at all, metaphysically, the interest that is, in every case, related to all beings and not merely to ourselves? The origin of anything like ground lies in the essence of existence defined as transcendental, i.e., in Dasein's being-carried-away into the for-the-sake-of itself. If for-the-sake-of is, as such, the primal phenomenon of ground, then ground transcends all beings according to all their various *modi essentiae* and *existentiae.*

The for-the-sake-of is not something adrift, but it temporalizes itself in *freedom.* As ecstatic self-projection on its own capacity-for-being, freedom understands itself from out of this capacity and at the same time holds this capacity before itself as responsibility. Freedom is consequently the *origin of anything like ground.* We can make this pithy by saying freedom is the metaphysical essence of transcending, existing Dasein. But freedom is qua transcendental freedom toward ground. To be free is to understand oneself from out of one's own capacity-to-be; but "oneself" and "one's own" are not understood individually or egoistically, but metaphysically. They are understood in the basic possibilities of transcending Dasein, in the capacity-to-be-with with others, in the capacity-to-be by extant things, in the factic existentiell capacity-to-be in each case toward oneself.

To understand oneself out of the for-the-sake-of means to understand oneself from out of ground. This self-understanding must have already made itself manifold into the basic possibilities of itself according to what I have termed the intrinsic bestrewal of Dasein (§ 10). The essence of ground differentiates itself into diverse sorts of "grounds" (e.g., the four causes), not because there are different beings, but because the metaphysical essence of Dasein as transcending has the possibility of first establishing world-access for diverse beings. And because Dasein transcends itself, Dasein is groundable for its own self-understanding along different possible directions in different ways, but never in a single way. As a being, factical Dasein has different possibilities for ontic understanding and knowing (historical, biological, psychological, cosmological). But the manifoldness of possible grounding, the variety of possible understandings of Dasein, must indeed be interpreted in itself still as manifoldness, and as a coherent manifoldness. It must be shown how the essence of Dasein as factical Dasein demands, not only with regard to itself but in the whole breadth of its possible transcendence, a variety of ways of inquiring, knowing, grounding, and proving.

This problematic will only then have a guiding clue, however, when it has become clear where the essence of ground is as such rooted, namely in the freedom of Dasein as the freedom toward ground. And only this freedom "is" and understands itself as the origin of responsibility. Because the for-the-sake-of is the recoiling for-the-sake-of-itself, freedom is, out of essential necessity, ultimately the *ground of ground.*

We even inquire about the why in this very form: Why the why? And so, it seems, one could ask further about the why of the why of the why, etc. Of itself such further questioning has the appearance of a radicality that never stops, but it is a semblance only and really thoughtlessness. For in the question about the why of the why, there are not simply two whys together in formal conjunction, which conjunction could then be reiterated in a correspondingly formal way. Rather, the why that questions, i.e., the first why that asks about the second why, is grounded as such in what is inquired about, i.e., in the why it puts into question. Thus, in the end, it is the questioning why that is to be defined, and that definition is nothing other than the essence of the why brought into question.

In generally clarifying the essence of ground as such, we have brought out two regions of problems: 1) clarification of the origin of the plurality of grounds, the forms of ground, i.e., the bestrewal of ground; 2) interpretation of the essential recoiling of ground back into one ground (thrownness in itself). This recoiling of ground, i.e., this turning round of Dasein, is a question connected in the closest way with the first question, as is shown by the "circle" of the understanding (cf. *Being and Time*). We cannot go into both groups of problems any further here. We are moreover attempting to clarify the essence of ground with one further step, so as to arrive at the goal of our course, which is insight into logic as the metaphysics of truth.

The primal phenomenon of ground is the for-the-sake-of, which belongs to transcendence. Maintaining itself in the for-the-sake-of and binding itself with it, freedom is freedom toward ground. Being-free, however, is understanding oneself out of possibility. It was said already, in the analysis of the concept of world, that there is, in the phenomenon of world, what we called an "overstepping." Freedom as the ecstatic being-toward-possibilities is thus, in itself, a swinging-over into possibilities. Insofar then as freedom (taken transcendentally) constitutes the essence of Dasein, Dasein, as existing, is always, in essence, necessarily "further" than any given factical being. On the basis of this upswing, Dasein is, in each case, beyond beings, as we say, but it is beyond in such a way that it, first of all, experiences beings in their resistance, against which transcending Dasein is powerless. The powerlessness is metaphysical, i.e., to be understood as essential; it cannot be removed by reference to the conquest of nature, to technology, which rages about in the "world" today like an unshackled beast; for this domination of nature is the real proof for the metaphysical powerlessness of Dasein, which can only attain freedom in its history.

N.B. To be sure, the natural and human sciences are not two different groups of sciences which differ in their development of concepts and methods of proof or differ in that the one occupies itself with sulphuric acid and the other with poems. Instead, they differ as basic possibilities of the free encounter of the metaphysical essence of Dasein with its world, which is, in itself, one and the same.

Only because, in our factical intentional comportment toward beings of every sort, we, outstripping in advance, return to and arrive at beings from possibilities, only for this reason can we let beings themselves be what and how they are. And the converse is true. Because, as factically existing, transcending already, in each case, encounters beings, and because, with transcendence and world-entry, the powerlessness, understood metaphysically, is manifest, for this reason Dasein, which can be powerless (metaphysically) only as free, must hold itself to the condition of the possibility of its powerlessness, to the freedom to ground. And it is for this reason that we essentially place every being, as being, into question regarding its ground.

We inquire into the why in our comportment toward beings of every sort, because in ourselves possibility is higher than actuality, because with Dasein itself this being-higher becomes existent. This being-higher of the possible, vis-à-vis the actual, is only existent when temporality temporalizes itself. If one, however, sees in the temporalization of temporality the being of what is more being than other beings, then it is true that πρότερον ἐνέργεια δυνάμεώς ἐστιν (Aristotle, *Metaphysics* Θ 8, 1049 b 5): "Actuality is prior to possibility"—namely, precisely because possibility is higher than actuality.

In its metaphysical essence, Dasein is the inquirer into the why. The human being is not primarily the nay-sayer (as Scheler said in one of his last writings), but just as little is the human being a yea-sayer. The human is rather the why-questioner. But only because man is in this way, can he and must he, in each case, say, not only yes or no, but essentially yes and no. In traditional academic logic the seemingly innocuous banalities found under the terms "positive and negative judgment" ultimately move in this dimension.

§ 14. *The Essence of ground and the idea of logic*

Logic is, we said at the beginning of these lectures, knowledge of the λόγος, the statement. Its basic characteristic is truth. It emerged further that the truth of statements is founded primarily on comportments which do not have the character of statements, such as intuiting and the like. The latter have the character of disclosing and, as ontic truth about beings, they are grounded in the understanding-of-being, i.e., in what makes the disclosability of beings possible. That is, however, world-entry, and that means the happening of a being-in-the-world. Understanding-of-being is transcendence; all understanding-of-being, whether unthematically pre-ontological, or thematic and conceptually ontological, is transcendental. This understanding-of-being and its essential basic modes is the disclosure that resides in the ecstatic unity of temporality, in the temporalizing breaking-open of horizons. This disclosure is the metaphysically primordial being-true, the truth, which is transcendence itself, *veritas transcendentalis*. It is the condition for the possibility of every ontic-intentional truth.

With the happening of transcendence, of transcendental truth, beings are already discovered as well, though we see, from the essence of truth as such and the metaphysical beginning of the happening of transcendence, that beings are, in the first instance and at length, concealed and that truth must be called unconcealedness with reference to this primary concealedness. Beings are generally concealed, as long as no world-entry happens as such. There is accordingly a deep insight in the Greek word for truth, ἀ-λήθεια. Beings must first of all be torn from concealment; concealment must be removed from beings, and it gets removed inasmuch as temporalizing temporality provides the occasion for world-entry. It can be shown everywhere in pre-Socratic philosophy and in Plato and Aristotle that this interpretation of the peculiarly privative, negative character of the Greek conception of truth is not etymological trifling. Let one statement of Heraclitus serve as reference, (Fragment 123): φύσις κρύπτεσθαι φιλεῖ, the being in itself and its essence loves to conceal itself and to remain in concealment.

Truth resides in the essence of transcendence; it is primordially transcendental truth. But if the basic theme of logic is truth, then logic itself is metaphysics if the problem of transcendence presents in another way the fundamental theme of metaphysics, as I have tried to show.

Only one thing is correct in the traditional and nowadays usual emphasis on the form of judgment as the center of logic, and that is that truth is shifted to the center. But then there must be a radical inquiry into the essence of truth. Metaphysics should not be transported into logic, or the converse. The point is not a division into disciplines, but the disciplines, moreover, are themselves the problem.

Now we saw that traditional logic is the science of propositions, of thinking, and its main purpose is to define the laws of thought and statement. The character of these laws (whether natural laws, norms, or laws of a wholly different sort) remains shaky. The usual laws in the usual sequence are: the principle of identity, the principle of non-contradiction, the principle of grounds [Grund]. And we saw that, for Leibniz, the primal truth is the *identitas* A=A, because he sees the essence of truth in identity.

Our claim is that the first grounding statement [Grundsatz— principle] of logic is the statement of ground. This claim, however, is not simply the reversal of the traditional order, but it is spoken out of the radicalization of logic toward metaphysics. The grounding statement of ground is not a rule and norm for making assertions; it is moreover the first grounding statement [Grundsatz] of logic as metaphysics. Now we saw that the primary theme of logic is transcendental truth, transcendence. What sense does this recourse to the statement of ground have? And correspondingly, what is the character of such "statements" which we call grounding statements [Grund-sätze].

These questions can only be answered by reference to the essence of ground. The primal phenomenon of ground is the for-the-sake-of. The origin of "ground" lies in freedom as the freedom for ground. The for-the-sake-of, however, is the primary character of world. World-projection in freedom is nothing other than the temporalization of the understanding-of-being. If ground qua for-the-sake-of is thus the primary character of world, and if world, however, is being, as it is understood in the understanding of being, and if being establishes world-entry for beings, i.e., lets beings be understood as beings, *then "ground" belongs essentially to being*. From this ensues the true metaphysical sense of the principle of ground. The principle states that the basic, grounding character [Grundcharacter] of ground as such belongs to the essence of being as such. And then from this the rule follows, in several phases of formulation, that making statements about beings must give grounds for itself because statements are disclosive assertions about beings.

The chains of proof in ontic argumentation do not primarily constitute the context of proof in the positive sciences, but they rather have their foundation in ontology. The primary grounds or, more exactly, the tendency to ground is here in the understanding-of-being. Science must offer grounds because it is ontic (treats beings).

Once the statement of ground has been provided with a transcendental exposition, its metaphysical contexts can be easily read off in retrospect from the common formulation of the principle of reason, *nihil est sine ratione: omne ens habet rationem*. "Every being has its ground" means that beings must, insofar as they disclose themselves as beings, ground themselves, because ground belongs to the being of beings. Nevertheless, "ground" is conceived here much further and much more radically than the traditional concept of *ratio*.

Now the statement-character of this statement also emerges from this. It is simply the first ground-statement [Grund-satz, principle], because it is the statement of ground. This means that all basic ground statements [Grund-sätze] are grounded in the statement of ground, and this is so in quite different ways and not only because they share the formal character with the principle of ground. But there can be, in particular, no thought here of any kind of linear deduction from the one principle (such as the deduction Fichte attempted from the principle of identity). Rather, if these principles are grounded in the principle of ground, this means these ground-principles too can only be interpreted from out of the ground of ground, i.e., from freedom, and that means from temporality.

Now already in first describing the true meaning of the principle of reason in Leibniz, we tried to show that the common formula emphasizes something important, the *potius quam* [rather than]. There is a preference-character in the principle of reason. What we have then been able to show, positively, concerning the essence and origin of ground out of freedom, out of transcendence, suggests the extent to which preference, in fact, belongs to the essence of ground. For this *potius* is only the expression of the surpassingness of world, of the upswing of freedom into possibility. How the *potius*-character of ground looks then in the concrete and how the modes then of ground, grounding, and giving-grounds each become manifold demand difficult considerations.

Ground belongs essentially to the essence of being. With concrete insight into this metaphysical connection I have only led you back to where Plato stood when he wrote the sentences in the *Republic* (*Politeia* VI, 509b 6–10), with which I close: Καὶ τοῖς γιγνωσκομένοις τοίνυν μὴ μόνον τὸ γιγνώσκεσθαι φάναι ὑπὸ τοῦ ἀγαθοῦ παρεῖναι, ἀλλὰ καὶ τὸ εἶναί τε καὶ τὴν οὐσίαν ὑπ᾽ ἐκείνου αὐτοῖς προσεῖναι, οὐκ οὐσίας ὄντος τοῦ ἀγαθοῦ, ἀλλ᾽ ἔτι ἐπέκεινα τῆς οὐσίας πρεσβείᾳ καὶ δυνάμει ὑπερέχοντος. And so you must say that knowing is not only present for and with known beings, present namely on the basis of the good (the good establishes for beings not only knownness and thereby world-entry) but also being and being-a-what is assigned to beings from that (namely the good). The for-the-sake-of, however, (transcendence) is not being itself, but surpasses being, and does so inasmuch as it outstrips beings in dignity and power.

SUPPLEMENT:
DISTANCE AND NEARNESS

To philosophize means to exist from ground. Philosophy is neither one science among others nor a production of world-views; it is more primordial than every science and, at the same time, more primordial than every world-view. The important thing is that we do it proper justice, that is, in philosophizing, we always transform each and every thing in ourselves and to ourselves. As long as we waiver back and forth on the surface by doubling theoretical and practical maxims, we are not yet in philosophy. Logic and metaphysics are grounded in the understanding-of-being that is determined by the ontological difference. The latter seems to us abstract, dry, and vacuous, and yet we must ask: What is the understanding-of-being?

The freedom toward ground is the outstripping, in the upswing, of that which carries us away and gives us distance.

The human being is a creature of distance! And only by way of the real primordial distance that the human in his transcendence establishes toward all beings does the true nearness to things begin to grow in him. And only the capacity to hear into the distance summons forth the awakening of the answer of those humans who should be near.

EDITOR'S EPILOGUE

The course of lectures edited here were given by Martin Heidegger, under the title "Logik," in the summer of 1928, his last semester at the University of Marburg/Lahn. Heidegger lectured four hours a week, Mondays, Tuesdays, Thursdays, and Fridays. The first lecture took place on May 1, and the last lecture, as a double period, on a Saturday, July 28. On Monday, May 21, 1928, Heidegger delivered the memorial for Max Scheler (p. 50 ff.), who died on May 19. He read the "summary" (p. 56f.) after the Pentecost break. The supplement "Distance and Nearness" (p. 220), which was not delivered, is a text for closing the lecture course.

Heidegger's manuscript of the lectures and the handwritten transcriptions of his former students, Hermann Mörchen and Helene Weiss, were available for this edition. The original manuscript has 73 (or, through a double numeration, 74) pages in folio format, written crosswise. About three-fourths of it contains, on the left side, continuous text formulated in sentences, with many insertions that are partially interlocked with one another and not always completely formulated. The right half of the page contains a great number of predominantly captionlike marginalia; to this is added a series of supplements with notes and additions. The first copy, which had already been reworked stylistically, had been prepared by Hildegard Feick. Her text, we thankfully mention, was a great help in first mastering the difficulty of deciphering Heidegger's handwriting, which was unusually small at the time. Hermann Mörchen's manuscript consists in captionlike notes of the entire lecture course. The text of Helene Weiss begins only after the part on Leibniz, near the end of § 9; aside from the first pages, it presents a development of her captionlike notes.

Both note transcriptions mirror throughout the flow and conceptual content of the lecture course very reliably, as is shown by a comparison with manuscript passages that Heidegger delivered unaltered. At the same time, as non-stenographic notes, they reproduce the trains of thought only in snatches. They therefore, inescapably lack the density of the handwritten manuscript. Also lost, to a great extent, is the tension in the movement of thought where, at the highpoints of the original text, Heidegger struggles for the decisive thoughts. Often, too, the lecture in delivery is much less complex than the written version. Our greatest effort was therefore expended on securing the total resources of the written manuscript; from the original manuscript, we took into account every caption and every suggestion of a thought that contained more than a mere repetition. In view of the condition of the text, it was also prohibitive to base the shaping of the text on passages from transcripts or on insertions in the text instead of on the original wording. But from the transcriptions we utilized the following: all thoughts from the manuscript which were expanded upon or additionally developed in the lectures; the summary repetitions insofar as they contain new concepts or new turns of thought; all completed formulations of supplements and marginalia mentioned only in captions in the manuscript; also the particularly felicitous variants of a formulation. As a whole our task was to take what was to be considered from the lectures delivered and adapt it to the more rigorous expository style of the written text.

The final text was put together according to the directives given by Heidegger himself. This means that the insertions, marginalia, and supplemental notes from the manuscript, the adoptions from the copies, as well as the variant formulations from the lecture recapitulations in the supplements or the copies, were worked into the continuous text with careful regard for the Heideggerian style of those years, so that the unity of the development of thought was reproduced as far as possible.

The lectures edited by Heidegger's own hand were our model in considerations of readability and clarity with respect to the line of thought. Stylistically we refrained from smoothing out the text of the manuscript any more than seemed necessary for an uninterrupted reading and for the elimination of misunderstandings. Fillers such as "now," "also," "however," etc., had to be preserved, for the most part, along with a certain peculiarly Heideggerian rhetorical idiom and unevenness, if his characteristic lecture style was to remain visible in the written text as well.

Heidegger had himself undertaken the division of the text into paragraphs. I am responsible for the divisions in the introduction and the subdivisions of § § 5, 9, and 11. The formulation of the title for § 10 was matched with the actual execution of the section. The division of the text into sections and the punctuation were largely left up to the editor, since Heidegger limited himself in the manuscript to dividing the text mostly into broad sections and to suggesting syntactical caesuras in individual sentences only by using short dashes between thoughts.

Citations in foreign languages which function purely as references are untranslated in Heidegger's manuscript. Where the wording of a quotation seems especially important for the line of thought, Heidegger provides at least a translation, usually one that adds commentary, but besides this he often provides the foreign-language quotation as well. These rules were adopted in this edition in connection with the manuscript and the transcripts.

Brackets "⟨ ⟩" designate Heidegger's additions within quotations and translations in the main text; the footnotes contain editor's notes [in italic brackets] regarding references to the literature.

The sections in the main text introduced by N.B. are side remarks, which Heidegger had himself so designated in the manuscript.

The lectures do not present a traditional or modern logic, but pursue the "metaphysical foundations of logic" in light of the being question. This was the title Heidegger himself chose for the main part of the course. This formulation was therefore chosen as the title of this volume. To uncover those foundations, Heidegger gives in the first half of the lectures an interpretation of Leibniz's metaphysics, spread throughout many individual texts and statements, an interpretation with regard to the function this metaphysics has as the foundation for Leibniz's logic and for traditional logic in general.

This first large interpretation of Leibniz by Heidegger is especially consequential for the latter's exposition of the modern metaphysics of subjectivity. The definition of substance as force and of the latter as (twofold) representation seemed so decisive to Heidegger that he repeatedly interpreted Leibniz, as he did Kant, in these lectures, in a treatise in the second volume of the book on Nietzsche, and in the lectures *Der Satz vom Grund*. Heidegger already published part of the interpretation given here (cf. § 5) in the *Festschrift* for Rudolf Bultmann on his 80th birthday (*Zeit und Geschichte*, edited by E. Dinkler, Tübingen 1964, pp. 491–507). The text printed at that time contains some passages Heidegger selected from the transcript by Hildegard Feick, which he lightly corrected and provided with a brief introduction. For the present edition, that text was once again proofed against the manuscript. In doing so, all the remaining deciphered insertions, marginalia, and notes not taken into account by Feick's transcription, and all the aids contained in the Mörchen transcription, which had not yet been available to Mrs. Feick, were used to complete the wording, to correct individual readings, and to organize a number of sentences and sections into a sequence that corresponds to the train of thought originally planned by Heidegger. It can be said that, at this time, we really have before us the complete main text of the first Leibniz interpretation by Heidegger.

The memorial for Max Scheler, which was shortened by

Heidegger and printed in a memorial volume edited by P. Good, *Max Scheler im Gegenwartsgeschehen der Philosophie*, (Bern and Munich, 1975, p. 9), was also dependent on Feick's transcription. This text is likewise given here in a complete form.

Besides the interpretation of Leibniz, the text of these lectures has significance for re-thinking Heidegger's pathway of thought, something which the *Gesamtausgabe* should facilitate. Especially significant in the second half are the discussions of transcendence and intentionality, and along with these the confrontation with Max Scheler, the guiding statements for understanding *Being and Time*, the introduction to the problem of time, the announcement of the conversion of fundamental ontology into a metontology, and the particularly detailed investigations of the concept of world in conjunction with the problem of ground. The treatise *Vom Wesen des Grundes* developed out of these investigations.

The present volume would not have come about without the cooperation of Dr. Heinrich Hüni, with whom I collated the text, and who carried out the necessary preparations before and afterwards with great care and dedication. For constructing the final text, which was often quite laborious, his thorough familiarity with Heidegger's thinking and language was indispensable. I am heartily grateful to him. My thanks also go to Mrs. Magdalena Prause, who did the typing.

Wuppertal, on the first anniversary
of the death of Martin Heidegger.   —Klaus Held

TRANSLATOR'S AFTERWORD

The Editor's Epilogue renders the German editor's account of the composition of the text and the principles employed in editing it for the Collected Edition (*Gesamtausgabe*) of Martin Heidegger's works in German. In this afterword, I will alert the reader to my approach to some of the problems peculiar to *The Metaphysical Foundations of Logic*.

It may soon be possible to translate Heidegger's texts into English by making use of electronic data retrieval systems. Computers will be able to sort out previous translational solutions and apply them to the text at hand in a technically consistent way. Scholarly exactitude might also require that we await eventual access to the complete archives of Heidegger's papers, notes, and letters; a philologically sound technical vocabulary for Heidegger's philosophy might be thus secured for the English language. Yet the present translation does not await those possibilities. The decision to produce an English-language version as soon as possible after the German publication was prompted by Heidegger's conception of the German Collected Edition of his writings, of which the present text is Volume 26 in the overall plan of the collection. Heidegger believed his writings have a peculiar timeliness for our particular juncture in history, and with that in mind he characterized the Collected Edition as "ways—not works" (*Wege—nicht Werke*); he refrained from using the monumental notion of "collected works." Pathways of thought for historically live options may need to be brought to light with a timely dispatch that precludes the polished exactitude of a timeless monument. A scholarly monument may need still another half century—if, indeed, there is to be one.

The urgency Heidegger felt about his Collected Edition appears in his unfinished foreword, cited in the Editor's Epilogue of the *Gesamtaugabe*, volume 1:

> The Collected Edition should in a variety of ways demonstrate a being-underway in the field of a self-transforming inquiry into the manifold meanings of the question of being. The Collected Edition should thus lead one to take up the question [of being] and ask it, especially to ask it in a more questioning way. To inquire more questioningly means to make the step back, back prior to reserve, back into a saying that names ("back" not in a temporal-historical sense, but "back" as the way-character of thinking).
>
> The purpose [of the Collected Edition] is to arouse discussion about inquiry into the matter of thinking (thinking as the relationship

to being as presentness; Parmenides, Heraclitus: νοεῖν, λόγος) and not about communicating the author's opinion, not about describing the writer's standpoint, and not about fitting him into the sequence of other historically ascertainable standpoints. These latter endeavors can, of course, be done at any time, especially in the age of information, but they are completely irrelevant for preparing a questioning access to the matter of thinking.

The large quantity of volumes testifies to the remaining questionableness of the question of being and provides many opportunities for self-examination. On the other hand, the endeavor collected in this edition remains but a weak echo of that beginning which withdraws ever more distantly: the self-retraction of ἀλήθεια. In a certain way it [the self-retraction of *aletheia*] is manifest and is being constantly experienced; yet its peculiarity remains necessarily unthought in the beginning, and this state-of-affairs places a unique restraint on all subsequent thinking. It would be a delusion to want now to construe what was initially recognized into something we now know.

The preceding remarks on urgency are by no means put forward as an excuse for translational inaccuracies or stylistic sloppiness. They intend, rather, to describe the spirit in which the translation was done, without the aid of computer coordination, without a research team, and with a minimum of *schole* or leisure. The resulting product has only that amount of wholeness a finite individual can design; the finished work is not a "philological-critical edition" in the European sense of those terms. I have aimed, then, at producing a translation that would as accurately as possible present the English-speaking reader with the contents of the German-language edition of 1978. My notes have been kept mininimal and, outside of a few minor printer's errata verified by the German editor, no attempt has been made to improve on the German edition by checking it against the manuscripts and transcriptions discussed in the Editor's Epilogue of the original edition.

In the original German edition, extended quotations in French, Latin, and Greek are usually run directly in the text without quotation marks or italics, a procedure consistent with the German university professor's custom of citing authors in the original tongue during classroom lectures. To avoid confusing the English-speaking reader, Latin and French quotations have been put in italics. Occasionally, where the original repeatedly uses a Latin word or phrase, the English cognate is used instead. For instance, a frequently used Latin *propositio* becomes simply the English "proposition." The Greek typescript distinguishes cita-

tions in that language, just as it does in the German text. Brackets
are reserved throughout for translator's interpolations or for English translations of the Greek or Latin. The symbols "⟨⟩" are used
to distinguish Heidegger's interpolations and comments within his
own translations or within citations of another author. Interpolations by other translators cited and by the editor of the German
edition are in italic brackets. Footnotes from the text are on the
bottom of the page and are numbered consecutively from the beginning of each major section; the translator's notes are at the foot
of the page and are designated by asterisks or daggers. It should
also be mentioned that quotations from Greek and Latin authors
have been translated from Heidegger's own German translation
wherever Heidegger did in fact make his own translation of the
text; where Heidegger did not put forward a German translation, I
made my own translation from the Greek and Latin, always, however, checking and assimilating the major English translations of
the text in question. The titles of German works referred to in the
text are usually given in German, with the exception of frequently
mentioned works that have classical status, such as the *Critique of
Pure Reason* and *Being and Time*.

Where the German terms were extremely difficult to translate, I
included the German in brackets or else noted the difficulties of
my translational choices at the bottom of the page. Some terms
remain inherently complex in Heidegger's German, and many
books and articles have been written in an attempt to elucidate his
creative use of language. The term *Grund,* for instance, suggests
English words such as "reason," "ground," "cause," "basis,"
"fundament," etc. Since the present text contains extensive passages concerning *der Satz vom Grund* (the principle of "reason"),
the best I can do is refer the reader to Terrence Malick's lengthy
and illuminating notes and preface to his translation of Heidegger's *Vom Wesen des Grundes, The Essence of Reasons,* (Evanston:
Northwestern University Press, 1969).

In general, my strategy has been to allow the context to determine a specific dimension of the meaning of a word, and thus I
have in no way sought to generalize a one-to-one equivalence between terms in the two languages; a certain artistic license is
needed here if the English is indeed to be English while nevertheless "rendering" the German original. The German pagination,
given in the running heads, allows the reader to refer to the original where the nuance I have chosen may be checked for appro-
priateness or where the scholar may find other semantic dimensions of interest. The reader with some German will find, I think,

that the translation can be followed word-for-word in the original without, I hope, any omissions or additions. The main difficulty in cross-checking with the original will occur in those passages where English syntax and sentence rhythms have prevailed over the complex hypotactics of the German language.

In this translation I have adopted Albert Hofstadter's approach to translating the central term "being" (*das Sein*). As Hofstadter has done in translating *The Basic Problems of Phenomenology* (Bloomington: Indiana University Press, 1982), "being" is not capitalized. I did this not merely for the sake of continuity in a series of translations. My rationale is based, moreover, on the changing needs of readers and the changing resources of language. It is possible to distinguish *das Seiende* from *das Sein* by rendering the former with the plural "beings" and the latter with "being" (no capital). It was once necessary in English to call attention to the German infinitive used as a noun, *das Sein*, and the capitalized "Being" served to alert readers to a locution which cannot be rendered precisely in English without forcing *das Sein* into "the to-be." But now that Heidegger's special focus on the question of being has become familiar, perhaps even all-too-familiar, it seems appropriate to permit the term to become naturalized in English, thus lessening the mythical, distant status of the term. De-mythologizing the question of being also implies that the question of the ontological difference, the difference between being and beings, will become more seriously problematic and more a matter for thought, once the mythic aura of capitalized "Being" has been removed and the suggestion eliminated that being is another name for the separate status of a divine Being—a suggestion which the English language, so sparing with its capitals, inevitably raises when "being" is capitalized. While any form of expression is as prone to trivialization as mythic forms are, the task of thinking seems to lie in devising strategies to distance us from the all-too-familiar.

Of the institutions that provided support for the timely publication of this volume, I should first mention the National Endowment for the Humanities; for seven months NEH freed me from my many teaching duties so I could devote energy to completing this project. The Research Division of the National Endowment also requested that I write a translator's introduction intended for English-speaking readers, and this has been made available separately. Inter Nationes, the German foundation, also offered support for the translation. I should like to thank the administration at Missouri Western State College, who granted me a leave of absence so I could devote full time to the project. I must also mention my gratitude to the funding institutions which made possible three years of advanced study in the German universities of Freiburg and Berlin; these include the U.S. Fulbright Commission, the German Academic Exchange (DAAD), and the direct exchange program of the President's Office of the Freie Universität Berlin.

Professors who were immediately helpful include John Sallis, whose comments and suggestions were insightful and based on admirable scholarship; Joseph Kockelmans, who generously went through first drafts of the entire translation with great care and made helpful comments; and Theodore Kisiel, who went over an early draft and made many useful suggestions. Albert Hofstadter, Manfred Frings, and David Lachterman each gave advice on scholarly questions. Friedrich-Wilhelm von Herrmann of the University of Freiburg provided invaluable help ten years ago when I studied Heideggers' work in Freiburg. Alphonso Lingis was the first to suggest I undertake this project. Susan Mango at the National Endowment for the Humanities offered valuable advice during the planning stages of the project. My colleagues at Missouri Western, James Mehl, Phil Mullins, and John Tapia, offered constant and friendly interest in the project; Gary Shapiro of the University of Kansas gave me friendly reminders that philosophy, and not the cello, is my first love. Of greatest personal importance was the presence of Joanna Popdan Heim and Michael Junior.

Index

abyss (Abgrund), 182

affirmation (κατάφασις): according to Aristotle, 23f.

ἀγαθόν (bonum, the good), 116f., 184, n.165

αἴσθησις, 183

αἰτία, 110

ἀ-λήθεια (unconcealment), 217

analysis: truth of statements as a result of, 34; Kantian a. and Leibniz's a. of notions, 36; of historical truths into identities, 48; and adequate knowledge, 62; and intuition, 63; existential a. and metaphysical history, 154; and finitude, 157f.

ἀνάμνησις (recollection) in Plato and the metaphysical recollection of being, 147

Anaxagoras, 11f.

Angst (anxiety), 167f.

anthropology: anthropological study of the "logic" of thinking, 18f.; and fundamental ontology, 136

anthropomorphism, 88

animism: as a misunderstanding of Leibniz's monadology, 88

Anwesenheit (presentness), 145f.; Anwesendes, 202

apperception, 95

appetition, 91; as the trend toward transition, 92

ἀρχή (origin, leading impulse), 110f.

Arnauld, Anton, 58

Aquinas, Thomas, 30, 44-47, 80-81, 146, 174; on judgment, 30, 44-47; on God's knowledge, 45.; on power (potentia), 80f.; on "world," 174

Aristotle, 4-6, 8, 9f., 21, 22f., 28, 30, 34f., 36, 51, 61, 80, 84, 110f., 125, 132, 142, 146, 149, 150f., 183, 184, 198, 204, 216, 217; the definition of philosophy according to, 9f.; description of λόγος as predication, 22f.

Augustine, 51, 134, 149, 173, 198f.

Barbarus, Hermolaus, 84

Basic Problems of Phenomenology, 200

Baumgarten, Alexander Gottlieb, 52, 174, 178

being (das Sein): and the definition of philosophy, 10f; philosophy as knowledge of, 12f., 148f.; and the theory of judgment, 70; Leibniz's interpretation of as monadological, 71; as the πρότερον (prior to), 146f.; "there is b." ("es gibt sich das Sein"), 147; the idea of and its regional variants, 151; the basic articulation of and the ontological difference, 152f.; and superior power, 165n.; and ground, 217f.